# Fritz Machlup • Kenneth Leeson
## and Associates

# INFORMATION THROUGH THE PRINTED WORD

## The Dissemination of Scholarly, Scientific, and Intellectual Knowledge

### Volume 3: Libraries

 PRAEGER PUBLISHERS
Praeger Special Studies

New York   •   London   •   Sydney   •   Toronto

Library of Congress Cataloging in Publication Data

Machlup, Fritz, 1902–
    Information through the printed word.

    CONTENTS: v. 1. Book publishing.--v. 2. Journals.--
v. 3. Libraries.
    1. Scholarly publishing--Collected works.
2. Book industries and trade--Collected works.
3. Scholarly periodicals--Collected works.
4. Libraries--Collected works. I. Leeson, Kenneth,
joint author. II. Title.
Z286.S37M3      658.8'09'070573              78–19460

The data used in the preparation
of this material were obtained
and processed with the support
of the National Science Foundation
Grant No. DSI 74-12756 and the
National Endowment for the
Humanities Grant No. AS-24510-76-155

PRAEGER PUBLISHERS
PRAEGER SPECIAL STUDIES
383 Madison Avenue, New York, N.Y. 10017, U.S.A.

Published in the United States of America in 1978
by Praeger Publishers,
A Division of Holt, Rinehart and Winston, CBS, Inc.

89    038    987654321

© 1978 by Praeger Publishers

Printed in the United States of America

PREFACE

This is a report on the findings of several years of research by a team of varying size, up to 16 persons at the peak of activities and, because of turnover in personnel and the use of occasional consultants, altogether 29 persons over the entire period. The project was financed chiefly by the National Science Foundation and the National Endowment for the Humanities through a series of grants to New York University, with considerable cost-sharing by New York University, funds from two other sources, and supplemental contributions of money and unpaid services by Professor Fritz Machlup, Principal Investigator, and Kenneth Leeson, Senior Research Associate.

The title of the project has changed over the years, partly in order to accommodate an expansion of its scope, and ultimately for the sake of euphony. In the first application for an NSF grant the project was called "The Production and Distribution of Scientific and Technological Information." When the scope of the research was extended to include scholarly knowledge in all disciplines, including the humanities, the title underwent a commensurate expansion: "The Dissemination of Scholarly Knowledge: A Study of the Economic Viability of the Publication of Books and Journals and of the Maintenance of Library Services and Associated Activities." This was more than a mouthful and badly in need of cosmetic surgery to meet higher standards of English composition. Hence the new title: *Information through the Printed Word: The Dissemination of Scholarly, Scientific and Intellectual Knowledge.* If any reader, addicted to the "S & T" label, misses the adjective "technical" (or more correctly "technological") as an additional modifier of the noun knowledge, or information, let him be assured that the three adjectives exhibited in the title fully cover all information generated by engineering sciences; indeed, any one of the adjectives would do.

This report will probably be read - partly or fully, cursorily or attentively - by persons in a variety of fields and with very different backgrounds. This makes it difficult to write in a manner that will not be regarded as too technical by some and too simplistic by others. Publishers may scoff at our "pedantic" explanations of practices, institutions, problems and word meanings customary in their industry, while economists may find these explanations too sketchy for an outsider. Librarians may be bored with details in the descriptions of library operations, while scholars and scientists

iii

in various fields may complain that we took too many things for granted and were inconsiderate of readers not familiar with the language and activities of librarians. There is no way to meet the needs of all readers; it is impossible to have the right pitch in an exposition addressed to readers in different fields and at different levels of sophistication. We appeal to our readers to bear this in mind if they find some terms or relations overexplained or underexplained from their own point of view.

The report is organized into the following six parts: One, General; Two, Book Publishing; Three, Journal Publishing; Four, Use of Journals; Five, General Appendix on the Economics of Statistical Sampling; Six, Libraries. The first volume contains Parts One and Two. The second volume contains Parts Three, Four, and Five. The third volume contains Part Six. Additional research is still under way and may yield findings to be reported eventually in a fourth volume.

For the record we are listing here the grants from the two sponsoring agencies:

*National Science Foundation*

GN42274     (Changed to SIS 74-12756-A01)
Division: Science Information
    Title: The Production and Distribution of Scientific
           and Technological Information
   Period: 7/1/74-12/31/75

DSI-74-12756-A02
Division: Science Information
    Title: The Production and Distribution of Scientific
           and Technological Information
   Period: 9/1/75-8/31/76

DSI-74-12756-A03
Division: Science Information
    Title: The Production and Distribution of Scientific
           and Technological Information
   Period: 9/1/76-8/31/77

IST-78-13383
Division: Science Information
    Title: An In-Depth Analysis of a Comprehensive Data
           Base on the Communication of Scientific/
           Scholarly Knowledge
   Period: 7/1/78-6/30/79 (for additional research not
           yet embodied in the three volumes)

*National Endowment for the Humanities*

AS-24510-76-155
Division:  Office of Planning and Analysis
   Title:  The Dissemination of Scholarly Knowledge:
           A Study of the Economic Viability of the
           Publication of Books and Journals
  Period:  12/1/75-5/31/77

AS-29910-77-1107
Division:  Office of Planning and Analysis
   Title:  Mining a Rich Deposit of Confidential Data on
           the Communication of Scholarly Knowledge
  Period:  9/1/77-8/31/78

*Earlier Grants for a Related Project*

The material contained in these three volumes on *Information Through the Printed Word* should not be confused with a related though separate undertaking by Fritz Machlup:  the updating of his book *The Production and Distribution of Knowledge in the United States* (Princeton University Press: 1962).  It contained 85 statistical tables, most of which terminated in 1958.  During the years 1971-1974 the National Science Foundation and the National Endowment for the Humanities had made various grants to Machlup to enable him to expand the material and bring the tables forward to 1970. When this research was completed, the project on book publishing, journal publishing, and library operations emerged as an undertaking more urgent than the writing of the second edition of the 1962 book.  Moreover, it was hoped that the research on books, journals, and libraries would enrich the material for the new edition of the more comprehensive work.  It is scheduled to appear, with all data brought forward to 1975, in a set of several volumes at various intervals between 1979 and 1982.

A preface usually includes a list of acknowledgements. Since the authors are indebted to so many persons and organizations that their listing extends over a good many pages, it was decided to relegate the acknowledgements to a separate chapter in Volume 1.

# CONTENTS

# List of Tables

PART 6


LIBRARIES

LIBRARIES AND LIBRARY STATISTICS

The role of libraries in the dissemination of knowledge through the printed word is difficult, perhaps impossible, to quantify if "information of all kinds" is to be included; but the task becomes easier if it is limited to intellectual, and especially scholarly and scientific knowledge.  In Chapter 2.1, in the discussion of the markets of the book-publishing industry, we presented figures for sales in dollars and in per cent indicating the shares in 1976 of various market outlets for different categories of books.  We found that "Sales to domestic libraries are largest (in terms of per cent of totals) for the category of professional books."  But "if we entertain the hypothesis that most of the professional books distributed through wholesalers go to domestic libraries, we find the sum of the sales to wholesalers and of direct sales to domestic libraries to be as large as 30.8 per cent."  The share of "trade books, adult" sold through wholesalers is even greater: 33.6 per cent.  If much of this goes to domestic libraries, which take another 9.0 per cent directly from the publisher, the portion of this category of books that is absorbed by libraries must be very substantial.

Since the number of readers per book in libraries is probably a multiple of that for books acquired by individuals or other institutions, one may say that libraries play an enormous role in the dissemination of knowledge embodied in professional books, that is, "technical, scientific, business, medical and other professional books," and in "trade books, adult," fiction and nonfiction, which in general qualify as conveyors of intellectual knowledge.

## TYPES AND NUMBERS OF LIBRARIES

When does a collection of books become a "library"?  According to the dictionary definition a library is "a place set

apart to contain books for reading, study, or reference."
However, the one-or-two-room libraries of private scholars
and collectors, or in the houses of rich families, do not
count as libraries in the sense used in a discussion of the
dissemination of knowledge where the library is supposed to
have the multiplier effect mentioned above.  Such an effect
can be expected only of a collection accessible to a multitude
of readers.  Should open access be regarded as a characteris-
tic of the library in this sense?  Not necessarily; it suf-
fices that the books collected are available to a large number
of people, say, the members of an institution, association, or
club, or the students and teachers of a school or institution
of higher education.  A workable definition would add also
the need for staff, at least one person to provide service.  A
listing of the types of libraries ordinarily recognized in
descriptions of the "library industry" will help circumscribe
the subject of inquiry in this chapter and will serve as a
basis for a statistic that reports the number of libraries in
the United States.

## Types of Libraries

The following distinctions are customary:  public libraries, college and university libraries, school libraries, and
special libraries.  To this short list several sources would
add State libraries and Federal libraries.  This classification, however, can become operational only if several boundary
questions are settled.  Should libraries of junior colleges
(community colleges) be regarded as a subclass of college
libraries (academic libraries)?  Should law libraries and
medical libraries that are connected with universities be
counted as academic or special libraries?  (The medical library
of a university may be separately housed and managed, and
even located in another city.)  Should special libraries of
the Federal government be counted as special or as Federal
libraries?  These questions seem trivial, and are surely not
crucial for any serious problems, but have to be settled if
we want unambiguous statistics.

## Numbers of Libraries

The statistics shown in Table 6.1.1 are based on the
American Library Directory, 1976-1977 (published by R. R.
Bowker, New York) and on The Bowker Annual of Library and Book-
trade Information, 1977.  It solves the questions asked in the

4

TABLE 6.1.1  Libraries in the United States, by Type
of Control or Function (except school libraries, and some
Federal libraries), 1976

| | |
|---|---:|
| Public libraries | 8,504 |
| Branch libraries of city, county, and regional systems | 5,477 |
| Sub total | 13,981 |
| University and college libraries | 1,696 |
| Junior college libraries | 1,129 |
| Sub total | 2,825 |
| Special libraries | 6,563 |
| Special libraries part of university and college systems | 1,252 |
| Special libraries within Armed forces installations | 85 |
| Sub total | 7,900 |
| Law libraries | 806 |
| Law libraries part of university and college systems | 147 |
| Sub total | 953 |
| Medical libraries | 1,955 |
| Medical libraries part of university and college systems | 157 |
| Sub total | 2,112 |
| Religious libraries | 996 |
| Religious libraries part of university and college systems | 19 |
| Sub total | 1,015 |
| Public libraries of armed forces | 559 |
| Total listed in AL Directory | 29,345 |
| Total of libraries not listed in this directory but on Bowker mailing lists: | |
| Public libraries in the United States with annual incomes of less than $2,000 or book funds of less than $500 approximately | 2,511 |
| Law libraries in the United States of less than 10,000 volumes | 170 |
| Grand total of libraries in the United States (except school libraries) | 32,026 |

Source:  The Bowker Annual of Library and Booktrade
Information, 1977.

preceding paragraph by enumerating the mixed types in separate lines. It excludes school libraries and a few kinds of State and Federal libraries; and it does not inform us whether such collections as hospital libraries, prison libraries, church-parish libraries, association, club and trade-union libraries are included among the public libraries.[1]

We can find divergent figures in different statistical compilations, but this is understandable since borderlines are differently drawn. Such questions as minimum size, open access, function and control are not uniformly answered, and there is also the question of nonresponse to questionnaires. Some directories and statistical tabulators, quite reasonably, omit nonrespondent libraries, while others persist in going after them if their existence is beyond doubt. For example, the same volume from which we take the figures for Table 6.1.1 contains a tabulation omitting libraries that failed to report to the *American Library Directory*. As a result, that tabulation contains only 7,394 public libraries rather than the 8,504 in the more inclusive table, or the 13,981 if branch libraries are counted separately.

For the same reason — failure to report — the tabulation in the *Bowker Annual* contains only 2,389 college and university libraries, as against the 2,825 given in the table from which we took our figures.

Another puzzle to the uninitiated is the absence, both from the summary statistics and the detailed tabulation, of the "more than 2,000 Federal libraries" about which one can read at various places. The answer is that most of them were classed as public, special, or academic libraries. Incidentally, the three largest libraries of the United States Government — the Library of Congress, the National Agricultural Library, and the National Library of Medicine — are called "National" libraries to distinguish them from the many Federal libraries.[2]

-------------------

[1]However, according to another source, "to be included in public library statistics, every agency must offer free services to everyone within some stipulated geographic area." Statistics Coordinating Project, *Library Statistics: A Handbook of Concepts, Definitions, and Terminology* (Chicago, Ill.: American Library Association, 1966), p. 30.

[2]Perhaps we ought to solve the "puzzle" of the Federal libraries. In a survey for Fiscal Year 1972 as many as 2,313 Federal libraries were identified and data on the size of their collections were received from 1,550 of them. Only 58 of the 2,313 were rated as large, that is, holding more than 100,000 volumes. The 1,550 libraries together held almost 60,000,000 titles, including nonbook titles (periodicals,

*Increase in the Number of Libraries*

Perhaps we should be more interested in statistics of changes over time than in those for a moment of time. For the construction of a time series it is essential to ascertain the consistency and comparability of the consecutive data, and these qualities are less likely to be found when the data pertain to a universe with uncertain boundaries. Thus, Donald King was probably right when he measured the growth of the library industry by using less comprehensive but more reliable figures, taken incidentally, from the same source, *The Bowker Annual*. We reproduce the series, from 1969 to 1976, for academic libraries and "all" libraries, from King's *Statistical Indicators of Scientific and Technical Information: Update 1977*.

|      | *Number of* | |
|------|-------------------------|-----------------|
|      | *Academic libraries* | *All libraries* |
| 1969 | 2,931 | 16,893 |
| 1970 | 2,968 | 17,308 |
| 1971 | 2,846 | 17,224 |
| 1972 | 2,723 | 17,139 |
| 1973 | 2,705 | 17,773 |
| 1974 | 2,686 | 18,407 |
| 1975 | 2,755 | 20,307 |
| 1976 | 2,825 | 22,208 |

The number of academic libraries in 1976 was slightly down from 1969, by 3.6 per cent, but the number of all, chiefly public and special libraries, was up by 31.5 per cent.

ON THE SCARCITY OF DETAILED LIBRARY STATISTICS

Several times in this report references are made to a shortage of data on the holdings and acquisitions of books and journals by libraries. Some of these references take the form

---

documents, audio-visual materials), over 36,305,000 volumes of books and bound periodicals, and 18,907,000 titles in the book stock. They received in 1972 a total of 558,000 periodicals. Table 6.1.2 presents the universe of Federal libraries by organization and type.

| Governmental organization | Number of libraries identified | Type of library | | | | Per cent of all Federal libraries |
|---|---|---|---|---|---|---|
| | | Special or technical[1] | General[2] | Educational[3] | Other[4] | |
| National libraries | 3 | 3 | | | | (5) |
| Legislative branch | 3 | 3 | | | | (5) |
| Judicial branch | 18 | 18 | | | | (5) |
| Executive Office of the President | 9 | 9[6] | | | | (5) |
| Department of Defense Headquarters | 20 | 13 | 2 | 5 | | (5) |
| Department of the Air Force | 266 | 38 | 152 | 64 | 12 | 11 |
| Department of the Army | 940 | 392[7] | 263 | 265 | 20 | 41 |
| Department of the Navy | 246 | 98 | 110 | 30 | 8 | 11 |
| Department of State | 2 | 2 | | | | (5) |
| Department of Justice | 31 | 5 | 24 | 2 | | 1 |
| Department of the Treasury | 2 | 2 | | | | (5) |
| Department of the Interior | 106 | 47 | 5 | 54 | | 5 |
| Department of Agriculture | 15 | 15 | | | | (5) |
| Department of Commerce | 38 | 36 | | 1 | 1 | 2 |
| Department of Labor | 2 | 2 | | | | (5) |
| Department of Health, Education and Welfare | 26 | 22 | 1 | 3 | | 1 |
| Department of Housing and Urban Development | 11 | 11 | | | | (5) |
| Department of Transportation | 14 | 12 | 1 | 1 | | (5) |
| Smithsonian Institution | 15 | 15 | | | | (5) |
| U. S. Information Agency | 133 | 1 | 132[8] | | | 6 |
| Veterans Administration | 321 | 160 | 159 | | 2 | 14 |
| Atomic Energy Commission | 4 | 4 | | | | (5) |
| National Aeronautics and Space Administration | 11 | 10 | | | 1 | (5) |
| Environmental Protection Agency | 28 | 28 | | | | 1 |
| General Services Administration | 10 | 4 | | | 6[9] | (5) |
| Federal Reserve System | 1 | 1 | | | | (5) |
| Other independent agencies | 33 | 30 | 1 | 1 | 1 | 1 |
| Boards, commissions | 3 | 3 | | | | (5) |
| Quasi-official agencies | 2 | 2 | | | | (5) |
| Totals | 2,313 | 986 | 850 | 426 | 51 | 100 |

[1] Includes health and medicine, engineering and science, and other special and technical libraries (special).
[2] Includes hospital, penal, and quasi-public libraries (other general).
[3] Includes academic and quasi-academic, and school libraries.
[4] Includes 45 systems headquarters and 6 Presidential libraries.
[5] Less than 1 per cent.
[6] Includes 4 libraries deleted from the survey at agency request.
[7] Includes 269 Army field law libraries deleted from the survey because data were unavailable.
[8] Overseas libraries of the U. S. Information Agency, deleted from the survey because data were unavailable.
[9] Presidential libraries.

Source:  United States Federal Library Committee, Survey of Federal Libraries: Fiscal Year 1972 (Washington: National Center for Education Statistics), p. 2.

of lamentations about the discrepancies between our ambitions to find ready answers to timely questions and our realization that most of these answers could not be obtained, because data were unavailable. Expressions of our disappointment may be mistaken for criticisms of library directors, and we wish to safeguard against this mistake.

In an article under the title "Our Libraries: Can We Measure Their Holdings and Acquisitions?" (American Association of University Professors, *Bulletin*, Vol. 62, October, 1976) the Principal Investigator made some unguarded statements which could be interpreted as criticisms of the libraries' lack of recording systems. Thus he wrote that "The keepers of the books in our libraries are not bookkeepers and the subscriptions they pay for learned journals are not entered into such lined journals and ledgers as are the bookkeepers' daily concern" (p. 304). And he expressed the conviction that "the old saying 'ignorance is bliss' does not apply any longer to [library] management techniques" (p. 307). The perpetrator of these snide remarks went out of his way to explain to librarians that no offense had been intended and no criticism implied. The thrust of such pronouncements and of the article as a whole was to convince the librarians of the thesis that good statistical records, broken down by field, are urgently needed for good library management at a time when available funds are far below what would be required for maintaining a balanced collection of the most indispensable books and journals.

The explanation of the lack of data on library holdings and acquisitions broken down by field is quite simple. As long as budgets were adequate for the acquisition of all the books and journals which the library wanted for its collection, there was no perceived need for detailed statistics.

Thus, in the case of a university library, if neither the president of the institution nor the provost ask for such information, if neither the trustees nor the library committees of the faculty are curious to know, the director of the library will not as a rule devote time and money to the compilation of statistical series which few, if any, might ever consult. Without a perceived need for such record-keeping and data-processing it would be unlikely for the information to be developed--which we now know to be important for present-day research and decisions.

Many libraries are now in the process of installing computerized systems for all sorts of library operations. The type of information we now lack may become available in the near future. The data, of course, will refer to years which for us lie in the future, not to the years on which our research has focused.

9

RESEARCH ON LIBRARY HOLDINGS AND ACQUISITIONS

While most libraries have periodically, perhaps even annually, taken stock of their holdings and recorded their acquisitions, such statistical efforts were ordinarily confined
to their total collection (or some special collections) without a breakdown by field or subject matter.  To obtain data
broken down by subject, a pioneering effort was made in 1966
by the University of Wisconsin at Madison, which made a
"shelflist count" of its holdings by groups and subgroups according to the classification system of the Library of Congress.  This count of titles was repeated every other year,
so that the growth of its collection by class can be seen for
the last ten years.  The General Library of the University of
California at Berkeley followed suit and later assumed leadership in a project called "National Shelflist Count," though
only 17 libraries participated in the first round in 1973, and
26 in the second round in 1975.
Before we report on these and similar projects, we shall
briefly discuss some of the problems involved in estimating or
measuring the size of a library collection and its growth.


UNITS OF MEASUREMENT

The most fundamental question relates to the choice of the
unit of measurement.  To measure the size of the collection at
a moment of time, the number of volumes and the number of
titles offer themselves as alternatives; to measure the growth
of the collection, the number of volumes and the number of
titles added during a period of time may be the crucial variables, but dollars spent on purchases of books and serials and
the dollar values of donated books and sets of journals may
also be acceptable indicators.  But there are conceptual difficulties involved in any one of the units of measurement.

## Volumes

One might think that physical units — volumes — would be the least troublesome to count. Unfortunately, the results would not be strictly comparable. The same book may have appeared in two or three volumes and in a one-volume edition; the same encyclopaedia may be available in eight fat volumes and in a one-volume edition; the same encyclopaedia may be available in eight fat volumes or in 15 slimmer ones; the same set of pamphlets or thin monographs may have been bound together into a hard-cover volume or shelved separately, making several volumes; the same issues of a periodical may have been bound into one, two, or three volumes; and so forth. Still, for a stock-taking in the library stacks, for a count of the books on the shelves — not a "shelflist count," which counts cards in the catalog rather than volumes on the shelves — the volume is the simplest unit of measurement. For several reasons, however, a count of the number of titles would yield more comparable measures of the size of a collection, especially in research libraries.

## Titles

There is plenty of trouble, too, with taking the title as the unit of measurement. We know of great works published in several books where the work has its title and each of the books has a title of its own. We know of many monographs, written by different authors, treating different subjects, and published with separate titles, but as parts of a series; most libraries catalogue each of these monographs as a separate title, but some libraries regard the title of the whole series as the one to catalogue. (These series are usually referred to as monographic series and, to the distress of many searchers, are sometimes treated as "serials" rather than books.) We know of many journals the names of which were changed, in some cases even more than once; are these as many titles as the names the journal has borne over the years or does it count as only one title? We know of many instances in which a library does not possess a complete set of a periodical; should this title be counted if the gaps are very wide or only if an occasional year is missing?

If each library answers these questions according to the best judgment of its own staff, the results of its title count will not be comparable with those of others. Only a national convention to which librarians adhere can secure comparability of the measurements. Such outside interference with local practice and possibly superior judgment is regrettable, but

12

comparable statistical records are important enough to sacrifice the freedom of idiosyncratic ideas about the best way of recording and reporting. (For similar reasons, one must not indulge in idiosyncratic reporting in making one's tax return or completing a census form.) Designers of questionnaires have fully understood this requirement and have formulated uniform instructions for their completion when they organized statistical surveys of different libraries.

In measuring the growth of library collections in subjects or subject groups one may, of course, simply compare the findings of consecutive measurements of the holdings. Until very recently, no such measurements have been available; the results of the first such collective undertaking, comparing the holdings of 17 libraries in 1973 and 1975, were released in 1976. It was based on shelflist counts of titles, not volumes. A very much simpler and cheaper way, however, to measure the annual increase of library holdings would be through adequate record-keeping of acquisitions.

## *Continuous Records of Acquisitions*

Records of expenditures for subscriptions to serial publications and for purchases of books and back-issues of periodicals could easily be compiled; unfortunately, few libraries have been keeping such records with a breakdown by subject matter or by the field (department) which the purchased materials were supposed to serve. Although the dollar as a unit of measurement is also deficient, especially in a period of inflation, it can still, in combination with appropriate index numbers, serve for approximate estimates.

An ideal system of information of library holdings and acquisitions would combine measurements in all units discussed: holdings of volumes, holdings of titles, and acquisitions in terms of volumes, titles, and money. The time may come when all this information will be available.

### SHELFLIST COUNTS

Only a relatively new library could have complete and consistent records of annual acquisitions adding up to a statement of its holdings at present. Libraries that have built their collections over many years cannot be expected to have records of all acquisitions since their inception. The only way of finding out what they possess — books, serials, and other materials in their stacks — is to count the volumes or titles on the shelves or to count the titles catalogued on the shelflists.


## *Shelflists*

Shelflists are ordinarily kept in the form of catalog cards in drawers classified by subject matter according to the classification system used. (Most research libraries use LC, the Library of Congress system; a good many use D, the Dewey Decimal system; a few use still other systems; and some special libraries use special systems, for example, NLM, National Library of Medicine, for medical collections, or various local systems for Law Libraries.) Actual counts of volumes on the shelves or of cards in the catalog drawers would be too expensive. Hence, various sampling techniques have been developed to lead to reasonably accurate estimates.


## *Techniques of Measurement*

Some readers may be interested in a description of one of the procedures used in an eminently successful shelflist count, directed by LeRoy D. Ortopan, Catalog Department, General Library, University of California, Berkeley. The technique consists essentially of three steps: first, to measure the number of *cards* in each of the subdivisions of the LC classification system; second, to estimate, with the help of sampling techniques, the number of *titles* catalogued on these cards; third, to take account of any special qualifications that have to be considered to arrive at valid findings, for example, regarding parts of the collection not yet processed or not catalogued, or catalogued by a system not converted into LC classification, or excluded for sundry reasons.

Measuring the number of cards is a relatively simple operation using a ruler, pulling "the cards forward in the drawer until they are vertical and packed tightly together" and reading in centimeters and millimeters the total length of the pack that belongs into the particular LC class. Translating the length of tightly packed cards into the number of titles calls for a sampling procedure. The drawers are numbered and random numbers are drawn for a random selection of drawers. In these randomly selected drawers, the first 10 centimeters and the next 2 centimeters of tightly packed cards are marked off with a marker card. These two centimeters (20 millimeters) of cards are then used as the sample for the count of titles

14

catalogued in 20 millimeters of cards; this implies that con-
tinuation cards (that is, cards relating to the same title)
are omitted; likewise, "spacer or divider cards" are omitted.
Titles of monographs "in an established series where each con-
stitutes a single, separately authored work" are included.[1]
The count of titles in the sample is then combined with the
analogous counts in the samples from all randomly selected
drawers, to yield the total of titles counted in all samples
together; it is divided by the "total number of centimeters in
all samples" (for example, 200 centimeters if exactly 100
drawers were sampled) to yield the "average number of titles
per centimeter." Multiplying this average by the length (in
centimeters) of the pack of cards in the particular subject
class or subdivision gives the number of titles in that class
or subdivision.

Some additional observations about exclusions or omissions
will be found in Chapter 6.3, where some of the findings of
the [Ortopan] *National Shelflist Count* will be reported and
discussed.

PUBLISHED REPORTS

The shelflist studies described in the preceding section
were published in two reports and a third one is in preparation. They were not the first of their kind, nor the only
ones that have been published. The reader may find it helpful
to have a brief survey of the literature on library statistics, although we cannot promise anything approaching compre-
hensiveness.

*The NCES Reports*

The U.S. Office of Education initiated in 1939 periodic
surveys of college and university libraries. In 1967, these
surveys became a part of the Higher Education General Information Survey (HEGIS) of the National Center for Education Sta-

---

[1] The parts of this explanation that are between quotation
marks are literally taken from the "Instructions for Data
Gatherers" formulated by Mr. Ortopan and his associates. See
*Titles classified by the Library of Congress Classification:
National Shelflist Count, 1975* (Berkeley, General Library,
University of California, 1976). We are greatly indebted to
Mr. Ortopan for lending us a copy of the report.

tistics (NCES).  The statistics obtained in these surveys
cover basic statistics on many library functions, including
the size of library collections and of library expenditures
broken down by type of institution, and by general purpose,
but not by subject or field.

Reports on the findings of these surveys have been published under the title *Library Statistics of Colleges and
Universities*, usually in two parts, one with the subtitle *In-
stitutional Data* (or *Data for Individual Institutions*), the
other *Analytic Report* (or *Summary Data*).  Mr. Frank L. Schick,
Chief of Library Branch, NCES, is in charge of this undertaking.  Analytic Reports with summary data were released for
1960, 1962, 1964, 1968, 1969, 1971, and 1973; and one for 1975
is forthcoming.  The 1973 Report contains the data for 2,887
institutions of higher education.

We have greatly profited from these reports, chiefly as
models for the design of our library questionnaire and for
some of the definitions of terms.  We shall also, in subsequent chapters, make use of the summary data.  However, to
the pursuit of our chief objective, the breakdown of all data
by subject, subject group or field, the NCES Statistics could
not contribute.


*The ARL Statistics*

The Association of Research Libraries (ARL) has compiled
statistical information from its member libraries since 1963.
It published the data on university libraries in annual reports under the title *Academic Library Statistics* from 1963/64
through 1973/74.  In 1974/75 it included eleven nonuniversity
libraries besides 88 university libraries, and in view of the
enlarged coverage changed the title of its report to *ARL Statistics*.  The latest issue, *ARL Statistics 1975-1976* (Washington: Association of Research Libraries, 1976), contains the
data for its 105 present members, 94 of which are university
libraries.  Suzanne O. Frankie, Associate Executive Director
of ARL, is in charge of the continuing undertaking.

The statistics comprise data on the collections in terms
of volumes (total stock, additions, gross and net), microform
units and current serials; on interlibrary loans (originals
and photocopies); on expenditures; and on personnel.  The
latest report contains also a historical series of the median
values of all these data for the eight years 1968/69 to
1975/76.

In subsequent chapters we shall make use of several of the
ARL Statistics, chiefly of the series of expenditures and
their breakdowns.  The availability of these data was very im-

16

portant for our own survey and analysis: directly, because
the published compilations served us as a control group,
against which we could check the findings from the figures we
had collected; and even more so indirectly, because the majority of the respondents to our questionnaire were members of
the ARL and their cooperation in supplying information to us
was so generous partly because they had a good many data
ready at hand from the annual statistical "census" for the
ARL Statistics.


## The Wisconsin Reports

In the first paragraph of this chapter we referred to the
pioneering achievement of the Memorial Library of the University of Wisconsin at Madison in making and publishing in 1966
the first shelflist count broken down by subject classes and
subclasses according to the LC system. The report was published as *Titles Classified, September 1954 to January 1966*.
It may well be called the first Ortopan report, since LeRoy D.
Ortopan was at the time Chief of Cataloging at Wisconsin; but
one may prefer to reserve this designation for the National
Shelflist Count, which he directed later (after 1972) from the
Catalog Department of the University of California at Berkeley.
The Wisconsin Shelflist Count was repeated every other
year. The second report, for the period January 1966 to January 1968, was released in 1968, the third report in 1970, the
fourth in 1972, the fifth and last[2] in 1974. In 1973 Wisconsin-Madison joined in the National Shelflist Count, first con-
ducted in March 1973 and to be repeated every odd year. With
all collections in every subject class and subclass measured
every other year, the additions made during every two-year
period are known and compared.


## The National Shelflist Count

We used the Ortopan reports for the brief description we
gave, in the preceding section, on the techniques employed in
the National Shelflist Count. The first report, on the 1973

---

[2]We are indebted to Ms. Jennifer A. Stephenson, Catalog Editor, University Libraries, University of Wisconsin-Madison,
for useful information on past and planned activities.

count, was published as *Titles Classified by the Library of Congress Classification: Seventeen University Libraries* (Berkeley: General Library, University of California, 1974), the second, on the 1975 count, as *Titles Classified by the Library of Congress Classification: National Shelflist Count, 1975* (Berkeley: General Library, University of California, 1977).

We shall devote all of chapter 6.3 to a discussion of the Ortopan reports and, in particular, to comparisons of their findings with some derived from our own research.


*Still Other Shelflist Counts*

Studies similar to Ortopan's were undertaken by other groups of libraries; there is a report for five libraries in New York State, another for 30 libraries in New Mexico and Texas. The New York State report was published under the title *Comparative Shelflist Measurement for FAUL Libraries, April 1975. Preliminary Edition of Titles Classified by the Library of Congress Classification Only* (Syracuse: Five Associated University Libraries, 1975). The report on the libraries in New Mexico and Texas appeared in two volumes, *Shelflist Measuring Project of the Southwest Academic Library Consortium/Council of New Mexico Academic Libraries* (Albuquerque: University of New Mexico, 1976).

A very ambitious project of measuring the sizes of collections in various subjects was started by the National Library of Canada in 1968. This was truly a national survey in that it included the libraries of all universities in Canada offering graduate studies in the humanities and the social sciences. It was also wider in scope than the surveys made in the United States in that the Canadian data are not only for titles, but for volumes too. On the other hand, they may be less suitable for studying the growth of the collections, because the shelflist counts at different libraries were not made at the same time but over several years. Two reports were published: *Research Collections in Canadian Libraries, Part I: Universities* (Ottawa: National Library of Canada, 1972-74) in six volumes, and *Research Collections in Canadian Libraries, Part 2: Special Studies* (Ottawa: National Library of Canada, 1973-74) in two volumes.

STUDIES OF THE ECONOMICS OF ACADEMIC LIBRARIES

A lament about the scarcity of library statistics would not be fair if it failed to pay due respect to the study by William Baumol and Matityahu Marcus.[3]  This was chiefly an analysis of two sets of statistical data:  one of these sets had been collected by the Association of Research Libraries for a sample of libraries at 58 institutions (23 private and 35 public) for the two decades 1949 to 1969, the other had been collected by the National Center for Education Statistics of the Office of Education for a sample of 678 four-year colleges and universities in 1967-68.  The long series yielded longitudinal findings, the other set yielded findings for a cross-section of academic libraries grouped by size and by control.

The limitations of the data restricted the scope of the statistical analysis.  There was no information on the collections of books measured by the number of titles, no separation of holdings into book volumes and journal volumes, no separation of either acquisitions of or expenditures for books and for periodicals (or serials), no classification of holdings, acquisitions, or expenditures by subjects or subject groups.  The analysts cannot be criticized for these lacunae in library statistics; they cannot be expected to analyze non-existing data.  They were able to analyze the distribution of library expenditures among personnel cost, materials cost, and other expenditures, using regression analysis to find significant relationships among these magnitudes and some such independent variables as size of library, enrollment, and so forth.

All findings were, of course, for the two decades to which the data referred, but some of the numerical relationships were expected to have validity for the future.  Actual developments in the 1970's have seriously disappointed such expectations.  For example, the analysts found expenditures for library materials increased more rapidly than personnel costs; that the number of volumes added to the collections increased faster than the size of the library personnel; and that the "growth patterns" over the two decades were "highly stable" and surely "not totally unchangeable in the future."[4] Alas, as we shall see in the chapters to come, the picture changed significantly in  the years subsequent to those for

_____

[3]William J. Baumol and Matityahu Marcus (Mathematica, Inc.), *Economics of Academic Libraries* (Washington, D.C.: American Council on Education, 1973).
[4]*Ibid.*, pp. 7, 15, 71, 72, respectively.

which the analysts had been furnished statistical data. One of the lessons to be learned from the Baumol-Marcus study is that statistics are always past history and that numerical relationships estimated for the past need not remain valid in the future. Of course, this is not the only lesson to be learned from the *Economics of Academic Libraries*. The booklet points to many interesting issues on which librarians should be informed. Moreover, the authors duly warned of "critical financial issues" to be faced in the future.

Perhaps we ought to mention another analysis of library planning and operation, from which we hoped to gain useful insights when we saw the enticing title, *Systematic Analysis of University Libraries: An Application of Cost-Benefit Analysis to the M.I.T. Libraries.*[5] What we found in this analysis, however, was only about carrels, stacks and storage, lounges, reserve rooms, and catalogues, Xeroxing, duplicates and microforms. Little was said about books and journals, and nothing about the composition of holdings and acquisitions, about the subjects and types of knowledge which a library is committed to communicate to researchers, teachers, students, or other interested readers.

---

[5]By Jeffrey A. Raffel and Robert Shishko (Cambridge, Mass.: The M.I.T. Press, 1969).

CHAPTER 6.3

AN EXAMINATION OF THE
NATIONAL SHELFLIST COUNT


In Chapter 6.2 we presented a brief review of reports
which various library groups had published on measurements of
their holdings and acquisitions.  We described the techniques
of shelflist counts, expecially those developed and applied by
librarians collaborating on a "National Shelflist Count" under
the leadership of LeRoy D. Ortopan of the General Library,
University of California, Berkeley.  The impressive document
that emerged from this undertaking proved to be a rich source
of information pertinent to our research.  A few additional
commentaries of descriptive character will be added here; then
we shall produce abstracts of some of the most relevant tabulations; and finally we shall discuss what these data contribute to our own research objectives.


THE SCOPE OF THE SHELFLIST PROJECT

Besides the description of the technique of shelflist
counts, which was given in the earlier chapter, we ought to
offer here essential information about the National Shelflist
Count, especially the samples obtained, the subject breakdown
provided, the exclusions or omissions that proved unavoidable,
and the objectives of the project.


*The Samples*

In the first round (1973) of the Ortopan study (as we
shall call it for the sake of brevity) twenty libraries volun-
teered to participate.  Four of these classified their collections to a large part or entirely by the Dewey Decimal system and only one of them, Pennsylvania State University, "was

21

able to provide a detailed breakdown under each of the class-number equivalents in the Library of Congress classification."[1] The other three of the would-be participants had to be excluded, which left a sample of seventeen libraries. These were Cornell University, Indiana University, Ohio State University, Pennsylvania State University, Rice University, Rutgers—The State University (New Jersey), the University of California at Berkeley, Davis, Irvine, Los Angeles, Riverside, San Diego, Santa Barbara, and Santa Cruz, the University of Chicago, the University of Michigan, and the University of Wisconsin-Madison.

Nine additional libraries joined the study in its second round (1975): the Library of Congress, Michigan State University, the State University of New York at Binghamton, Buffalo, and Stony Brook, Syracuse University, the University of California at San Francisco, the University of Rochester, and the University of Texas at Austin.[2] This increased the sample to 26 libraries. In order to use the data of the 1975 survey for a measure of the growth of the collections, we shall use the 1975 data for the seventeen libraries that composed the 1973 sample. Because the collection of the Library of Congress is so much larger than any of the academic libraries in the sample of 26, we shall in our tables show the data for the Library of Congress separately. Thus we shall divide the sample of 26 into three parts: the Library of Congress, the other 25 libraries with data for 1975, and the 17 libraries for which also 1973 data are available. Size and composition of the collections can be shown for all three groups, separately as well as combined; growth and changes in composition over two years can be shown only for the group of 17.


*The Breakdown by Field*

The Ortopan Report shows the composition of the collections on which the participating libraries reported by a *summary breakdown* into 44 subject classes, designated by only one or two letters of the classification system of the Library of Congress (LC), and a *detailed breakdown* into 482 subject groups, designated by both letters and numbers of the LC system.

---

[1] *Titles Classified by the Library of Congress Classification: National Shelflist Count, 1975* (Berkeley: General Library, University of California, 1977), p. v.

[2] The University of Rochester was mistakenly omitted in the list on p. v of the Ortopan Report.

These breakdowns are largely compatible with the classification system that we had adopted for our research project. (We explained in Chapter 1.4 why we did not adopt the LC classification in its entirety: it differed not only from the systems used by many libraries, but especially from the subject classifications used by book publishers, wholesalers, various NSF reports, and the departmental organizations of universities.) Through some rearrangements we were able to fit the data of the Ortopan Report into our subject breakdown of 32 groups, with the following exceptions: our subject groups Physical Education (Code No. 18), Occupational Education (Code No. 19) and Education (Code No. 20) had to be merged in order to correspond to the LC class "Education" (L-LT); our subject group English Composition, Communications, Speech and Drama (Code No. 23) had to be omitted, with the eligible titles distributed among various parts of the LC class "General Literature" (PN); our subject group General, Adult (Code No. 28), of considerable importance in the classification systems of the book trade, had to be omitted, with eligible titles distributed over various LC classes, including History, Social Sciences, Literature, and others. Our group "Other" had to be omitted because every title in the catalogued collections had been entered into some LC class.

Thus, we managed to accommodate the 482 subject groups of the Ortopan study into a breakdown that corresponds to 27 of our 32 fields. In order to avoid losing much valuable information, we subdivided several of our fields into their most important components. For example, in our Table 6.3.2, we have 6 subdivisions of the Life Sciences, 4 of the Physical Sciences, 14 of Engineering, 13 of Language and Linguistics, 8 of Art and Art History, and so forth. Hence, the 27 fields of our classification are organized with the more detailed breakdown into 88 subdivisions.

## The Exclusions

The shelflist count does not include every title on the shelves of the reporting libraries. Exclusions were inevitable for several reasons, the most important of which are the following:

1. Libraries often have large stacks of uncatalogued materials.
2. They have parts of their collections catalogued by systems other than LC and could not undertake to convert all their holdings into the detailed breakdown of LC subject groups.

3. They have backlogs of unprocessed materials.
4. They may not have catalogued the separate titles of monographs that form parts of a series.
5. They may not have catalogued pamphlets (usually defined as soft-cover booklets of less than 60 pages).
6. They may not have counted serial titles (though the respondents were asked to report both titles and volumes of periodicals, and whether or not their holdings of listed periodicals were complete). But, according to the director of the project, "no effort has been made in this study to count serial titles in the reporting libraries" (p. xiv).

As a result, "the main report . . . excludes title counts for many substantial collections, such as microform, sound recordings, pamphlets, manuscripts, and maps, unless these materials are classified by the Library of Congress classification and included in the shelflists measured" (*ibid.*).

The participating libraries were asked to provide "information about inclusions, omissions, or local shelflisting practices." To supply examples of "reported exclusions we may note that the University of California, Berkeley, excluded 36,151,703 manuscripts, 234,181 maps, and 833,552 pamphlets from the count of its library holdings (*ibid.*, p.xxxix); that the University of Texas at Austin reported only 291,809 titles classified by the LC system, omitting thereby the bulk of its collection, namely, 928,967 titles classified in Dewey; and that several of the participating libraries omitted the holdings of their Law Libraries and Medical Libraries, again because they were not classified in LC.

## *The Objectives*

Regarding any major research project requiring huge statistical labors and producing reams of statistical data, some critics are apt to question the usefulness of the undertaking to the participants, the sponsors, or the public. Since such criticisms may be leveled against the Ortopan study, we wish to give it our strong endorsement and to express our appreciation and respect for all who contributed to its success. The effort at periodic stock-taking should be continued, with the particpation of many more libraries, at least until electronic recording systems, continuously keeping track of all accretions to the libraries, are in place.

Instead of formulating our appraisal of the project and its merits, we may reproduce here Mr. Ortopan's own description of the objectives of the program he has directed:

"A primary objective of this report is to
provide information about the distribution
of holdings among research libraries.
It fulfills another objective for those
libraries which participated in the 1973
study by showing the areas of growth within the classified collections, providing
the collection development or subject
specialist with a tool for studying patterns of growth and a means of evaluating
collection growth in the various subject
areas.
Each library fulfills its own needs first,
and within large institutions this often
consists of satisfying a variety of demands which are often conflicing.  In-
structional needs must be met without over-
looking the long-range objectives of developing and maintaining adequate research
collections in the various subject areas.
Cooperation between institutions is becom-
ing an essential part of this effort,
whether or not they are organizationally
or geographically bound.  In this respect,
it is important to understand one's own
strengths as well as those of one's associates.  While direct comparison between
libraries is difficult, if not impossible,
in recognizing the existence of other collections in areas where a library is strong
or weak, and assessing the growth rates
of those collections, a library may derive
more benefit from the utilization of its
acquisition funds.
This report is intended as a means for ac-
complishing that purpose.  It represents
the initial step in an effort to supply
data on the distribution of research library collections by subject, with the long-
range goal of developing a coordinated
national program of collection and collecting evaluation.  Achievement of this objective will insure the continuing development of resources which reflect the needs
of the library patron, both in areas of
current acquisitions and in new fields as
they evolve." (p. xv).

## ABSTRACTS OF SUMMARY TABLES

The Ortopan Report has almost 600 pages of statistical data. It goes without saying that the two tables which we shall produce here cannot do justice to the colossal amount of labor embodied in the Report. Yet, they will distill the information we deem most important for our purposes.

### Breakdown by 27 Fields

In the "summary" produced in Table 6.3.1 we present the breakdown of the reported titles by 27 fields corresponding to the classification scheme adopted for our survey and explained in Chapter 1.4. The table records the number of titles in the reported parts of the 1975 collections by (1) 26 libraries, (2) the Library of Congress, (3) the 25 libraries without the Library of Congress, (4) the 17 libraries for which also counts of their 1973 collections were available. In the remaining columns the table shows (5) the number of titles these 17 libraries held in 1973, (6) the increases in their holdings between 1973 and 1975 in absolute numbers, and (7) the same increases in per cent of their 1973 holdings.

In each of the first six columns the distribution of titles among the fields is shown also by its percentage share in the total. This allows quick comparisons: for example, the composition of the 1975 holdings of the 25 university libraries shown in column (3) can be easily compared with that of the Library of Congress in column (2); or the composition of the 1975 holdings of the 17 university libraries shown in column (4) can be readily compared with that of their 1973 holdings in column (5); and the composition of the new acquisitions between 1973 and 1975 can be compared with that of any of the holdings shown in the first five columns.

### The Library of Congress and 25 University Libraries

Let us begin with a comparison of the composition of the 1975 holdings by 25 university libraries with that of the collection of the Library of Congress. We shall not be deceived by the differences in the shares of titles in medicine and in law, because these shares are largely affected by the cataloguing systems in the medical and law libraries of the participating universities, that is, whether the librarians concerned had or had not taken the time for converting their classification systems into the LC system. (It happens that

26

TABLE 6.3.1  Shelflist Count of Titles, by 27 Fields in the Ortopan Samples of 26 and 17 Libraries, 1973 and 1975

| Our code | Field | 26 Libraries 1975 | Per cent of total | Library of Congress 1975 | Per cent of total | 25 Libraries 1975 | Per cent of total | 17 Libraries 1975 | Per cent of total | 17 Libraries 1973 | Per cent of total | 17 Libraries increase 1973-1975 | Per cent of total | 17 Libraries per cent increase 1973-1975 |
|---|---|---|---|---|---|---|---|---|---|---|---|---|---|---|
| 01 | Life sciences | 715,934 | 3.1 | 115,516 | 2.4 | 600,418 | 3.3 | 501,616 | 3.3 | 464,034 | 3.4 | 47,582 | 2.6 | 10.5 |
| 02 | Physical sciences | 786,345 | 3.4 | 146,448 | 3.0 | 638,897 | 3.5 | 521,239 | 3.5 | 470,771 | 3.5 | 50,468 | 2.7 | 10.7 |
| 03 | Environmental science and technology | 49,715 | 0.2 | 12,969 | 0.3 | 36,746 | 0.2 | 30,547 | 0.2 | 22,405 | 0.2 | 8,142 | 0.4 | 36.3 |
| 04 | Mathematics | 372,929 | 1.5 | 47,295 | 1.0 | 325,634 | 1.8 | 242,070 | 1.6 | 216,257 | 1.6 | 25,813 | 1.4 | 11.9 |
| 05 | Statistics | 68,439 | 0.3 | 16,311 | 0.3 | 52,128 | 0.3 | 43,550 | 0.3 | 38,809 | 0.3 | 4,741 | 0.3 | 12.2 |
| 06 | Engineering | 903,144 | 3.9 | 317,602 | 6.5 | 585,542 | 3.2 | 481,068 | 3.2 | 413,221 | 3.1 | 67,847 | 3.7 | 16.4 |
| 07 | Medical sciences | 692,333 | 3.0 | 131,176 | 2.7 | 561,157 | 3.0 | 457,413 | 3.0 | 343,072 | 2.6 | 114,341 | 6.2 | 33.3 |
| 08 | Other applied sciences and tool subjects | 1,322,676 | 5.7 | 340,171 | 6.9 | 982,505 | 5.3 | 827,394 | 5.5 | 730,017 | 5.5 | 97,377 | 5.3 | 13.3 |
| 09 | Psychology | 235,446 | 1.0 | 35,470 | 0.7 | 199,976 | 1.1 | 163,183 | 1.1 | 122,049 | 0.9 | 31,134 | 1.7 | 25.5 |
| 10 | Economics | 1,869,736 | 8.0 | 450,988 | 9.2 | 1,418,768 | 7.8 | 1,178,696 | 7.8 | 994,131 | 7.5 | 184,565 | 10.0 | 18.6 |
| 11 | Business administration | 180,490 | 0.8 | 41,755 | 0.9 | 138,735 | 0.8 | 108,686 | 0.7 | 100,660 | 0.8 | 8,026 | 0.4 | 8.0 |
| 12 | Political science | 746,749 | 3.2 | 161,549 | 3.3 | 585,200 | 3.3 | 490,865 | 3.2 | 432,189 | 3.2 | 58,676 | 3.2 | 13.6 |
| 13 | Law | 290,786 | 1.2 | 74,945 | 1.5 | 215,841 | 1.2 | 190,406 | 1.2 | 109,795 | 0.8 | 80,611 | 4.4 | 73.4 |
| 14 | Philosophy & religion | 1,433,683 | 6.1 | 306,449 | 6.1 | 1,127,234 | 6.1 | 950,050 | 6.1 | 862,673 | 6.5 | 87,377 | 4.8 | 10.1 |
| 15 | History & archaeology | 3,879,778 | 16.6 | 755,480 | 15.4 | 3,124,298 | 16.9 | 2,628,332 | 17.4 | 2,348,100 | 17.7 | 280,232 | 15.2 | 11.9 |
| 16 | Geography | 335,489 | 1.4 | 166,350 | 3.4 | 169,139 | 0.9 | 143,314 | 0.9 | 133,484 | 1.0 | 9,830 | 0.5 | 7.4 |
| 17 | Anthropology, sociology, urban studies | 926,217 | 4.0 | 161,531 | 3.3 | 764,686 | 4.2 | 619,099 | 4.1 | 515,953 | 3.9 | 103,146 | 5.6 | 20.0 |
| 18 19 20 | Education, including physical and occupational | 709,894 | 3.0 | 127,911 | 2.6 | 581,983 | 3.2 | 469,057 | 3.1 | 413,621 | 3.1 | 55,436 | 3.0 | 13.4 |
| 21 | Home economics | 96,810 | 0.4 | 36,222 | 0.7 | 59,588 | 0.3 | 50,653 | 0.3 | 48,779 | 0.4 | 1,874 | 0.1 | 3.8 |
| 22 | Language & linguistics | 1,579,853 | 6.8 | 327,483 | 6.7 | 1,251,370 | 6.8 | 1,071,752 | 6.8 | 923,203 | 7.1 | 148,549 | 8.1 | 16.1 |
| 24 | Literature, English and foreign, including drama | 3,573,748 | 16.3 | 481,649 | 9.8 | 3,092,099 | 16.8 | 2,493,560 | 16.5 | 2,289,318 | 17.2 | 204,242 | 11.1 | 8.9 |
| 25 | Music | 859,218 | 3.7 | 243,632 | 5.0 | 615,686 | 3.3 | 445,537 | 3.0 | 382,867 | 2.9 | 62,670 | 3.4 | 16.4 |
| 26 | Art and art history | 835,876 | 3.6 | 153,890 | 3.1 | 681,986 | 3.7 | 554,132 | 3.7 | 479,042 | 3.6 | 75,090 | 4.1 | 15.7 |
| 27 | Fiction | 138,013 | 0.6 | 40,859 | 0.8 | 97,154 | 0.5 | 69,507 | 0.5 | 59,359 | 0.4 | 10,148 | 0.6 | 17.1 |
| 29 | General, juvenile | 105,129 | 0.5 | 75,393 | 1.5 | 29,736 | 0.2 | 25,830 | 0.2 | 41,162 | 0.3 | -15,332 | (-0.8) | (-37.3) |
| 30 | Games and sports | 124,587 | 0.5 | 39,786 | 0.8 | 84,801 | 0.4 | 67,840 | 0.4 | 61,258 | 0.5 | 6,582 | 0.4 | 10.7 |
| 32 | Interdisciplinary | 483,361 | 2.1 | 100,595 | 2.0 | 382,756 | 2.0 | 325,905 | 2.2 | 296,710 | 2.2 | 29,195 | 1.6 | 9.8 |
| | Total | 23,313,366 | 100% | 4,909,405 | 100% | 18,403,961 | 100% | 15,141,300 | 100% | 13,302,839 | 100% | 1,838,361 | 100% | 13.8% |

Source: LeRoy D. Ortopan, Titles Classified by the Library of Congress Classification: National Shelflist Count (Catalog Department, University of California, Berkeley, 1973 and 1975).

the 25 academic libraries reported larger shares in medicine and smaller shares in law relative to those in the collection of the Library of Congress. These variances cancel each other and thus cannot affect the relative shares of all other fields.)

No one can be surprised that the academic libraries have relatively smaller collections in fields that play small roles, if any, in higher education and scholarly research. Thus, the shares of titles in Home Economics, Fiction, General Juvenile, and Games and Sports are smaller in the academic collections than in the Library of Congress. If we add the percentage shares of the holdings in these five fields, we find that the academic libraries hold only 1.4 per cent of their total collection as against 3.8 per cent held by the Library of Congress. At the opposite end of the distribution are fields in which academic teaching and research is most intensive. Thus, the shares of the Life Sciences, Physical Sciences, Mathematics, and Psychology are larger in the academic libraries than in the Library of Congress, the combined shares being 9.7 per cent in the 25 academic libraries but only 7.1 per cent in the Library of Congress.

On the other hand, the academic libraries report smaller shares in Economics, Business Administration, Political Science, and Geography, with a combined 12.7 per cent as against 16.8 per cent held by the Library of Congress. The largest portion of this difference is due to the holdings in Geography (0.9 per cent compared with 3.4 per cent), which may be explained not only by the relatively small role this field nowadays plays in most university curricula, but also by large numbers of maps which many academic libraries either do not possess or have not catalogued by the LC system. There are two fields that do much better, in terms of their relative shares in the total collection, in academic libraries than at the Library of Congress: Education (3.2 per cent as against 2.6 per cent) and Anthropology and Sociology (4.2 per cent as against 3.3 per cent). This may be a matter of multiple copies held at different locations of some university libraries; or it may be merely a coincidence, true just for the particular sample.

Some similarities in the relative shares of certain fields are quite remarkable: Philosophy and Religion (6.1 per cent in the 25 university libraries, 6.2 per cent at the Library of Congress), History and Archaeology (16.9 and 15.4), Language and Linguistics (6.8 and 6.7), Interdisciplinary (2.0 and 2.0). A disparity in the shares of Music and Art may strike us as odd: in Music the university libraries had a smaller share (3.3 against 5.0), but in Art their share was larger (3.7 against 3.1). The disparity may be a matter of art titles being catalogued by LC classes much more than titles in Music; an alternative reason may be that Music collections are often separated from the general university libraries and omitted from the shelflist count; or Art may play a greater role than Music in university teaching and research.


## Seventeen Libraries in 1973 and 1975

Comparing the composition of the holdings of the 17 academic libraries in 1975 and in 1973, we notice that there were no changes in relative shares in seven fields, increases by only 0.1 per cent in six fields, and decreases by only 0.1 per cent in seven fields. Of the remaining seven fields with changes by more than 0.1 per cent, four had their shares in the total increased and three had their shares reduced. The increased shares were those of Anthropology, Sociology and Urban Studies by 0.2 per cent, of Economics by 0.3 per cent, of Medical sciences by 0.4 per cent, and of Law by 0.5 per cent. The shares were reduced for Philosophy and Religion by 0.2 per cent, for History and Archaeology by 0.3 per cent, and Literature by 0.7 per cent. These changes seem to confirm the complaints of friends of the humanities about adverse discrimination in the recent acquisition policy of libraries.

The arithmetic of these changes can be checked in two ways: by comparing the relative shares of the acquisitions made in the two years between the two counts with relative shares in the holdings in 1973, and by comparing the percentage increases in the various fields with the percentage increase of the total collection. Thus, using the first way to check, we see that the share of Economics in the total increase of titles was 10.0 per cent, which is *much greater* than the 7.5 per cent which had been the share of Economics in the total holdings in 1973. Likewise, we see that the share of Literature in the total increase of titles was 11.1 per cent, which is *much less* than the 17.2 per cent which had been the share of Literature in the total holdings in 1973. Now, using the second way to check the finding, we notice that the holdings of titles in Economics increased from 1973 to 1975 by 18.6 per cent, which compares rather *favorably* with the total increase in the entire holdings of the libraries by 13.8 per cent. Likewise, we notice that the holdings in Literature increased in the two years by only 8.9 per cent, which compares quite *unfavorably* with the 13.8 by which the entire holdings of the libraries increased.

This second kind of comparison is the easiest method of separating the well-treated fields from the ill-treated ones. If the total holdings of the libraries increased by 13.8 per cent, this is the "average increase," which divides the privi-

29

leged from the underprivileged fields.  Among the latter we
find Home Economics at the bottom of the list with an increase
by only 3.8 per cent, followed by Geography with an increase
by 7.4 per cent and Business Administration, by 8.0 per cent.
Among the biggest gainers we find Law with an increase by 73.4
per cent followed by Environmental Science and Environmental
Technology with 36.3 per cent, Medicine with 33.3 per cent,
and Psychology with 25.5 per cent.  Whether these great differences in the rates of growth of the holdings in different
fields were the results of conscious policies of those in
charge of budgets and acquisitions in the academic libraries
cannot be seen from the statistical data.  Other types of
survey research are needed to answer this question.

Incidentally, we notice that the holdings of titles in
Juvenile Literature have been reduced by 37.3 per cent.  We
do not know whether these books were removed from the collection or only reclassified.

## A MORE DETAILED BREAKDOWN

Early in this chapter we mentioned that we had managed to
convert the detailed breakdown of the Ortopan tabulation, with
its 482 subject groups, into one that corresponds to 27 of
our 32 fields and into a more detailed one with 88 subdivisions.  We announced that Table 6.3.2 would present the data
from the participating libraries in these 88 subdivisions.  We
shall now briefly describe this table, and add some observations about what it can tell us.

### *Breakdown by 88 Subjects*

In the first column we show the LC code for the subject
or subject group, in some cases in a single letter (such as J
for Political Science or K for Law), but mostly in two letters
(such as QL for Zoology and PC for Romance Languages) and for
a few subjects in two letters plus numbers used in the LC subdivisions (such as HF 5001-6351 for Business Administration).
In the second column we show our own code number, the same
that was given for the 27 fields in Table 6.3.1.

The third column lists the subjects, first with their more
detailed designations and then, between horizontal lines,
their summation into the field according to our own classifi-

TABLE 6.8.2  Shelflist Count of Titles, by 88 Fields in the Octopus Samples of 36 and 17 Libraries, 1973 and 1975

| LC code | Our code | Subjects | 36 Libraries 1975 | Per cent of field total | Library of Congress 1975 | Per cent of field total | 36 Libraries 1973 | Per cent of field total | 17 Libraries 1975 | Per cent of field total | 17 Libraries 1973 | Per cent of field total | Librarian change 1973-1975 | Per cent of field total | 17 Libraries per cent change |
|---|---|---|---|---|---|---|---|---|---|---|---|---|---|---|---|
| QH | | Natural history | 171,812 | 24.0 | 25,843 | 22.4 | 145,969 | 24.3 | 117,437 | 22.9 | 106,879 | 22.5 | 10,558 | 22.2 | 10.0 |
| QK | | Botany | 139,705 | 19.5 | 23,333 | 20.2 | 116,312 | 19.4 | 99,741 | 19.9 | 90,670 | 20.0 | 9,071 | 19.1 | 10.0 |
| QL | | Zoology | 211,067 | 29.5 | 37,850 | 33.8 | 173,217 | 28.8 | 148,404 | 29.6 | 135,412 | 29.8 | 12,992 | 27.1 | 9.6 |
| QM | | Human anatomy | 16,389 | 3.5 | 4,945 | 4.3 | 20,434 | 3.4 | 17,612 | 3.6 | 15,791 | 3.6 | 1,921 | 3.9 | 11.5 |
| QP | | Physiology | 128,211 | 17.9 | 8,316 | 15.8 | 109,993 | 18.3 | 89,287 | 17.8 | 80,406 | 17.7 | 8,961 | 16.6 | 11.0 |
| QR | | Microbiology | 39,950 | 5.6 | 6,157 | 4.5 | 34,793 | 5.8 | 29,154 | 5.8 | 24,778 | 5.5 | 4,378 | 8.2 | 17.7 |
| | 01 | Life sciences | 715,934 | 100.0 | 115,516 | 100.0 | 600,418 | 100.0 | 501,815 | 100.0 | 454,034 | 100.0 | 47,581 | 100.0 | 10.5% |
| QB | | Astronomy | 86,795 | 11.1 | 17,315 | 11.8 | 69,480 | 10.9 | 59,386 | 11.4 | 53,012 | 11.0 | 7,273 | 14.4 | 14.0 |
| QC | | Physics | 296,818 | 37.8 | 61,708 | 35.3 | 245,110 | 38.4 | 193,013 | 37.0 | 183,040 | 38.9 | 9,973 | 19.8 | 6.5 |
| QD | | Chemistry | 203,707 | 26.0 | 35,376 | 24.2 | 168,331 | 26.2 | 133,647 | 25.6 | 123,839 | 26.1 | 10,008 | 21.4 | 8.8 |
| QE | | Geology | 198,025 | 25.2 | 43,049 | 28.7 | 155,976 | 24.4 | 136,394 | 26.0 | 113,880 | 24.0 | 22,414 | 44.4 | 19.9 |
| | 02 | Physical sciences | 786,345 | 100.0 | 146,449 | 100.0 | 638,897 | 100.0 | 531,239 | 100.0 | 470,771 | 100.0 | 50,468 | 100.0 | 10.7% |
| TD | 03 | Environmental technology | 49,718 | 100.0 | 13,969 | 100.0 | 36,748 | 100.0 | 30,547 | 100.0 | 22,405 | 100.0 | 8,142 | 100.0 | 26.3% |
| QA | 04 | Mathematics | 375,929 | 100.0 | 47,896 | 100.0 | 326,694 | 100.0 | 243,070 | 100.0 | 216,257 | 100.0 | 26,813 | 100.0 | 11.9% |
| BA | 05 | Statistics | 68,439 | 100.0 | 16,311 | 100.0 | 52,129 | 100.0 | 43,650 | 100.0 | 38,909 | 100.0 | 4,741 | 100.0 | 12.2% |
| T | | Technology general | 64,517 | 8.4 | 25,182 | 7.9 | 59,335 | 10.1 | 50,076 | 10.4 | 49,488 | 12.0 | 588 | 0.9 | 1.2 |
| TA | | Engineering general | 113,669 | 12.6 | 31,853 | 10.0 | 81,716 | 14.0 | 64,981 | 13.5 | 27,672 | 6.7 | 37,309 | 55.0 | 134.8 |
| TC | | Hydraulic engineering | 36,739 | 4.1 | 14,633 | 4.5 | 23,116 | 4.0 | 11,594 | 4.0 | 18,818 | 4.6 | 676 | 0.8 | 3.1 |
| TE | | Highway engineering | 13,648 | 1.5 | 6,719 | 1.8 | 7,959 | 1.4 | 6,970 | 1.4 | 6,648 | 1.6 | 332 | 0.5 | 4.8 |
| TF | | Railroad engineering | 17,137 | 1.9 | 9,666 | 2.7 | 6,521 | 1.5 | 7,704 | 1.8 | 7,346 | 1.8 | 358 | 0.5 | 4.9 |
| TG | | Bridge engineering | 10,354 | 1.1 | 3,084 | 1.0 | 7,350 | 1.2 | 6,330 | 1.3 | 8,030 | 1.9 | (-1,700) | (-2.5) | (-21.2) |
| TH | | Building construction | 39,663 | 4.4 | 18,638 | 5.9 | 20,937 | 3.6 | 17,541 | 3.6 | 15,804 | 3.8 | 1,737 | 2.6 | 11.0 |
| TJ | | Mechanical engineering | 75,738 | 8.4 | 28,639 | 9.0 | 47,097 | 8.0 | 39,378 | 8.2 | 33,412 | 8.1 | 5,966 | 8.6 | 17.5 |
| TK | | Electrical engineering | 120,822 | 14.5 | 41,290 | 13.0 | 89,532 | 15.3 | 70,087 | 14.6 | 62,660 | 16.2 | 7,377 | 10.9 | 11.8 |
| TL | | Motor vehicles, aeronautics, astronautics | 96,896 | 10.8 | 39,067 | 12.3 | 56,939 | 9.7 | 46,360 | 9.6 | 49,498 | 12.0 | 3,794 | 5.6 | 8.1 |
| TN | | Mining engineering | 100,191 | 11.1 | 37,677 | 11.9 | 62,514 | 10.7 | 53,700 | 11.2 | 54,601 | 13.3 | (-901) | (-1.3) | (-1.7) |
| TP | | Chemical technology | 87,090 | 9.6 | 27,808 | 8.8 | 59,282 | 10.1 | 49,950 | 10.3 | 43,203 | 10.6 | 6,747 | 9.5 | 13.3 |
| TR | | Photography | 30,702 | 3.4 | 7,793 | 2.5 | 23,613 | 3.9 | 17,744 | 3.7 | 14,505 | 3.5 | 3,239 | 4.8 | 22.3 |
| TS | | Manufactures | 67,060 | 7.4 | 27,669 | 8.7 | 39,491 | 6.7 | 31,613 | 6.6 | 28,278 | 6.9 | 3,335 | 5.2 | 12.5 |
| | 06 | Engineering | 903,144 | 100.0 | 317,602 | 100.0 | 585,543 | 100.0 | 481,068 | 100.0 | 413,221 | 100.0 | 67,847 | 100.0 | 16.4% |
| R-RZ | 07 | Medical sciences (medicine) | 698,333 | 100.0 | 131,176 | 100.0 | 567,157 | 100.0 | 467,413 | 100.0 | 343,072 | 100.0 | 124,341 | 100.0 | 36.3% |
| S | | Agriculture | 441,828 | 33.4 | 114,478 | 33.7 | 327,350 | 33.3 | 287,931 | 34.8 | 249,014 | 34.0 | 38,917 | 41.0 | 16.1 |
| Z | | Bibliography | 690,195 | 52.2 | 160,316 | 46.3 | 539,879 | 54.9 | 441,434 | 53.4 | 394,874 | 54.0 | 47,660 | 49.8 | 12.1 |
| U-V | | Military and naval sciences | 100,653 | 14.4 | 76,377 | 22.2 | 115,276 | 11.7 | 89,039 | 11.8 | 89,129 | 12.1 | 9,900 | 10.2 | 11.2 |
| | 08 | Other applied sciences and tool subjects | 1,388,676 | 100.0 | 340,171 | 100.0 | 982,505 | 100.0 | 827,394 | 100.0 | 730,017 | 100.0 | 97,377 | 100.0 | 13.3% |
| BF | 09 | Psychology | 235,446 | 100.0 | 35,470 | 100.0 | 199,976 | 100.0 | 163,183 | 100.0 | 132,049 | 100.0 | 31,134 | 100.0 | 25.5% |
| HB-HJ | 10 | Economics (excluding | 1,889,736 | 100.0 | 460,968 | 100.0 | 1,516,788 | 100.0 | 1,178,696 | 100.0 | 994,131 | 100.0 | 184,565 | 100.0 | 18.6% |
| HF 5001-6351 | 11 | Business administration | 180,490 | 100.0 | 41,765 | 100.0 | 138,735 | 100.0 | 108,696 | 100.0 | 100,660 | 100.0 | 8,036 | 100.0 | 8.0% |
| J | 12 | Political science | 746,749 | 100.0 | 161,449 | 100.0 | 585,300 | 100.0 | 490,865 | 100.0 | 482,189 | 100.0 | 58,676 | 100.0 | 8.0% |
| K | 13 | Law | 290,786 | 100.0 | 74,945 | 100.0 | 215,941 | 100.0 | 180,406 | 100.0 | 109,796 | 100.0 | 60,931 | 100.0 | 73.4% |
| B-BX | 14 | Philosophy and religion (excluding Psychology BF) | 1,423,683 | 100.0 | 306,449 | 100.0 | 1,127,234 | 100.0 | 960,060 | 100.0 | 869,673 | 100.0 | 97,377 | 100.0 | 10.1% |

Source: LeRoy D. Octopus, Titles Classified by the Library of Congress Classification: National Shelflist Count (Catalog Department, University of California, Berkeley, 1973 and 1975).

31

TABLE 6.3.3  Shelflist Count of Titles, by 88 Fields in the Ortopan Samples of 26 and 17 Libraries, 1973 and 1976
(Continued)

| LC code | Our code | Subjects | 26 Libraries 1975 | Per cent of field total | Library of Congress 1975 | Per cent of field total | 26 Libraries 1976 | Per cent of field total | 17 Libraries 1975 | Per cent of field total | 17 Libraries 1976 | Per cent of field total | 17 Libraries change 1973-1976 | Per cent of field total | 17 Libraries per cent change |
|---|---|---|---|---|---|---|---|---|---|---|---|---|---|---|---|
| C-CT | | Auxiliary sciences of history | 236,359 | 6.1 | 65,466 | 8.7 | 171,473 | 5.5 | 147,962 | 5.6 | 140,272 | 6.0 | 7,690 | 2.7 | 5.5 |
| D-DX | | History: general and old world | 2,373,338 | 61.2 | 469,505 | 62.1 | 1,903,833 | 60.0 | 1,577,413 | 60.0 | 1,441,027 | 61.4 | 136,386 | 48.7 | 9.5 |
| E-F | | History: American | 1,848,081 | 32.2 | 216,549 | 28.7 | 1,031,532 | 33.0 | 888,359 | 33.8 | 754,677 | 32.1 | 133,742 | 47.7 | 17.7 |
| GN 100-875 | | Prehistoric archaeology | 21,418 | 0.6 | 33,960 | 0.5 | 17,468 | 0.6 | 14,718 | 0.6 | 12,330 | 0.5 | 2,388 | 0.9 | 19.4 |
| | 15 | History & archaeology | 3,879,776 | 100.0 | 785,480 | 100.0 | 3,134,306 | 100.0 | 3,668,332 | 100.0 | 2,348,100 | 100.0 | 280,232 | 100.0 | 11.9 |
| | | *(per cent of total)* | *16.6%* | | *16.6%* | | *15.4%* | | *16.9%* | | *17.4%* | | *16.2%* | | |
| G | | Geography, general | 257,907 | 76.9 | 148,454 | 89.3 | 109,453 | 64.7 | 93,141 | 65.0 | 91,386 | 68.4 | 1,815 | 18.5 | 2.0 |
| GA | | Mathematical geography | 12,379 | 3.7 | 2,914 | 1.8 | 9,465 | 5.6 | 8,149 | 5.7 | 7,204 | 5.4 | 945 | 9.6 | 13.1 |
| GB | | Physical geography | 38,191 | 11.4 | 10,991 | 6.2 | 27,200 | 16.5 | 23,613 | 16.5 | 19,981 | 15.0 | 3,632 | 36.9 | 18.2 |
| GC | | Oceanography | 18,761 | 5.6 | 3,025 | 1.8 | 15,756 | 9.3 | 13,581 | 9.5 | 10,749 | 8.1 | 2,832 | 28.8 | 26.4 |
| GF | | Anthropogeography | 8,231 | 2.5 | 1,666 | 1.0 | 6,565 | 3.9 | 4,830 | 3.4 | 4,234 | 3.2 | 606 | 6.2 | 14.4 |
| | 16 | Geography | 335,469 | 100.0 | 166,350 | 100.0 | 169,139 | 100.0 | 143,314 | 100.0 | 133,484 | 100.0 | 9,830 | 100.0 | 7.4 |
| | | *(per cent of total)* | *1.4%* | | *1.4%* | | *0.8%* | | *0.9%* | | *1.0%* | | *0.5%* | | |
| GN | | Anthropology (excluding Prehistoric archaeology GN-100-875) | 80,896 | 8.8 | 8,986 | 5.6 | 71,910 | 9.4 | 68,873 | 9.4 | 60,761 | 9.8 | 7,612 | 7.3 | 14.8 |
| GR | | Folklore | 47,782 | 5.2 | 7,328 | 4.5 | 40,454 | 5.3 | 34,729 | 5.6 | 31,051 | 6.0 | 3,678 | 3.6 | 11.9 |
| GT | | Manners and customs | 21,544 | 2.4 | 4,493 | 2.8 | 18,051 | 2.4 | 14,866 | 2.4 | 12,368 | 2.4 | 2,498 | 2.4 | 20.2 |
| HM-HX | | Sociology | 774,995 | 83.7 | 140,724 | 87.1 | 634,271 | 82.9 | 511,941 | 82.6 | 481,783 | 81.7 | 89,458 | 86.7 | 21.2 |
| | 17 | Anthropology, sociology, urban studies | 925,217 | 100.0 | 161,531 | 100.0 | 764,686 | 100.0 | 619,099 | 100.0 | 815,963 | 100.0 | 103,146 | 100.0 | 20.0 |
| | | *(per cent of total)* | *4.0%* | | *3.4%* | | *3.5%* | | *4.2%* | | *4.1%* | | *3.9%* | | |
| L-LC, L8, L9 | 20 | Education (including physical education & occupational education & tional education) | 708,994 | 100.0 | 137,911 | 100.0 | 581,993 | 100.0 | 489,057 | 100.0 | 413,631 | 100.0 | 55,436 | 100.0 | 13.4 |
| | | *(per cent of total)* | *3.0%* | | *3.0%* | | *2.6%* | | *3.2%* | | *3.1%* | | *3.0%* | | |
| LT | | Handicrafts | 31,333 | 28.9 | 10,507 | 29.0 | 11,498 | 18.2 | 9,336 | 18.4 | 7,871 | 16.1 | 1,455 | 77.6 | 18.6 |
| TX | | Home economics | 73,877 | 77.1 | 25,715 | 71.0 | 48,162 | 80.1 | 41,427 | 81.6 | 40,908 | 83.9 | 419 | 22.4 | 1.0 |
| | 21 | Home economics | 95,810 | 100.0 | 36,222 | 100.0 | 59,589 | 100.0 | 50,853 | 100.0 | 48,779 | 100.0 | 1,874 | 100.0 | 3.8 |
| | | *(per cent of total)* | *0.4%* | | *0.7%* | | *0.3%* | | *0.3%* | | *0.4%* | | *0.1%* | | |
| P | | Philology and linguistics, general | 72,312 | 4.6 | 8,012 | 2.4 | 64,300 | 5.1 | 51,849 | 4.8 | 42,777 | 4.8 | 8,472 | 5.7 | 19.8 |
| PA | | Classical languages and literature | 257,843 | 16.3 | 42,098 | 12.9 | 215,745 | 17.2 | 182,860 | 17.0 | 169,168 | 18.3 | 13,492 | 9.1 | 8.0 |
| PB | | Modern European; Languages, general | 19,169 | 1.2 | 3,388 | 1.0 | 15,601 | 1.3 | 13,761 | 1.2 | 11,994 | 1.3 | 767 | 0.5 | 6.4 |
| PC | | Romance languages | 108,732 | 6.9 | 21,990 | 6.7 | 86,742 | 6.9 | 71,622 | 6.7 | 62,690 | 6.8 | 8,932 | 6.0 | 14.3 |
| PD | | Germanic languages | 26,001 | 1.6 | 3,257 | 1.0 | 22,744 | 1.8 | 19,977 | 1.9 | 17,121 | 1.9 | 2,856 | 1.9 | 16.7 |
| PE | | English | 88,788 | 5.6 | 20,679 | 6.3 | 69,109 | 5.4 | 54,375 | 5.1 | 47,695 | 5.2 | 6,680 | 4.5 | 14.0 |
| PF | | West Germanic | 46,195 | 2.9 | 7,538 | 2.3 | 38,657 | 3.1 | 31,933 | 3.0 | 27,080 | 2.9 | 4,853 | 3.3 | 17.9 |
| PG | | Slavic | 375,069 | 23.8 | 73,647 | 22.5 | 301,442 | 24.1 | 257,131 | 24.0 | 223,248 | 24.2 | 33,883 | 22.8 | 15.2 |
| PH | | Finno-Ugrian, Basque | 33,436 | 2.1 | 8,826 | 2.7 | 24,610 | 2.0 | 23,669 | 2.1 | 19,348 | 2.1 | 3,330 | 2.2 | 17.2 |
| PJ | | Oriental languages and literature; Indo-Iranian | 138,125 | 8.1 | 26,219 | 8.0 | 101,906 | 8.1 | 89,922 | 8.4 | 76,654 | 8.3 | 13,268 | 8.9 | 17.3 |
| PK | | Indo-Iranian | 171,877 | 10.8 | 45,114 | 13.8 | 126,763 | 10.1 | 111,703 | 10.4 | 91,224 | 9.9 | 20,479 | 13.8 | 22.5 |
| PL | | Languages and literature of Eastern Asia | 237,103 | 15.0 | 65,295 | 19.3 | 173,808 | 13.9 | 167,189 | 14.7 | 126,562 | 13.7 | 30,637 | 20.6 | 24.2 |
| PM | | American Indian languages | 14,113 | 0.9 | 3,439 | 1.1 | 10,674 | 0.9 | 8,572 | 0.8 | 7,662 | 0.8 | 910 | 0.6 | 11.9 |
| | 22 | Language and linguistics | 1,678,852 | 100.0 | 327,463 | 100.0 | 1,351,370 | 100.0 | 1,075,753 | 100.0 | 923,303 | 100.0 | 148,549 | 100.0 | 16.1 |
| | | *(per cent of total)* | *6.9%* | | *6.9%* | | *6.7%* | | *6.9%* | | *7.1%* | | *8.1%* | | |

Source: LeRoy D. Ortopan, Titles Classified by the Library of Congress Classification: National Shelflist Count (Catalog Department, University of California, Berkeley, 1973 and 1976).

32

TABLE 6.3.2 Shelflist Count of Titles, by 88 Fields in the Ortopom Samples of 26 and 17 Libraries, 1973 and 1975 (Continued)

| LC code | Our code | Subjects | 26 Libraries 1975 | Per cent of field total | Per cent of total | Library of Congress 1975 | Per cent of field total | Per cent of total | 25 Libraries 1975 | Per cent of field total | Per cent of total | 17 Libraries 1975 | Per cent of field total | Per cent of total | 17 Libraries 1973 | Per cent of field total | Per cent of total | 17 Libraries change 1973-1975 | Per cent of field total | Per cent of total | 17 Libraries per cent of total change |
|---|---|---|---|---|---|---|---|---|---|---|---|---|---|---|---|---|---|---|---|---|---|
| PN | | Literary history and collections | 446,459 | 12.5 | | 73,442 | 15.2 | | 373,017 | 12.1 | | 292,909 | 11.7 | | 261,087 | 11.4 | | 31,822 | 15.6 | | 12.2 |
| PQ | | Romance literatures | 1,085,872 | 30.4 | | 150,123 | 31.2 | | 935,749 | 30.3 | | 752,758 | 30.2 | | 662,449 | 28.9 | | 90,309 | 44.2 | | 13.6 |
| PR | | English literature | 911,796 | 25.5 | | 88,570 | 18.4 | | 823,226 | 26.6 | | 661,212 | 26.5 | | 644,374 | 28.1 | | 16,838 | 6.2 | | 2.6 |
| PS | | American literature | 612,034 | 17.1 | | 80,089 | 16.6 | | 531,945 | 17.2 | | 488,390 | 17.2 | | 395,330 | 17.3 | | 33,060 | 16.5 | | 8.4 |
| PT | | Germanic literature | 517,687 | 14.5 | | 89,435 | 18.6 | | 488,162 | 13.8 | | 368,391 | 14.4 | | 326,078 | 14.2 | | 32,213 | 15.8 | | 9.9 |
| | 24 | Literature | 3,573,748 | 100.0 | 16.3% | 481,649 | 100.0 | 9.5% | 3,092,099 | 100.0 | 16.5% | 2,493,560 | 100.0 | 16.5% | 2,289,318 | 100.0 | 17.2% | 204,242 | 100.0 | 11.1% | 8.9% |
| M | | Music | 441,785 | 51.4 | | 121,115 | 49.7 | | 320,670 | 52.1 | | 224,715 | 50.4 | | 184,562 | 48.2 | | 40,153 | 64.1 | | 21.8 |
| ML | | Literature of music | 317,847 | 37.0 | | 78,771 | 32.3 | | 239,076 | 38.8 | | 184,830 | 41.5 | | 162,287 | 42.4 | | 22,543 | 36.0 | | 13.9 |
| MT | | Music instruction & study | 99,586 | 11.6 | | 43,746 | 18.0 | | 55,840 | 9.1 | | 35,992 | 8.1 | | 36,018 | 9.4 | | (-26) | (-0.4) | | (-0.1) |
| | 25 | Music | 859,218 | 100.0 | 3.7% | 243,632 | 100.0 | 5.0% | 615,586 | 100.0 | 3.3% | 445,537 | 100.0 | 3.0% | 382,867 | 100.0 | 2.9% | 62,670 | 100.0 | 3.4% | 16.4% |
| N | | Visual arts | 229,932 | 27.5 | | 37,857 | 24.6 | | 192,075 | 28.2 | | 154,932 | 28.0 | | 132,787 | 27.7 | | 22,145 | 29.5 | | 16.7 |
| NA | | Architecture | 160,381 | 19.2 | | 28,272 | 18.4 | | 132,109 | 19.4 | | 112,227 | 20.3 | | 97,067 | 20.2 | | 15,160 | 20.2 | | 15.6 |
| NB | | Sculpture | 50,422 | 6.0 | | 8,110 | 5.3 | | 42,312 | 6.2 | | 34,539 | 6.2 | | 30,393 | 6.3 | | 4,146 | 5.5 | | 13.6 |
| NC | | Drawing, design | 55,478 | 6.6 | | 13,512 | 8.8 | | 41,966 | 6.2 | | 33,415 | 6.0 | | 28,268 | 5.9 | | 5,157 | 6.9 | | 18.3 |
| ND | | Painting | 206,916 | 24.8 | | 35,568 | 23.1 | | 171,348 | 25.1 | | 138,058 | 24.6 | | 119,587 | 25.0 | | 18,471 | 21.9 | | 13.7 |
| NE | | Print media | 37,126 | 4.4 | | 9,045 | 5.9 | | 28,081 | 4.1 | | 22,348 | 4.0 | | 19,021 | 4.0 | | 3,327 | 4.4 | | 17.5 |
| NK | | Decorative arts | 85,764 | 10.3 | | 19,486 | 12.7 | | 66,278 | 9.7 | | 54,729 | 9.9 | | 48,329 | 10.1 | | 6,400 | 8.5 | | 13.2 |
| NX | | Arts in general | 9,857 | 1.2 | | 2,040 | 1.3 | | 7,817 | 1.1 | | 5,984 | 1.1 | | 3,600 | 0.8 | | 2,284 | 3.0 | | 63.4 |
| | 26 | Art and art history | 835,876 | 100.0 | 3.6% | 163,890 | 100.0 | 3.3% | 681,986 | 100.0 | 3.7% | 564,132 | 100.0 | 3.7% | 479,042 | 100.0 | 3.6% | 75,090 | 100.0 | 4.1% | 15.7% |
| | 27 | Fiction | 138,013 | 100.0 | 0.6% | 40,859 | 100.0 | 0.8% | 97,154 | 100.0 | 0.5% | 69,507 | 100.0 | 0.5% | 59,359 | 100.0 | 0.4% | 10,148 | 100.0 | 0.6% | 17.1% |
| PZ 5-799 | 28 | General juvenile (juvenile literature) | 105,129 | 100.0 | 0.5% | 75,393 | 100.0 | 1.5% | 29,736 | 100.0 | 0.2% | 25,830 | 100.0 | 0.2% | 41,162 | 100.0 | 0.3% | (-15,332) | 100.0 | (-0.8%) | -37.3% |
| GV | 29 | Games and sports (recreation) | 124,687 | 100.0 | 0.5% | 39,786 | 100.0 | 0.8% | 84,801 | 100.0 | 0.8% | 67,840 | 100.0 | 0.4% | 61,258 | 100.0 | 0.5% | 6,582 | 100.0 | 0.4% | 10.7% |
| A-AZ | | General works | 289,120 | 55.7 | | 59,710 | 59.4 | | 209,410 | 54.7 | | 180,832 | 55.5 | | 166,637 | 56.2 | | 14,195 | 48.6 | | 8.5 |
| H | | Social science, general | 60,609 | 12.5 | | 9,058 | 9.0 | | 51,551 | 13.5 | | 44,083 | 13.5 | | 39,456 | 13.3 | | 4,627 | 15.8 | | 11.7 |
| Q | | Science, general | 153,632 | 31.8 | | 31,827 | 31.6 | | 121,795 | 31.8 | | 100,990 | 31.0 | | 90,617 | 30.5 | | 10,373 | 35.5 | | 11.5 |
| | 32 | Interdisciplinary | 463,361 | 100.0 | 2.1% | 100,595 | 100.0 | 2.0% | 382,766 | 100.0 | 2.0% | 325,905 | 100.0 | 2.0% | 296,710 | 100.0 | 2.2% | 29,195 | 100.0 | 1.6% | 9.8% |
| | | All fields | 23,313,366 | 100.0% | | 4,909,405 | 100.0% | | 18,403,961 | 100.0% | | 16,141,300 | 100.0% | | 13,302,939 | 100.0% | | 1,838,361 | 100.0% | | 13.8% |

Source: LeRoy D. Ortopom, Titles Classified by the Library of Congress Classification: National Shelflist Count (Catalog Department, University of California, Berkeley, 1973 and 1976).

cation. Not all fields are subdivided in this fashion; there are some where subdivisions would hardly increase our insights.

The remaining seven columns accommodate the data for the same samples, sub-samples, etc. that were summarized in Table 6.3.1; that is to say, for (1) the 26 libraries in 1975, (2) Library of Congress, 1975, (3) 25 libraries (without the Library of Congress), 1975, (4) 17 libraries, 1975, (5) 17 libraries, 1973, (6) 17 libraries, increase 1973-1975, (7) 17 libraries, per cent increase 1973-1975.

Next to each of the columns with the absolute numbers of titles (reported to be held in the collections) we show two figures indicating the percentage distribution among the subjects. The first of these columns gives the percentage share of each subject in the total number of titles in the particular *field*, the second gives the percentage share of the field in the *grand total*.

Most of this detailed information may not be of interest to the general observer of library services, but only to representatives of particular fields. Engineers, for example, may be interested in the relative shares of the 14 engineering subjects, and linguists may be interested in the distribution of the collections in their field among different languages and language groups. Some apparent disparities, however, among figures in different columns or different rows may be of interest even to outsiders. We shall illustrate this by a few observations.


*Natural Sciences and Engineering*

In the Life Sciences one may be curious to see how the more descriptive or taxonomic subjects compare with the more theoretical or experimental ones. If we put Natural History, Botany, Zoology, and Human Anatomy into the former category, and Physiology and Microbiology into the latter, we may point to the fact that the 25 university libraries had 24.1 per cent of their Life Sciences collections in Physiology and Microbiology, while the analogous share in the collection of the Library of Congress was only 20.3 per cent. Moreover, the collections of the university libraries in these two subjects seem to grow faster than those in the other category of subjects. Thus, if we compare the shares of the various subjects in the 1973 *holdings* of the 17 libraries and in their *increases* over the two years, we find that the shares in increases exceeded those of holdings in Physiology and Microbiology, but not in the more descriptive subjects. While the

34

collections in all Life Sciences together grew by 10.5 per
cent, the collection in Microbiology grew by 17.7 per cent
    In the Physical Sciences, we notice that the collections
of the 25 academic libraries, compared with the Library of
Congress, were relatively stronger in Physics and Chemistry,
and weaker in Astronomy and Geology.  On the other hand, the
17 libraries seem to be anxious to add to the collections in
which they were relatively weaker.  Thus, we see a remarkable
turnabout in the percentage shares of their 1973 holdings and
of their two-year increases:  the latter are now greater in
Astronomy and Geology.  The rate of increase was especially
high in Geology:  19.9 per cent, as against a 10.7 per cent
increase in all Physical Sciences together.
    In the field of Engineering the most striking figure is
the change in the holdings of titles in "Engineering, General."
The share of this subject in the total increase for the 17
libraries was no less than 55.0 per cent, which contrasts with
the low share of 6.7 per cent which this subject commanded of
the 1973 holdings.  The two-year rate of increase in "Engineering, General" was a whopping 134.8 per cent.  While we are
talking about Engineering, we may point to the anomaly of
absolute reductions in the holdings in two subjects, "Bridge
Engineering" and "Mining Engineering."  This could conceivably be a matter of reclassification or of accidental discrepancies in the shelflist count.
    The subdivisions of our field "Other Applied Sciences and
Tool Sciences" include Military and Naval Sciences.  We are
hardly surprised to see that the shares of these subjects in
the academic libraries are very much smaller than in the Library of Congress, 11.7 per cent compared with 22.2 per cent.


*Social Sciences and Humanities*

    A curious reader of the data on History and Archaeology
may be struck by the large acquisitions in Prehistoric
Archaeology.  While the absolute numbers in this subject are
quite small, it seems odd that the rate of increase between
1973 and 1975 was 19.4 per cent, compared with only 11.9 per
cent in all History and Archaeology together.
    We mentioned in the discussion of the breakdown by 27
fields that the holdings by academic libraries in the field
of Geography were so much smaller than those of the Library of
Congress.  Now that we see the data for five subdivisions of
Geography, we find some of the differences even more striking.
Thus, again comparing the academic libraries with the Library
of Congress, we notice that the former are weaker in "Geography, General," but stronger in such subjects as Mathemati-

cal Geography, Physical Geography, Oceanography, and Anthropogeography.  As far as acquisitions between 1973 and 1975 are concerned, the relative shares are especially high in Physical Geography and Oceanography, very much higher than in Human Geography.

In the field Anthropology, Sociology, and Urban Studies, we may comment on differences between the distribution of acquisitions and that of the 1973 holdings.  For example, the share in acquisitions was lower than that in holdings in Anthropology, but higher in Sociology.  This contributed to the order of magnitude in which these subjects are represented in the total.  The titles in Sociology are nine times as numerous as those in Anthropology.

In the vast field of Language and Linguistics, we find that in Classical Languages and Literature the academic libraries are relatively much stronger than the Library of Congress; but they are weaker in Indo-Iranian and Eastern-Asian Languages and Literature.  However, they seem to be trying to make up for this disparity in holdings:  the percentage increases in these two subject groups for the academic libraries for the period 1973-1975 were the highest observed in the entire field of Language and Linguistics.

The field of Art and Art History is broken down into eight subdivisions.  What strikes the eye is that the new acquisitions seem to be concentrated in "Arts in General."  The percentage increase in this line is shown as 63.4 per cent, while that for the entire group of Art and Art History is only 15.7 per cent.


CONCLUSIONS


Can any conclusions be drawn from what we have observed in the statistical comparisons based on the National Shelflist Count?  The one conclusion we may confidently draw is that interesting differences in the composition of collections between different groups of libraries and different years can be derived from the results of shelflist counts by subjects and subject groups.  But whether the same interesting differences can be assumed to hold for larger sectors of the population of libraries is an open question.  To be really informative of the national situation and national trends, the shelflist count would have to become really national or, at least, it would have to include many more of the large research libraries of the country.  To say this is not to criticize the undertaking.  It was a successful beginning and the organizers and participants deserve the gratitude of all who want information on the holdings and acquisitions of our libraries.

CHAPTER 6.4

DESCRIPTION OF OUR "SURVEY OF COLLECTION DEVELOPMENT"

As we reported in an early chapter, our efforts at obtaining data from libraries were expended chiefly in three
consecutive surveys:  (1) a questionnaire sent to the (then)
99 members of the Association of Research Libraries (ARL), designed to find out what kind of data would be readily available or obtainable at reasonable cost; (2) a questionnaire
sent to a selected sample of 778 libraries of all categories,
designed to obtain information on expenditures, book purchases, periodical purchases, collection assessment, etc.; and
(3) a request for detailed quantitative data to a small number
of libraries that had indicated that such data (on expenditures,
holdings and acquisitions) classified by subject groups would
be available.  Copies of the first and second questionnaire
can be found in the Appendix to Part Six, pp. 6.A.1 and 6.B.1.
In this chapter we shall furnish a description of the
second of these surveys, officially called "A Survey of Collection Development in Libraries" but colloquially referred to
as the "Pink Questionnaire Package."  This description will be
preceded by an account of the deliberations and negotiations
that had gone on for more than a year and influenced the design of the questionnaire in several ways.

THE PREPARATIONS

The story of this Survey is one of frustrations.  It
should be told, partly for the sake of the lessons one can
learn from it, partly for the explanations it can offer for
expressions of dissatisfaction by both respondents and researchers.

*Designing the Questionnaire*

From the 70 replies received in our first survey we had
learned that only very few libraries would be able to supply
the data really needed for our purposes:  dollar expenditures,
holdings and acquisitions of books, and holdings of and
changes in subscriptions to professional journals, all classified by field or subject group.  Questionnaires asking for
such information would be useless because an overwhelming
majority of the libraries did not have the kinds of records
required for answering the questions.  We had also learned
that in many libraries staff personnel is overburdened and
could not be expected to cooperate with researchers making undue demands on their time.

While we were working on questionnaire forms for a less
demanding survey of collection development we learned that
another group of researchers, under the direction of Dean
Bernard Fry of Indiana University, had just mailed questionnaires to several hundred libraries to collect information,
chiefly on journal subscriptions and related matters.  It
would be unwise, so we were told, to impose upon the librarians with another set of questionnaires.  The decision was for
us to wait for a year.  When we thought our time had come, we
learned that Dean Fry's group was planning to send another
questionnaire to the libraries of his sample and that in addition, King Research, Inc., the organization headed by Donald
King, was also about to send questionnaires to librarians.
Surely we must spare the librarians that triple threat.  We
should avoid their getting caught under the cross-fire of
three batteries of data-hungry troops bombarding these help-
less civilians with deadly questionnaires.  It was agreed that
the three task forces should combine their wits and produce a
single joint questionnaire.

This decision resulted in a series of meetings of the
data-seeking researchers, each trying to shape the joint
questionnaire in a way most favorable to his objectives, even
if this were to put the questions important to the other
groups out of focus, and if it meant duplication of some
questions in different sections of the questionnaire.  Each
group considered some of the questions of the other groups
misleading and/or superfluous ballast that should be discarded.  After some rounds of bickering, a spirit of concilia-
tion prevailed and the outline of a joint questionnaire package to be sent to the same libraries was agreed upon.

After all these labors, problems of timing arose.  We were
anxious to get on with the job without further delay.  Alas,
one of the allies in the joint enterprise was held up by funding problems — and the whole idea of the joint questionnaire
had to be given up.  There was not enough time to reformulate

"our" questions and to make "our" questionnaire optimal for our purposes. Thus the pink questionnaire package went out to the libraries scientifically selected by the researchers at King Research, Inc.


*Selecting the Sample*

The population of libraries in the United States (over 21,000 in 1976) can be stratified in several ways — by function, by ownership or affiliation, by size of budget, etc. The most customary grouping distinguishes (1) academic (over 3,000 in 1976), (2) public (8,300), (3) special (8,500), and (4) Federal (1,400) libraries. This nomenclature does not sound quite consistent, in as much as Federal libraries are surely public — if public means the opposite of private rather than the opposite of restricted, that is, publicly operated but not necessarily open to the public — and special libraries may be academic, public, or Federal. However, it is understood that customarily one means by public libraries chiefly the municipal (not Federal) libraries maintained for the benefit of local readers; that Federal libraries are, besides the Library of Congress, a number of collections maintained by various departments and agencies of the Federal government; and that special libraries are those serving particular "specialties" or particular interests but are neither academic, nor municpal, nor Federal.

The separate category "research libraries" cuts across the four types; most of them are academic libraries, in that they are part of the large universities, but some are public (such as the New York Public Library), some are special (such as the John Crerar Library in Chicago) and at least one is Federal (the Library of Congress). Our first thought was that we should be interested only in the research libraries, because they are the ones that bulk largely as buyers of professional books and journals and as providers of information services of the kind most pertinent to our research. It is chiefly the research library (academic, public, special, or Federal) that plays a crucial role in the dissemination of scientific-scholarly-intellectual knowledge. Hence, we thought, an inquiry limited to the (approximately 100) research libraries would give us the insights we were seeking.

We were disabused of this preconception. Library specialists and researchers convinced us that findings regarding the role of libraries in knowledge production could not reasonably be based on a sample that excludes all but the members of the ARL; we would have to go beyond these narrow confines. Moreover, while most libraries not qualifying as research librar-

39

ies may have small budgets for acquiring professional books and journals, they are so numerous that the combined total of their expenditures for materials of a scientific and scholarly nature may be so large that it cannot be omitted if a realistic picture of the situation is to be obtained. Our objection that small libraries usually have small personnel budgets and may not be equipped to tackle the completion of long questionnaires was overridden. We were persuaded that we needed a sample that included libraries of all four types and that only a scientifically selected random sample would be appropriate to our purposes.

*TABLE 6.4.1 Total Number of Libraries, by Type, Numbers Selected for Random Sample, Numbers of Responses, and Relative Response Rates, 1976-1977*

|  |  | (1)<br>Total<br>number | (2)<br>Number<br>in sample | (3)<br>Number<br>responding | (4)<br>Response<br>rate |
|---|---|---|---|---|---|
| 1. | Academic | 3,030 | 329 | 131 | 39.8% |
| 2. | Public | 8,310 | 243 | 64 | 26.3% |
| 3. | Special | 8,510 | 83 | 13 | 15.7% |
| 4. | Federal | 1,430 | 123 | 15 | 12.2% |
|  | Total | 21,280 | 778 | 223 | 28.7% |

*Sources: For columns (1) and (2) King Research, Inc. For columns (3) and (4) Machlup, Leeson, and Associates.*

Such a random sample was selected at considerable cost. It included, as we show in Table 6.4.1, 329 academic libraries, 243 public libraries, 83 special libraries, and 123 Federal libraries, altogether 778 libraries. Alas, its randomness was destroyed by the substantial differences in the response rates. Only 223 usable responses were received, 131 from academic libraries, 64 from public libraries, 13 from special libraries, and 15 from Federal libraries. The response rates were 39.8, 26.3, 15.7 and 12.2 per cent, respectively. Thus, the objectives of a scientifically selected random sample were largely frustrated. We should point to the superior

40

response on the part of research libraries. From the 105 members of the ARL 75 usable responses were received, which amounts to a response rate of 71.4 per cent.

This result taught us a lesson which we believe is of importance to research undertakings of many types and in many fields. We learned that the use of procedures designed to make research findings more accurate or more reliable may, by absorbing too large a part of the available resources, reduce the scope of the findings. In other words, prospective benefits should be compared with prospective costs. If the choice is between six most accurate findings and ten only approximate ones, it should be considered whether the increased accuracy of the six is worth the sacrifice of the other four approximate ones. We secured an opinion of a mathematical consultant, who furnished us with a paper "On the Economics of Statistical Sampling." The paper is included as a chapter of this Report in Part Eight and we commend it to the attention of fellow researchers working with statistical samples.

## THE QUESTIONNAIRE

The questionnaire, as sent to the 778 libraries in the sample, consists of the following five sections: I. Library Expenditures (4 pages), II. Book Purchases (7 pages), III. Periodical Purchases (6 pages), IV. Collection Assessment (1 page), and V. Availability of Automated Files (2 pages). Since each of the sections has an additional page or two with definitions and instructions, the entire package consists of 26 pages. Each section could be assigned to the appropriate member of the staff.

## *Definitions*

The three sections on expenditures and purchases had the same set of definitions of terms. We reproduce them here:

Book: All catalogued monographs and catalogued government documents. Excludes bound volumes of periodicals and newspapers, annuals, society journals, and proceedings.

Serial: An inclusive term for publications issued in successive parts bearing numerical or chronological designations and intended to be continued indefinitely. Includes periodicals, newspapers, annuals, society journals and proceedings.

Periodical: A serial publication usually published at regular or stated intervals over an indefinite period, each issue of which contains separate articles. Includes society journals, excludes newspapers, annuals, and proceedings.

Microform: Material that has been photographically reduced in size and which is too small to be read without magnification. Includes microfilm, microfiche, microcard and microtext.

Other Materials: Includes audio recordings, film strips, movies, slides, maps, charts, etc. Excludes books, serials and microforms.

Title: A bibliographic unit, whether issued in one or several volumes, reels, discs, slides or parts.

Volume: A physical unit that has been catalogued. Excludes microforms and "other materials."

Domestic Publication: Book or serial published in the United States.

Foreign Publication: Book or serial published outside the United States.

A few additional definitions were provided in connection with particular questions in some of the sections. They are not of sufficient importance to warrant reproduction here. One question was common to each of the five sections (No. 12 in Section I, No. 17 in Section II, No. 12 in Section III, No. 1 in Section IV, and No. 3 in Section V). It inquired about the number of organizational units with collections that were part of the library or "library system" and whether all of them, or how many of them, were included and which units were excluded from the coverage in the answers to the questionnaire.

*Questions on Library Expenditures*

In Section I, twelve questions on expenditures were asked. Question 1 requested a breakdown of total library expenditures in the years 1970 to 1976 into five items: (a) books, serials, microforms, and other materials, (b) salaries and wages, including fringe benefits, (c) binding, (d) plant operation and maintenance, (e) all other (supplies, equipment, etc.), and (f) total. Question 2 asked for a further breakdown of the expenditures for materials into five categories: (g) books, (h) periodicals, (i) other serials, (j) total serials, (k) microforms (of both books and serials), and (l) other materials. Question 3 asked how "numbered monographic serials" were treated in the preceding breakdown, that is, whether they were treated as books, periodicals, or other serials. Question 4 requested a breakdown of the expenditures for microforms into those of microform books and microform serials.

Question 5 was essentially about the age of the library; it asked for how many years the library had been regularly purchasing library materials. Question 6 asked for an estimate of the per cent of the library's book expenditures in 1976 for books published before 1970. Question 7 asked for an estimate of the per cent of the periodical expenditures in 1976 for back issues of periodicals, that is, for issues published prior to 1976.

Question 8 inquired whether the library experienced in 1976 "budget pressures which had an impact on [the library's] collection development and maintenance activities" and, if so, what kind of actions it took in response to those pressures. To facilitate answering the question, specific "actions" were listed for possible check marks; for example, "dropped duplicate subscriptions to periodicals," "dropped the only subscription to indexing/abstracting services," "purchased microform of periodical in lieu of original," "reallocated budget to periodicals at the expense of books," and so forth, with a total of 19 enumerated kinds of action, and some space for specifying other actions. As a sequel to this, Question 9 requested an indication of which of the cost-reducing actions taken in 1976 proved to be the most effective in reducing budget pressures.

Question 10 asked the librarians to "indicate for which years they can generate a breakdown of total materials expenditures by subject field" designated by a formal classification system, such as Dewey, LC or any other. (This was not a request for the actual breakdown, but only for an indication of the year or years for which such a breakdown *could* be obtained.) If the librarian could not generate such a subject breakdown according to a formal classification system, Question 11 asked whether they could provide any other kind of breakdown of expenditures for materials, for example, by academic division or by library department.


*Questions on Book Purchases*

In Section 2, 16 questions were asked on the library's purchases of books. Question 1 related to "book collection trends" by requesting data, possibly from 1970 to 1976, on holdings and acquisitions of books. The question distinguished between the total number of (a) book *volumes* and (b) book *titles*; likewise, the number of book volumes added and the number of book titles added, with a possible separation of acquisition through purchase and through gift and exchange.

Question 2 asked for an estimate of the per cent of total *expenditures* for books in 1976 that went for the purchase of volumes published outside the United States. Question 3 asked the analogous question for the total number of book *volumes*.

Question 4 was an attempt at getting some approximation to a breakdown of book volumes by subject matter (a) for the 1976 holdings and (b) for the 1976 acquisitions. The breakdown was not by any of the customary detailed classifications, but only by rather broad subject groups such as Natural Sciences, Engineering and Technology, Social Sciences, Humanities, Law, etc. Question 5 attempted to get information on "Changes in Book-Buying Patterns by Subject, 1970-1976." The answers did not require any sophisticated measuring procedures, but merely a rough comparison of general buying patterns in 1976 with those in 1970, expressed through circling for each subject one of six numbers, (1) meaning "buying significantly more," (2) "buying slightly more," (3) "no change," (4) "buying slightly less," (5) "buying significantly less," (6) "not applicable." There were 36 subjects listed, with several additional ones provided in the form to be specified by the respondent.

In Question 6 we asked the librarians to select and rank the three subjects for which they were buying significantly more and the three subjects for which they were buying significantly less than in the past. Thus, the question would add to the information obtained from the preceding one. Question 7 in turn enlarged on Question 6 by inquiring into the reasons for the changes in book-buying patterns that were ranked as significant in Question 6. Twelve possible reasons were suggested for buying more or buying fewer books in four of the subjects singled out in Question 6; and space for additional reasons was provided in the form.

Question 8 aimed at a rather different kind of information, namely, it asked for an estimate of the percentages of books acquired in 1976 that were published by (a) commercial publishers, (b) university presses, (c) societies and associations, (d) federal and state governments, and (e) others. Question 9 asked for estimates of the per cent of books purchased from different distributors, that is, directly from the publisher, through wholesalers, book stores, etc. Question 10 asked whether the library was purchasing books by advance-selection procedures such as approval plans or standing orders (blanket orders). Question 11 attempted to enlarge on this information by asking for estimates of the per cent of domestic book purchases made through such purchasing plans (as compared with ordering individual titles, individually selected). Question 12 asked for the analogous estimates for books pub-

lished abroad.  In Question 13 the librarian was asked to name
the wholesaler or wholesalers who handle his approval plans.
Question 14 was related to the preceding one in that it asked
to name the wholesalers who had handled such approval plans
for the library in the past, with plans discontinued during
the last five years.

The next two questions attempted to inquire into the capacity of the library to generate a *breakdown by subject* of the
number of *book volumes added* during any or all years between
1970 and 1976, where the subject breakdown could be in Dewey,
LC, or any other classification system.  For libraries that
could not obtain any such breakdown by subject classes, Question 16 suggested an alternative, in that it asked librarians
whether they could supply information on the book volumes
added broken down by academic division, library department, or
any other kind of departmentalization that could serve as a
substitute for the customary type of classification.


## Questions on Periodical Purchases

The section on periodicals contained only 11 substantive
questions, most of which were analogous to the questions on
books of the previous section.  Thus, Question 1 on "periodical
collection trends" asked for data on periodical subscriptions
for the period 1970-1976.  It distinguished between (a) the
number of *subscriptions* and (b) the number of *periodical titles*
excluding duplicate copies.  The next two columns ask for (c)
the number of subscriptions cancelled, and (d) the number of
periodical titles cancelled.  Further columns invited information on the number of subscriptions and periodical titles added in each of the years.  Question 2 asked for an estimate of
the percentage of total expenditures for periodicals in 1976
that went for subscriptions of periodicals published abroad.
Question 3 asked the analogous question, not in terms of expenditures, but in terms of numbers of subscriptions.

Our attempt at getting a breakdown by subjects was pro-
moted by Question 4, which asked the librarian to estimate for
the periodical subscriptions effective in 1976 a percentage
breakdown into broad subject classes.  The proposed breakdown
was the same as in Question 4 of the section on books.  Question 5 did for periodical subscriptions what Question 5 in the
previous section had done for books, that is, to ask for a
circling of numbers that would indicate the degree to which
the number of subscriptions in each of some 36 subjects had
changed significantly or slightly.  Question 6 asked for a
statement of the most significant changes in subscriptions by
singling out and ranking the three subjects in which acquisi-

45

tions of periodicals were most significantly increased or reduced. Question 7, fully analogous to what was asked about
books, inquired into the reasons for changes in subscriptions
in the subjects most significantly affected.

Question 8 inquired about the types of publishers of the
domestic periodicals to which the library had subscriptions in
1976, to wit (a) commercial publishers, (b) university presses, (c) societies and associations, (d) governments, and (e)
other publishers. Question 9 asked whether these subscriptions were directly with the publisher or through an inter-
mediary.

Question 10 inquired into the capacity of the library to
generate a breakdown of the number of periodical titles newly
subscribed to in any or all of the years since 1970, where the
breakdown should be by one of the customary classification
systems such as Dewey, LC, etc. For libraries that could not
provide such a classification, Question 11 suggested alternative breakdowns, such as by academic division or library department, and asked for what years this could be made available.

## Questions on Collection Assessment

Only a single substantive question was asked to obtain the
librarians's assessment of the collection level in some 36
subjects. For each of the subjects the librarian was requested
to circle one of six possible symbols: (1) standing for "comprehensive (virtually exhaustive)," (2) for "research level,"
(3) for "study level," (4) for "basic level," (5) for "minimal
level," and (6) for "not applicable."

A set of definitions was supplied for each of these designations.

## Questions on Availability of Automated Files

Question 1 asked whether the library used, on a regular
basis, automated systems for (a) ordering books, (b) ordering
serials, (c) cooperative cataloguing, (d) circulation, (e)
accounting controls, (f) inventory controls (for example,
an automated shelflist). In each case, we asked for the first
year in which the system was in operation.

Question 2 asked whether any of eleven lists could be
generated from data kept in machine-readable form. Included
were such lists as book titles by date of publication with the
number of times circulated, new book titles acquired (by sub-

ject), current serial titles (by subject), all book titles in the collection (by subject), circulation by type of borrower, etc. For each such list we asked also for the earliest year for which the data would be obtainable.

## RESPONSES

The response rates to the different questions varied substantially from library to library. As we said early in this chapter, of the 778 libraries selected for the random sample, only 223 usable responses were received; but there were not many questions that were answered by all 223 respondents. Although some questions were answered by as many as 211 libraries, there were also some questions answered by as few as five.

Our report on the findings from the data received and analyzed will not be presented in exactly the order in which the question appeared in the questionnaire. Instead, we shall present our analysis in a way that will combine the findings with an examination of information obtained from different segments of our own research as well as data from other sources.

CHAPTER 6.5

LIBRARY EXPENDITURES

     As in most parts of our survey and analysis, the problem
of a trade-off between the size of the sample and the amount
of information (number of observations) was very much in
evidence in our inquiry into library expenditures.  If we were
to insist on reporting the data supplied by the <u>same</u> group of
libraries in response to <u>all</u> our questions on expenditures,
the sample would consist of only a handful of libraries.
Virtually none of our respondents, for example, had separate
data on their expenditures for microforms, let alone, on the
breakdown of these expenditures by microform books and microform serials.  The most sensible thing to do in these circumstances was to insist neither on the sameness of the sample
for different questions nor on completeness in coverage.  Instead, wherever questions or subquestions made sense independent of other questions or subquestions we tried to use most
of the replies we got, even if this meant 206 respondents in
one instance, 157 in another, and 119 in the case of the statistic on total expenditures broken down by only some of the
categories we had distinguished in our questionnaire for
separate reporting.

EXPENDITURE STATISTICS

     Before we discuss the expenditure statistics compiled from
the answers received, we have a few comments to offer regarding the sample into which the libraries sorted themselves by
supplying usable data.

From the replies by 119 libraries to our Question I-2, we found that in 1976 these libraries together spent $61,782,000 for materials. Of this total 47.3 per cent was for books, 46.3 per cent for serials, and 6.4 per cent for other materials. Average expenditure for all materials was $519,176 per library.

The group, that is, the responding portion of the selected sample (119 out of 778), was composed of 74 academic libraries, 37 public libraries, 2 special libraries, and 6 Federal libraries. The data from the academic libraries overwhelm those from the other three types. In order to convey an idea of the relative influence of the inclusion of the other types of libraries we show in Table 6.5.1 a breakdown of the 1976 expenditures for books and for serials by the four types. ("Other Materials" are not included in this breakdown.)

The combined expenditures of all 119 libraries for books and serials together were $57,855,000; the 74 academic libraries accounted for $49,678,000, or 85.9 per cent. They accounted for 79.7 per cent of the total expenditures for books and for 92.1 per cent of the total for serials. The 37 public libraries accounted for 18.5 per cent of the total spent for books and for only 5.2 per cent of the total spent for serials. The special libraries and the Federal libraries made hardly any difference to the total purchases, the latter because there are only so few among the respondents, the former because of both their minimal representation and their small size. We may recall that the selected random sample had included 83 special libraries and 123 Federal libraries; but only two special libraries and six Federal libraries (2.4 and 4.9 per cent, respectively) complied with our request to report their expenditures for books and serials for all years, 1970-1976. If the few Federal libraries that did report are representative of their type —which we do not know — some important information has been missed, especially about expenditures for serials. This is suggested by the fact that the "average Federal library" in our small group of six spent as much as $123,733 for serials in 1976, or 51 per cent of what the "average library" in the sample of 119 spent for serials, but more than three times the amount spent by the "average public library."

In order to check whether the public libraries in our sample were typical of the entire population of public libraries we examined the statistics of "Public Library Acquisitions Expenditures" in the *Bowker Annual of Library and Booktrade Information, 1977.* According to this source, the 7,394 public libraries spent in 1976 $130,511,000 for books and $13,630,000 for serials, or 90.5 per cent for books and 9.5 per cent for

TABLE 6.5.1 Expenditures for Books and Serials by 119 Libraries,
Totals and Averages, by Type of Library, 1976
(In dollars and per cent)

| Types of library | Academic | Public | Special | Federal | Total |
|---|---|---|---|---|---|
| Number in sample | 74 | 37 | 2 | 6 | 119 |
| Spent for books | $23,299,000 | $5,394,500 | $2,600 | $529,000 | $29,225,100 |
| Spent for serials | $26,379,000 | $1,507,000 | $1,400 | $742,400 | $28,629,800 |
| Spent for books and serials | $49,678,000 | $6,901,500 | $4,000 | $1,271,400 | $57,854,900 |
| Per cent for books | 46.9% | 78.2% | 65.0% | 41.6% | 50.5% |
| Per cent for serials | 53.1% | 21.8% | 35.0% | 58.4% | 49.5% |
| Books per cent of $29,225,100 | 79.7% | 18.5% | 0.0% | 1.8% | 100.0% |
| Serials per cent of $28,629,100 | 92.1% | 5.2% | 0.0% | 2.6% | 100.0% |
| Both per cent of $57,854,900 | 85.9% | 11.9% | 0.0% | 2.2% | 100.0% |
| Spent for books, average per library | $314,851 | $145,797 | $1,319 | $ 88,167 | $245,589 |
| Spent for serials, average per library | $356,473 | $ 40,730 | $ 710 | $123,733 | $240,587 |
| Spent for both, average per library | $671,324 | $186,527 | $2,029 | $211,900 | $486,176 |

Source: Machlup, Leeson, and Associates.

serials. This compares with 78.2 per cent and 21.8 per cent shown for our 37 public libraries in Table 6.5.1. That the share of serials acquired by these members of our sample is more than twice that of the average public library in the nation is easily explained by the fact that our respondents are much larger libraries than the national average. The public libraries in our sample spent in 1976 $186,527 for books and serials on the average per library, while the average for all public libraries in the United States was only $19,494. Thus, "our" public libraries were almost ten times the size of the national average.

We must suppose that similar distortions, due mainly to uneven response rates by different types of libraries, may affect the findings derived from the data, especially concerning the breakdown of expenditures for library materials. But this cannot be helped and, with due warning, we shall proceed.

## *Total Expenditures of the 119*

Table 6.5.2 summarizes the data on total expenditures by the 119 libraries from 1970 to 1976, broken down into only three categories: for reading materials, for personnel, and for other things (such as supplies, binding, equipment, plant operation, etc.). In current dollars, total expenditures in-increased from year to year, and so did the expenditures for materials and personnel. The rates of increase, however, differed: thus, personnel expenditures increased by 65.4 per cent over the period, while materials expenditures increased by only 39.1 per cent (probably less than the prices of books and serials).

With the different rates of increase over the years, the relative shares of the three expenditure categories in the total changed. Expenditures for materials were 28.5 per cent of total expenditures in 1970, but only 25.3 per cent in 1976. The share of personnel expenditures increased from 59.3 to 62.6 per cent. Other expenditures were a rather stable percentage of the total.

## *Their Purchases of Materials*

In Table 6.5.3 we see how the expenditures for materials acquired by the 119 libraries were divided among books, serials, and other materials. We did not obtain adequate data for dividing the expenditures for serials into those for periodicals and other serials (such as daily or weekly newspapers, annuals, etc.); nor did we get a breakdown of expenditures for other materials into those for microforms, audiovisual, tapes, phonograph records, and other materials. Even the division

*TABLE 6.5.2 Expenditures for Materials, Personnel, and All Other, by 119 Libraries, 1970-1976*

| | Total expenditures | Books, serials, microforms and other materials | Per cent of total | Wages and salaries | Per cent of total | All other | Per cent of total |
|---|---|---|---|---|---|---|---|
| 1970 | 155,898,000 | 44,419,000 | 28.5 | 92,485,000 | 59.3 | 18,994,000 | 12.2 |
| 1971 | 167,163,000 | 44,572,000 | 26.7 | 101,611,000 | 60.8 | 20,981,000 | 12.5 |
| 1972 | 175,313,000 | 45,393,000 | 25.9 | 108,801,000 | 62.1 | 21,119,000 | 12.0 |
| 1973 | 188,455,000 | 48,381,000 | 25.7 | 116,395,000 | 61.8 | 23,679,000 | 12.5 |
| 1974 | 207,539,000 | 52,835,000 | 25.4 | 128,640,000 | 62.0 | 26,064,000 | 12.6 |
| 1975 | 228,363,000 | 56,311,000 | 24.7 | 141,844,000 | 62.1 | 30,208,000 | 13.2 |
| 1976 | 244,241,000 | 61,782,000 | 25.3 | 152,951,000 | 62.6 | 29,805,000 | 12.1 |
| Per cent change 1970-1976 | +56.7% | +39.7% | | +65.4% | | +55.4% | |

*Source: Machlup, Leeson, and Associates.*

53

TABLE 6.5.3  Expenditures for Books, Periodicals, and Other Materials, by 119 Libraries, 1970-1976

| | Total purchases | Books | Per cent of total | Serials | Per cent of total | Other materials | Per cent of total |
|---|---|---|---|---|---|---|---|
| 1970 | 44,419,000 | 28,007,000 | 63.1 | 14,236,000 | 32.0 | 2,176,000 | 4.9 |
| 1971 | 44,571,000 | 26,338,000 | 59.1 | 15,797,000 | 35.4 | 2,435,000 | 5.5 |
| 1972 | 45,393,000 | 25,669,000 | 56.6 | 17,434,000 | 38.4 | 2,290,000 | 5.0 |
| 1973 | 48,382,000 | 26,744,000 | 55.3 | 18,649,000 | 38.5 | 2,989,000 | 6.2 |
| 1974 | 52,835,000 | 27,388,000 | 51.8 | 22,333,000 | 42.3 | 3,114,000 | 5.9 |
| 1975 | 56,311,000 | 27,433,000 | 48.7 | 24,938,000 | 44.3 | 3,940,000 | 7.0 |
| 1976 | 61,782,000 | 29,225,000 | 47.3 | 28,631,000 | 46.3 | 3,926,000 | 6.4 |
| Per cent change 1970-1976 | +39.1% | +4.3% | | +101.1% | | +80.4% | |

Source: Machlup, Leeson, and Associates.

between books and serials is not quite reliable, because libraries follow different practices with regard to numbered monographic series. These are separate books on different topics written by different authors, but in the same general area, often with an editor or editorial committee in charge of selecting and refereeing the manuscripts. (Examples: Studies in Philology, Studies in Physical Anthropology, Essays in International Finance.) These monographic series are treated differently in the cataloguing and bookkeeping departments of different libraries. We asked in our questionnaire for an indication of the adopted practice, and learned from 101 libraries (all of which are included in our sample of 119) that six of them treated these publications as "periodicals," 21 as "other serials," while another 21 included them indiscriminately among total serials, and 53 catalogued and counted them as books.

Despite these obstacles to additivity and comparability, the breakdown into broad categories of expenditures for materials provides useful insights. Table 6.5.3 reveals a highly important development of the 1970-1976 period: the crowding-out of book purchases by the expansion and inflation of the budget for serials. The relative share of library expenditures for books fell year after year, from 63.1 per cent of total purchases of materials in 1970 to 47.3 per cent in 1976. The share of serials purchases, on the other hand, increased from 32.0 per cent in 1970 to 46.3 per cent. These drastic budget shifts were associated with the very different rates of increases in purchases over the period. Total purchases increased by 39.1 per cent; purchases of serials, however, increased by 101.1 per cent, purchases of "other materials" by 80.4 per cent, and purchases of books by only 4.3 per cent.

The doubling of expenditures for serials with almost a freezing of expenditures for books is such a trenchant course of action that it is hard to believe that it was the result of deliberate policy decisions. The ordering departments of the libraries may just have skidded into this long-term trend by a series of short-term decisions, thinking that they could temporarily postpone the purchase of books for the sake of uninterrupted subscriptions to ever more expensive journals deemed indispensable for teaching and research in the sciences, especially the natural sciences. Thus, the librarians financed the subscriptions to increased numbers of more expensive journals by cutting down their purchases of books. The expenditures for books were cut not only relatively and not only in real terms (that is, in the number of books acquired) but also in absolute terms of money. The dollar amounts spent for books were below the 1970 level in every year from 1971 to 1975.

To say that the dollar allocations to book purchases increased by only 4.3 per cent from 1970 to 1976, compared with an 101.1 per cent increase (more than a doubling) of the expenditures for serials, is to understate the discriminatory starving of the book collection, in that it disregards the even worse allocations in the intervening years. If we add the expenditures during the six years 1971-1976 — despite the risk of being misled by adding current dollars of declining purchasing power — we find that the aggregate six-year outlays were $162,797,000 for books and $127,782,000 for serials. The average annual dollar outlays for the period were $27,133,000 for books and $21,297,000 for serials. Compared with the expenditures in 1970 ($28,007,000 for books, $14,236,000 for serials) the average annual spending for books fell to 96.9 per cent of 1970's expenditures, while the average annual spending for serials rose to 149.6 per cent. Whether the gaps in the library collections of books will ever be filled is highly doubtful. What a library missed acquiring in a year or two can perhaps be made up in subsequent years. It is hard to believe, however, that libraries will be able to fill gaps resulting from underspending during six years (and probably more years, since the underallocations to book-buying have probably continued beyond 1976).

## A Sample of 75 Academic Libraries

The libraries in the sample of 119 were not subdivided according to the size of their budgets. We were interested, however, in possible differences in the allocation of funds by *libraries of different size*. Data received from 75 academic libraries allowed us to assemble them into budget strata, or size brackets of their total expenditure in 1976.

We decided to distinguish four brackets: (1) $4,000,000 or more, (2) $2,000,000 to $3,999,999, (3) $1,000,000 to $1,999,999, and (4) less than $1,000,000. The findings from such a stratification of the sample depend considerably on the choice of the dividing lines between the size brackets. In a first attempt we had, in imitation of other studies, chosen relatively small budgets for stratifying the sample, with the result that the top strata were overcrowded and the low strata underpopulated, which gave us misleading clues. The four size brackets now employed afford us a more reasonable distribution of the 75 libraries, with 15 in the highest stratum and 22 as the largest number of members in any of the strata.

Table 6.5.4 summarizes for the 75 libraries the data on total expenditures, broken down into expenditures for materials, wages and salaries, and other things. The absolute figures mean little — since they depend on the number and size of the respondents in each budget bracket — and are presented only because we do not want to withhold information. We might have divided them by the number of libraries included in the respective bracket, to obtain the expenditures of the average library in each stratum. Thus, for example, the 15 libraries in the top bracket had total expenditures of $55,753,000 in 1970 and, therefore, an average of $3,717,000 per library; and the 20 libraries in the lowest bracket had total expenditures of $4,564,000 and, therefore, an average of $228,200 per library.

What is really interesting in the data presented in Table 6.5.4 is the percentage distribution among purchases of materials and wages and salaries, and the changes in these relative shares for different size brackets and over the years. Thus we notice that the *largest and the smallest* libraries spent consistently a larger percentage of their total expenditures for wages and salaries than the medium-sized libraries did. This was true in every one of the seven years in the series. Students of economics may be exhilarated at this illustration of a U-shaped cost curve, exhibiting higher labor cost for the smallest and the largest producers of library services and lower cost for the (evidently "more efficient") producers of medium size. Yet we should warn against putting too much confidence in such mixed statistical data. Before drawing conclusions regarding the lowest-cost size, or optimal size, of an academic library, one would need a fine breakdown of the cost into such subdivisions as ordering departments, catalog departments, and all the rest.

Incidentally, we notice also that in 1970 the percentage spent for personnel was lower in the smallest libraries than for the largest (56.2 against 58.3 per cent) but the difference became smaller and smaller until it reversed itself; in 1976, the personnel cost in the smallest libraries absorbed a larger percentage of total expenditures than it did in the largest libraries (63.1 against 61.9 per cent). We shall presently come back to this observation.

In general, the 75 academic libraries had the same experience as the 119 libraries whose data were summarized in Table 6.5.2: the share of personnel expenditures increased for the first two or three years of the period, and remained relatively stable afterwards. The share of expenditures for materials declined from 1970 to 1975 from 32.8 to 28.4 per cent, and stood at 29.2 per cent in 1976. The changes in

57

TABLE 6.5.4 Expenditures for Materials, Personnel, and All Other by 75 Academic Libraries, Classified by Size of Total Expenditures, 1970-1976

| Year | Size brackets of libraries by total expenditures | Number of libraries | Total expenditures | Books, serials, microforms and other materials |
|------|--------------------------------------------------|---------------------|--------------------|-------------------------------------------------|
| 1970 | $4,000,000 or more | 15 | 55,753,000 | 17,003,000 |
| | $2,000,000 to $3,999,999 | 22 | 42,716,000 | 14,591,000 |
| | $1,000,000 to $1,999,999 | 18 | 14,664,000 | 5,205,000 |
| | Less than $1,000,000 | 20 | 4,564,000 | 1,758,000 |
| | All sizes | 75 | 117,697,000 | 38,557,000 |
| 1971 | $4,000,000 or more | 15 | 59,147,000 | 17,030,000 |
| | $2,000,000 to $3,999,999 | 22 | 44,075,000 | 14,340,000 |
| | $1,000,000 to $1,999,999 | 18 | 16,211,000 | 5,172,000 |
| | Less than $1,000,000 | 20 | 5,061,000 | 1,870,000 |
| | All sizes | 75 | 124,494,000 | 38,413,000 |
| 1972 | $4,000,000 or more | 15 | 61,416,000 | 16,197,000 |
| | $2,000,000 to $3,999,999 | 22 | 45,829,000 | 14,295,000 |
| | $1,000,000 to $1,999,999 | 18 | 17,643,000 | 6,125,000 |
| | Less than $1,000,000 | 20 | 5,741,000 | 2,103,000 |
| | All sizes | 75 | 130,629,000 | 38,720,000 |
| 1973 | $4,000,000 or more | 15 | 67,472,000 | 17,829,000 |
| | $2,000,000 to $3,999,999 | 22 | 47,786,000 | 15,007,000 |
| | $1,000,000 to $1,999,999 | 18 | 18,451,000 | 5,922,000 |
| | Less than $1,000,000 | 20 | 6,144,000 | 2,293,000 |
| | All sizes | 75 | 139,853,000 | 41,051,000 |
| 1974 | $4,000,000 or more | 15 | 74,359,000 | 19,526,000 |
| | $2,000,000 to $3,999,999 | 22 | 53,314,000 | 16,467,000 |
| | $1,000,000 to $1,999,999 | 18 | 20,301,000 | 6,705,000 |
| | Less than $1,000,000 | 20 | 6,711,000 | 2,338,000 |
| | All sizes | 75 | 154,685,000 | 45,036,000 |
| 1975 | $4,000,000 or more | 15 | 81,967,000 | 21,231,000 |
| | $2,000,000 to $3,999,999 | 22 | 57,708,000 | 17,410,000 |
| | $1,000,000 to $1,999,999 | 18 | 22,084,000 | 6,879,000 |
| | Less than $1,000,000 | 20 | 7,610,000 | 2,616,000 |
| | All sizes | 75 | 169,369,000 | 48,136,000 |
| 1976 | $4,000,000 or more | 15 | 86,919,000 | 22,892,000 |
| | $2,000,000 to $3,999,999 | 22 | 61,986,000 | 20,049,000 |
| | $1,000,000 to $1,999,999 | 18 | 24,539,000 | 7,407,000 |
| | Less than $1,000,000 | 20 | 7,938,000 | 2,631,000 |
| | All sizes | 75 | 181,382,000 | 52,979,000 |
| 1970-1976 per cent change | $4,000,000 or more | | +55.9% | +34.6% |
| | $2,000,000 to $3,999,999 | | +45.1% | +37.4% |
| | $1,000,000 to $1,999,999 | | +67.3% | +42.3% |
| | Less than $1,000,000 | | +73.9% | +49.7% |
| | All sizes | | +54.1% | +37.4% |

| Year | Per cent of total | Wages and salaries | Per cent of total | All others | Per cent of total | Total per cent |
|---|---|---|---|---|---|---|
| 1970 | 30.5 | 32,518,000 | 58.3 | 6,232,000 | 11.2 | 100 |
| | 34.2 | 23,184,000 | 54.2 | 4,941,400 | 11.6 | 100 |
| | 35.5 | 7,912,000 | 54.0 | 1,547,000 | 10.5 | 100 |
| | 38.5 | 2,563,000 | 56.2 | 243,000 | 5.3 | 100 |
| | 32.8 | 66,177,000 | 56.2 | 12,963,000 | 11.0 | 100 |
| 1971 | 28.8 | 35,706,000 | 60.4 | 6,411,000 | 10.8 | 100 |
| | 32.5 | 25,058,000 | 56.9 | 4,677,000 | 10.6 | 100 |
| | 31.9 | 9,278,000 | 57.2 | 1,761,000 | 10.9 | 100 |
| | 36.9 | 2,971,000 | 58.7 | 220,000 | 4.3 | 100 |
| | 30.9 | 73,013,000 | 58.6 | 13,069,000 | 10.5 | 100 |
| 1972 | 26.4 | 38,474,000 | 62.6 | 6,745,000 | 11.0 | 100 |
| | 31.2 | 26,488,000 | 57.8 | 5,046,000 | 11.0 | 100 |
| | 34.7 | 9,780,000 | 55.4 | 1,738,000 | 9.9 | 100 |
| | 36.7 | 8,400,000 | 59.2 | 238,000 | 4.1 | 100 |
| | 29.6 | 78,142,000 | 59.9 | 13,767,000 | 10.5 | 100 |
| 1973 | 26.4 | 41,495,000 | 61.5 | 8,148,000 | 12.1 | 100 |
| | 31.4 | 27,590,000 | 57.7 | 5,189,000 | 10.9 | 100 |
| | 32.1 | 10,668,000 | 57.8 | 1,861,000 | 10.1 | 100 |
| | 37.3 | 3,658,000 | 59.6 | 193,000 | 3.1 | 100 |
| | 29.4 | 83,411,000 | 59.6 | 15,391,000 | 11.0 | 100 |
| 1974 | 26.3 | 46,389,000 | 62.3 | 8,444,000 | 11.4 | 100 |
| | 30.9 | 30,361,000 | 56.9 | 6,486,000 | 12.2 | 100 |
| | 33.0 | 11,596,000 | 57.1 | 2,000,000 | 9.9 | 100 |
| | 34.8 | 4,168,000 | 62.1 | 205,000 | 3.1 | 100 |
| | 29.1 | 92,514,000 | 59.8 | 17,135,000 | 11.1 | 100 |
| 1975 | 25.9 | 50,762,000 | 61.9 | 9,974,000 | 12.2 | 100 |
| | 30.2 | 33,533,000 | 58.1 | 6,765,000 | 11.7 | 100 |
| | 31.1 | 13,036,000 | 59.1 | 2,169,000 | 9.8 | 100 |
| | 34.4 | 4,726,000 | 62.1 | 268,000 | 3.5 | 100 |
| | 28.4 | 102,057,000 | 60.3 | 19,176,000 | 11.3 | 100 |
| 1976 | 26.3 | 53,760,000 | 61.9 | 10,267,000 | 11.8 | 100 |
| | 32.3 | 36,064,000 | 58.2 | 5,873,000 | 9.5 | 100 |
| | 30.2 | 14,477,000 | 59.0 | 2,655,000 | 10.8 | 100 |
| | 33.1 | 5,008,000 | 63.1 | 299,000 | 3.8 | 100 |
| | 29.2 | 109,309,000 | 60.3 | 19,094,000 | 10.5 | 100 |
| | | +65.3% | | +64.7% | | |
| | | +55.6% | | +18.9% | | |
| | | +83.0% | | +71.6% | | |
| | | +95.4% | | +23.0% | | |
| | | +65.2% | | +47.3% | | |

Source: Machlup, Leeson, and Associates.

59

relative shares are reflections of the different rates of increase over the years. From 1970 to 1976, total expenditures by the 75 academic libraries increased by 54.1 per cent, expenditures for library materials increased by only 37.4 per cent (which is about the same as the increase in prices), while wages and salaries increased by 65.2 per cent, and other expenditures (for such things as binding, supplies, equipment, repairs, etc.) increased by 47.3 per cent. These rates of increase relate to the entire sample of 75 libraries, but we find large disparities if we break it down by size strata.

We see, for example, that the lowest stratum — the 20 academic libraries spending less than $1,000,000 in 1976 — increased total expenditures by 73.9 per cent over the 1970 level, compared with 55.9 per cent by the highest stratum and with only 45.1 per cent by the second stratum (that is, the 22 libraries spending between $2 and 4 million in 1976). The enlarged budgets of the smallest libraries allowed them to increase both the purchases of materials and the personnel expenditures by more than any of the larger libraries did. The smallest libraries increased their purchases of materials by 49.7 per cent (as against 34.6 per cent for the top stratum), and their expenditures for wages and salaries by 95.4 per cent (as against 65.3 per cent for the top stratum and 55.6 per cent by the second stratum). The increase — almost a doubling — of personnel expenditures by the smallest libraries explains the previously mentioned observation that the smallest libraries now spend the largest part of their budgets on personnel. (We have not looked into the question whether they increased their staffs or raised wages, but this information is available in the NCES publications.)

One may be puzzled by the uneven rates of increase in "all other expenditures" and by the large differences in the relative shares of these items in the total budgets. Thus, the 1970-1976 increase was only 23.0 per cent for the smallest libraries (compared with 71.6 per cent for the neighboring stratum) and the relative shares of "other expenditures" in total expenditures in 1976 was only 3.8 per cent (compared with 10.8 per cent for the neighboring stratum). A partial explanation, we suppose, may be that the smallest libraries are rarely housed in special buildings that require repairs, may not have much equipment and furnishing that require replacement, may not send books to binderies, and so forth. The small rate of increase in "other expenditures" by libraries in the second-highest stratum, 18.9 per cent from 1970 to 1976, is really puzzling. Since there had been an increase by 36.9 per cent from 1970 to 1975, we suspect that the sharp drop in "other expenditures" in 1976 may be traceable to a reporting error. We did not take the time to look for it.

Table 6.5.5 subdivides the expenditures for materials into those for books, serials, and other materials.  A look at the column "other materials" makes us wonder why, from 1971 (not in 1970) to 1976 the smaller libraries (with total expenditures less than $2 million) spent consistently much higher percentages of total materials purchases for these "other materials" than the larger libraries did.  This item includes audiovisual tapes, phonograph records and other nonprint materials, which are perhaps considered indispensable, or priority purchases, for libraries; this would explain the larger share they assume in the smaller budgets.

The column for serials reveals an interesting regularity for the relative shares which serials purchases by libraries of different size absorb of their total purchases.  In every one of the seven years, the largest libraries (in the top stratum) spent a lower percentage for serials than the libraries in the second stratum.  Our hypothesis is that the libraries in the budget bracket between $2 and 4 million regard their purchases of periodicals and other serials as so important that, under budget pressures, they stint much more on their book purchases than the largest libraries have to do.  In other words, with serials being accorded a higher priority than books, the libraries with the second-largest budgets spend higher percentages for serials (and lower percentages for books) than do the richest libraries, which can still afford to buy *some* more of the books they want.  The comparison of the second stratum with the third shows the opposite; we suppose that libraries in the third stratum cannot afford to maintain collections on a research level and hence do not aspire to subscribe to all the costly periodicals that the larger libraries regard as necessary.  Thus, the percentage spent on serials was consistently lower for the third stratum; indeed, except in 1973 and 1975, it was the lowest percentage of all four strata of libraries.  (The two exceptions are probably explained by extraordinarily large expenditures by the smallest libraries for "other materials," which evidently cut into the funds available for serials.)

We come last to the expenditures for books, because we strongly suspect that most libraries allocated to book acquisitions the funds that they had left over after they had met the "requirements" in the acquisition of serials and other materials.  This suspicion is strongly suggested by the increasing percentage shares of material purchases going to serials and declining percentage shares of the budget allocations to book purchases.  The share of serials purchases, for all 75 libraries together, increased year after year from 34.2 per cent in 1970 to 49.9 per cent in 1976; the share of book

61

TABLE 6.5.5  *Expenditures for Books, Serials, and Other Materials,*
*by 75 Academic Libraries, Classified by Size of Total Expenditures 1970-1976*

| Year | Size brackets of libraries by total expenditures | Number of libraries | Total purchases | Books |
|------|--------------------------------------------------|---------------------|-----------------|-------|
| 1970 | $4,000,000 or more | 15 | 17,003,000 | 10,945,000 |
| | $2,000,000 to $3,999,999 | 22 | 14,591,000 | 8,517,000 |
| | $1,000,000 to $1,999,999 | 18 | 5,205,000 | 3,186,000 |
| | Less than $1,000,000 | 20 | 1,758,000 | 1,079,000 |
| | All sizes | 75 | 38,557,000 | 23,727,000 |
| 1971 | $4,000,000 or more | 15 | 17,030,000 | 10,204,000 |
| | $2,000,000 to $3,999,999 | 22 | 14,340,000 | 7,483,000 |
| | $1,000,000 to $1,999,999 | 18 | 5,172,000 | 3,080,000 |
| | Less than $1,000,000 | 20 | 1,870,000 | 1,035,000 |
| | All sizes | 75 | 38,412,000 | 21,802,000 |
| 1972 | $4,000,000 or more | 15 | 16,197,000 | 8,876,000 |
| | $2,000,000 to $3,999,999 | 22 | 14,295,000 | 7,428,000 |
| | $1,000,000 to $1,999,999 | 18 | 6,125,000 | 3,599,000 |
| | Less than $1,000,000 | 20 | 2,103,000 | 1,087,000 |
| | All sizes | 75 | 38,720,000 | 20,990,000 |
| 1973 | $4,000,000 or more | 15 | 17,829,000 | 9,794,000 |
| | $2,000,000 to $3,999,999 | 22 | 15,007,000 | 7,405,000 |
| | $1,000,000 to $1,999,999 | 18 | 5,922,000 | 3,253,000 |
| | Less than $1,000,000 | 20 | 2,293,000 | 1,161,000 |
| | All sizes | 75 | 41,051,000 | 21,613,000 |
| 1974 | $4,000,000 or more | 15 | 19,526,000 | 10,265,000 |
| | $2,000,000 to $3,999,999 | 22 | 16,467,000 | 7,482,000 |
| | $1,000,000 to $1,999,999 | 18 | 6,705,000 | 3,352,000 |
| | Less than $1,000,000 | 20 | 2,338,000 | 1,089,000 |
| | All sizes | 75 | 45,036,000 | 22,188,000 |
| 1975 | $4,000,000 or more | 15 | 21,231,000 | 10,569,000 |
| | $2,000,000 to $3,999,999 | 22 | 17,410,000 | 7,202,000 |
| | $1,000,000 to $1,999,999 | 18 | 6,879,000 | 3,229,000 |
| | Less than $1,000,000 | 20 | 2,616,000 | 1,173,000 |
| | All sizes | 75 | 48,136,000 | 22,173,000 |
| 1976 | $4,000,000 or more | 15 | 22,892,000 | 10,805,000 |
| | $2,000,000 to $3,999,999 | 22 | 20,049,000 | 8,209,000 |
| | $1,000,000 to $1,999,999 | 18 | 7,407,000 | 3,290,000 |
| | Less than $1,000,000 | 20 | 2,631,000 | 1,163,000 |
| | All sizes | 75 | 52,979,000 | 23,467,000 |
| 1970-1976 | $4,000,000 or more | | +34.6% | -2.5% |
| per cent | $2,000,000 to $3,999,999 | | +37.4% | -3.6% |
| change | $1,000,000 to $1,999,999 | | +42.3% | +3.3% |
| | Less than $1,000,000 | | +49.7% | +7.8% |
| | All sizes | | +37.4% | -1.1% |

*(Table continued)*

| Year | Per cent of total | Serials | Per cent of total | Other materials | Per cent of total | Total per cent |
|------|------|------|------|------|------|------|
| 1970 | 64.4 | 5,683,000 | 33.4 | 375,000 | 2.2 | 100 |
|  | 58.4 | 5,280,000 | 36.2 | 794,000 | 5.4 | 100 |
|  | 61.2 | 1,603,000 | 30.8 | 416,000 | 8.0 | 100 |
|  | 61.4 | 624,000 | 35.5 | 55,000 | 3.1 | 100 |
|  | 61.5 | 13,190,000 | 34.2 | 1,640,000 | 4.3 | 100 |
| 1971 | 59.9 | 6,338,000 | 37.2 | 488,000 | 2.9 | 100 |
|  | 52.2 | 6,048,000 | 42.2 | 809,000 | 5.6 | 100 |
|  | 59.6 | 1,693,000 | 32.7 | 399,000 | 7.7 | 100 |
|  | 55.2 | 700,000 | 37.4 | 135,000 | 7.2 | 100 |
|  | 56.7 | 14,779,000 | 38.5 | 1,831,000 | 4.8 | 100 |
| 1972 | 54.8 | 6,866,000 | 42.4 | 455,000 | 2.8 | 100 |
|  | 52.0 | 6,441,000 | 45.0 | 426,000 | 3.0 | 100 |
|  | 58.8 | 2,110,000 | 34.4 | 416,000 | 6.8 | 100 |
|  | 51.6 | 855,000 | 40.7 | 161,000 | 7.7 | 100 |
|  | 54.2 | 16,272,000 | 42.0 | 1,458,000 | 3.8 | 100 |
| 1973 | 54.9 | 7,240,000 | 40.6 | 795,000 | 4.5 | 100 |
|  | 49.3 | 6,978,000 | 46.5 | 624,000 | 4.2 | 100 |
|  | 54.9 | 2,208,000 | 37.3 | 461,000 | 7.8 | 100 |
|  | 50.6 | 845,000 | 36.9 | 287,000 | 12.5 | 100 |
|  | 52.6 | 17,271,000 | 42.1 | 2,167,000 | 5.3 | 100 |
| 1974 | 52.6 | 8,493,000 | 43.5 | 768,000 | 3.9 | 100 |
|  | 45.4 | 8,301,000 | 50.4 | 684,000 | 4.2 | 100 |
|  | 50.0 | 2,808,000 | 41.9 | 545,000 | 8.1 | 100 |
|  | 46.6 | 1,017,000 | 43.5 | 232,000 | 9.9 | 100 |
|  | 49.3 | 20,619,000 | 45.8 | 2,229,000 | 4.9 | 100 |
| 1975 | 49.8 | 9,642,000 | 45.4 | 1,020,000 | 4.8 | 100 |
|  | 41.3 | 9,220,000 | 53.0 | 988,000 | 5.7 | 100 |
|  | 46.9 | 3,009,000 | 43.8 | 641,000 | 9.3 | 100 |
|  | 44.9 | 1,089,000 | 41.6 | 354,000 | 13.5 | 100 |
|  | 46.1 | 22,960,000 | 47.7 | 3,003,000 | 6.2 | 100 |
| 1976 | 47.2 | 11,176,000 | 48.8 | 911,000 | 4.0 | 100 |
|  | 40.9 | 10,619,000 | 53.0 | 1,221,000 | 6.1 | 100 |
|  | 44.4 | 3,385,000 | 45.7 | 732,000 | 9.9 | 100 |
|  | 44.2 | 1,280,000 | 48.7 | 188,000 | 7.1 | 100 |
|  | 44.3 | 26,460,000 | 49.9 | 3,052,000 | 5.8 | 100 |
| 1970-1976 |  | +96.7% |  | +142.9% |  |  |
| per cent |  | +101.1% |  | +53.8% |  |  |
| change |  | +111.2% |  | +76.0% |  |  |
|  |  | +105.1% |  | +241.8% |  |  |
|  |  | +100.6% |  | +86.1% |  |  |

Source: Machlup, Leeson, and Associates.

purchases fell year after year from 61.5 per cent in 1970 to
44.3 per cent. It also fell for every one of the four strata
of libraries: in the top stratum from 69.4 per cent in 1970
to 47.2 per cent in 1976; in the lowest stratum from 61.4 per
cent to 44.2.

The changes in the distribution of purchases among the
three categories of library materials reflect the changes in
annual expenditures over the years. From 1970 to 1977 total
purchases by the 75 academic libraries increased by 37.4 per
cent; this breaks down into an increase of purchases of serials by 100.6 per cent, an increase of purchases of other nonbook materials by 86.1 per cent, and a reduction of expenditures for books by 1.1 per cent. This reduction in the dollar
outlays for books by all 75 libraries is composed of reductions by 2.5 per cent and 3.6 per cent, respectively, for the
two upper strata of libraries, and increases by 3.3 per cent
and 7.8 per cent, respectively, for the two lower strata. The
reduction in dollar outlays was especially drastic for the
larger libraries in the years 1970 to 1972; in the top stratum, dollar outlays for books fell from $10,945,000 to
$8,876,000. The reductions in expenditures for books do not
tell the whole story, in as much as the prices of books increased throughout the period. According to our calculations
(see Chapter 2.3.) book prices increased from 1970 to 1976
by 50 per cent.


*A Comparison with Nationwide Statistics*

We can again check how the figures derived from our sample
of 75 academic libraries compare with nationwide statistics
published by the National Center for Education Statistics
(NCES) in *Library Statistics of Colleges and Universities*.
Data were published for the fall of 1960, 1964, 1968, 1969,
1971, and 1973, and are about to be published for the fall of
1975 (and were kindly released to us). Comparisons with our
data would thus be possible for 1971, 1973 and 1975, though
not for all expenditure items.

The NCES statistics emcompass all college and university
libraries at least one year old in the fall of the year for
which the data are compiled. This involves an increasing
population of libraries from 1,951 academic libraries in 1960,
to 2,431 in 1969, and 2,972 in 1975. Aggregate expenditures
by an increasing number of libraries have to be adjusted for
that increase if we are interested in changes relevant to the
average library. On the other hand, no such adjustment is
needed if we only wish to compare the proportions between expenditures for library materials and personnel or if we want

64

to find out the increase in the libraries' purchases of books, serials and other library materials over the years.

Table 6.5.6 presents these statistics of college and university libraries for the years for which they were collected by the NCES. In the last line of the table the percentage changes from 1969 to 1975 are shown, in the hope that they permit valid comparisons with the analogous changes computed for our sample of 75 academic libraries that made up our Table 6.5.4. Total expenditures of our 75 academic libraries increased from 1970 to 1976 by 54.1 per cent; total expenditures by 2,972 academic libraries in 1975 exceeded those by 2,431 libraries in 1969 by 81.0 per cent. If we correct for the increase in the number of libraries by comparing the average expenditures per library in 1975 and 1969, we find the increase to be 48.1 per cent. This is not a valid procedure, however, since libraries "born" only in the last seven years are surely not of the size of mature ones and their expenditures are most likely far below average. Average expenditures per library in 1975 were $356,242 for the population of 2,972 libraries, compared with $2,418,427 for the average per library in our sample of 75. Let us bear in mind that 55 members of our group were in the upper three budget strata and only 20 had expenditures below a million dollars in 1976. An altogether different kettle of fish!

The expenditures for books, serials and other materials increased for the whole population of academic libraries by 54 per cent from 1969 to 1975. Corrected for the increase in the number of libraries, the increase was only 26 per cent but, again, this small percentage increase over a six-year period partly reflects the addition of new libraries with understandably small budgets. In any case, the increase in purchases of library materials from 1970 to 1976, by the 75 academic libraries of our own sample, 37.4 per cent, lies in the middle of the unadjusted and the adjusted percentage figure for the universe of university and college libraries, which is a plausible position.

We now turn to the relative shares of the various expenditure items in the total of the libraries' expenditures. In the national statistic, purchases of library materials in 1975 accounted for 31.0 per cent, and personnel cost for 61.8 per cent of total expenditures. In our sample of 75 academic libraries, purchases of materials accounted for 29.2 per cent, and personnel cost for 60.3 per cent of expenditures in 1976. The closeness of the percentages in our diminutive sample to those in the entire population of academic libraries reinforces our confidence in the data we obtained. (Evidently the distribution between library materials and personnel cost is less seriously affected by the average size of the library.)

TABLE 6.5.6  Expenditures for Materials, Personnel and All Other, by All Academic Libraries in the United States, 1960, 1964, 1968, 1969, 1971, 1973, 1975

| Year | Number of libraries | Total expenditures excluding capital outlays | Books, serials, and all other materials | Per cent of total | Wages and salaries | Per cent of total | All other | Per cent of total |
|---|---|---|---|---|---|---|---|---|
| 1960 | 1,951 | $ 137,200,000 | $ 40,700,000 | 29.7 | $ 84,100,000 | 61.3 | $12,400,000 | 9.0 |
| 1964 | 2,140 | $ 246,000,000 | $ 79,000,000 | 32.1 | $145,000,000 | 59.0 | $22,000,000 | 8.9 |
| 1968 | 2,370 | $ 509,798,000 | $187,914,000 | 36.9 | $274,057,000 | 53.8 | $47,827,000 | 9.3 |
| 1969 | 2,431 | $ 584,848,000 | $212,891,000 | 36.4 | $317,485,000 | 54.3 | $54,471,000 | 9.3 |
| 1971 | 2,535 | $ 737,533,000 | $247,668,000 | 33.6 | $417,347,000 | 56.6 | $72,518,000 | 9.8 |
| 1973 | 2,887 | $ 866,838,000 | $282,194,000 | 32.6 | $496,545,000 | 57.3 | $88,097,000 | 10.1 |
| 1975 | 2,972 | $1,058,750,000 | $327,904,000 | 31.0 | $654,042,000 | 61.8 | $76,804,000 | 7.2 |
| Per cent change 1969-1975 | +22.3% | +81.0% | +54.0% | | +106.0% | | +41.0% | |

Source:  NCES, Library Statistics of Colleges and Universities, Analytical Reports and Summary Data.

The NCES data for purchases of library materials were not further broken down in the earlier surveys, but for 1973 and 1975 we were given a breakdown. The nationwide outlays in 1973 were $191,739,000 for books, $78,483,000 for periodicals, and $11,972,000 for other materials (audiovisual and other nonprint materials); and in 1975 $200,431,000 for books, $111,945,000 for periodicals, and $15,528,000 for other materials. The percentage shares of these three categories of purchases were 67.9, 27.8, and 4.2 per cent in 1973, and 61.1, 34.1, and 4.8 per cent in 1975. For our 75 libraries, Table 6.5.5 gave the shares as 44.3, 49.9 and 5.8 per cent in 1976, sufficiently different from the national distribution to call for an explanation.

The explanation is not difficult to find if we remember the differences in the average size of the libraries in question. The existence of many mini-libraries in the population of academic libraries — over a thousand community colleges (junior colleges) with funds devoted largely to acquiring basic books and hardly any journals — fully explains that book purchases constitute a larger share, and serial subscriptions a smaller share, of the acquisitions of library materials.

From our examination of the NCES data we derived an "economic indicator" of possible significance: a sizable change of relative shares of book and periodical purchases from 1973 to 1975. Despite the large component of mini-libraries and infant-libraries (libraries born in the last six or seven years), the relative share of book purchases dropped within two years from 68 to 61 per cent and the share of periodical subscriptions rose from 28 to 34 per cent, a drastic transfer of funds from books to periodicals. This need not mean that the libraries subscribed to more periodicals; it may merely reflect the large increases in subscription rates but certainly a reduction in the acquisition of books.


*A Comparison with Statistics of Research Libraries*

The sample of 75 academic libraries scrutinized carefully in this chapter included a large contingent of research libraries. The availability of *ARL Statistics* makes it almost imperative for us to check our results against the analogous data compiled for the 94 university libraries that are members of the Association of Research Libraries.

The results are very close. In 1975/76 the 94 university libraries in the ARL spent 30.2 per cent of their total operating expenditures for acquisition of library materials, 58.4 per cent on personnel, and 11.4 per cent on other things (including binding). The corresponding distribution for the

75 academic libraries in our sample was 29.2, 60.3, and 10.5 per cent. The distributions of library materials are not so easily compared, because ARL Statistics has no separate figures for books but only totals (with and without binding) and, for the first time in 1975/76, for periodicals (defined to include all serials, from daily papers to monographic series appearing with intervals exceeding a year.)[1] Although a statistic of total microform holdings is included in the ARL tables, expenditures for microform and other materials that are neither books nor serials (disks, tapes, manuscripts, etc.) are not separately shown; they are evidently included in the total. The ARL shows expenditures for current periodicals amounting to 40.4 per cent of total materials expenditures (without binding); the corresponding figure in our sample was 49.9 per cent. Since we had a narrower definition of periodicals, the difference in relative outlays is unexplained. That acquisitions of back issues of periodicals were included in our statistic but not in ARL's, could explain at best a very small fraction of the difference. To look for the sources of the discrepancy should perhaps be among the tasks still to be performed.

BUDGET PRESSURES

What we found from the expenditure statistic about the discriminatory treatment of books and serials is of course well known to librarians. This is quite evident from the answers to our question on the libraries' reactions to budget pressures. We had asked them in Question I-8:

> "During 1976, your library may have experienced budget pressures which had an impact on your collection development and maintenance activities. If this is so, please circle the code

---

[1]Footnotes in the libraries' report forms, reproduced in ARL Statistics 1975-1976, indicate that not all libraries conformed with the definition given in the questionnaire. Some libraries excluded government publications, and at least one excluded newspapers. And we know that practices regarding monographic series are far from consistent.

numbers of the items below which correspond
to the specific actions your library took to
relieve this budget pressure."

The question was answered by 210 libraries.  Of these, no less
than 90, or 42.9 per cent, circled the code number next to
this action: "Reallocated budget to periodicals at the expense
of books."
    In the following we shall examine the full set of replies
received to our question about the libraries' reactions to
budget pressures in 1976.


## Economies, Cuts, and Reallocations

    Table 6.5.7 lists 22 possible "actions" which libraries
may have taken in response to budget pressures.  One of the
alternatives — the only one that excluded the other 21 possibilities — was "no action taken," which evidently signified
that the libraries which circled this code number did not experience any budget pressure in 1976 and had all the money
they wanted.  There were 58 libraries, or 27.6 per cent of the
sample of 210, in this fortunate position.  The other 152 respondents to the question marked several of the codes signify-
ing money-saving or money-diverting actions of various sorts;
altogether 885 such marks were counted.  This implies that the
152 libraries reporting some actions had taken an average of
5.8 of the actions indicated in our questionnaire or specified
by the respondent on the blank lines provided for this purpose.
    The action most frequently mentioned in the answers from
the 210 libraries was: "dropped the only subscription to
periodicals."  No less than 99 libraries, or 47.1 per cent of
the 210, reported that they had done so.  The next-frequent
economy measure taken was "added fewer new subscriptions to
periodicals" — 94 libraries, or 44.8 per cent.  The report that
they had "reallocated budget to periodicals at the expense of
books" came, as we had mentioned above, from 90 libraries.
Next in frequency — 80 libraries, or 38.1 per cent — was the
statement that they had "dropped duplicate subscriptions to
periodicals."  Every one of the actions listed in the ques-
tionaire was taken by *some* of the 210 libraries, and 26 libraries reported that they had taken other actions besides
those listed by us.  One library reported that the action
taken to fight the budget pressure was a "budget increase."
Most of the libraries were less fortunate and reported cost
reductions through "reduced binding," "cheaper type of binding," "dropped current services," "joined consortium," "closed
undergraduate library," "reduced buying duplicate copies,"

69

TABLE 6.5.7  Cost-Reducing Actions Taken by 210 Libraries
under Budget Pressure in 1976, Absolute and Relative Frequencies

| Code no. | Action | Yes Number | Yes Per cent | No Number | No Per cent |
|---|---|---|---|---|---|
| 1 | Dropped duplicate subscriptions to periodicals | 80 | 38.1 | 130 | 61.9 |
| 2 | Dropped duplicate subscriptions to newspapers | 21 | 10.0 | 189 | 90.0 |
| 3 | Dropped duplicate subscriptions to indexing/ abstracting services | 30 | 14.3 | 180 | 85.7 |
| 4 | Dropped the only subscriptions to periodicals | 99 | 47.1 | 111 | 52.9 |
| 5 | Dropped the only subscriptions to newspapers | 37 | 17.6 | 173 | 82.4 |
| 6 | Dropped the only subscriptions to indexing/ abstracting services | 32 | 15.2 | 178 | 84.8 |
| 7 | Added fewer new subscriptions to periodicals | 94 | 44.8 | 116 | 55.2 |
| 8 | Added fewer new subscriptions to newspapers | 59 | 28.1 | 151 | 71.9 |
| 9 | Added fewer new subscriptions to indexing/ abstracting services | 44 | 21.0 | 166 | 79.0 |
| 10 | Added no new subscriptions to periodicals | 16 | 7.6 | 194 | 92.4 |
| 11 | Added no new subscriptions to newspapers | 45 | 21.4 | 165 | 78.6 |
| 12 | Added no new subscriptions to indexing/ abstracting services | 29 | 13.8 | 181 | 86.2 |
| 13 | Purchased microform of periodical in lieu of original | 20 | 9.5 | 190 | 90.5 |
| 14 | Purchased microform of periodical in lieu of binding | 54 | 25.7 | 156 | 74.3 |
| 15 | Reallocated budget to periodicals at the expense of books | 90 | 42.9 | 120 | 57.1 |
| 16 | Reallocated budget to periodicals at the expense of binding | 24 | 11.4 | 186 | 88.6 |
| 17 | Reallocated budget to periodicals at the expense of supplies/equipment | 15 | 7.1 | 195 | 92.9 |
| 18 | Reallocated budget to periodicals at the expense of salaries | 7 | 3.3 | 203 | 96.7 |
| 19 | Reallocated budget to periodicals at the expense of other | 5 | 2.4 | 205 | 97.6 |
| 20/21 | Other actions taken | 26 | 12.4 | 184 | 87.6 |
| 22 | No action taken | 58 | 27.6 | 152 | 72.4 |
| | Total | 885 | 20.1 | 3,525 | 79.1 |

Source:  Machlup, Leeson, and Associates.

TABLE 6.5.8   Cost-Reducing Actions Regarded
as the Most Effective by 127 Libraries,
Absolute and Relative Frequencies

| Code no. | Action taken | Number of libraries | Per cent of total |
|---|---|---|---|
| 1 | Dropped duplicate subscriptions to periodicals | 11 | 8.6 |
| 2 | Dropped duplicate subscriptions to newspapers | 3 | 2.3 |
| 3 | Dropped duplicate subscriptions to indexing/abstracting services | 0 | 0.0 |
| 4 | Dropped the only subscription to periodicals | 37 | 29.1 |
| 5 | Dropped the only subscription to newspapers | 2 | 1.5 |
| 6 | Dropped the only subscription to indexing/abstracting services | 1 | 0.8 |
| 7 | Added fewer new subscriptions to periodicals | 20 | 15.7 |
| 8 | Added fewer new subscriptions to newspapers | 1 | 0.8 |
| 9 | Added fewer new subscriptions to indexing/abstracting services | 0 | 0.0 |
| 10 | Added no new subscriptions to periodicals | 2 | 1.6 |
| 11 | Added no new subscriptions to newspapers | 0 | 0.0 |
| 12 | Added no new subscriptions to indexing/abstracting services | 1 | 0.8 |
| 13 | Purchased microform of periodical in lieu of original | 2 | 1.6 |
| 14 | Purchased microform of periodical in lieu of binding | 5 | 4.0 |
| 15 | Reallocated budget to periodicals at the expense of books | 26 | 20.5 |
| 16 | Reallocated budget to periodicals at the expense of binding | 1 | 0.8 |
| 17 | Reallocated budget to periodicals at the expense of supplies/equipment | 2 | 1.6 |
| 18 | Reallocated budget to periodicals at the expense of salaries | 1 | 0.8 |
| 19 | Reallocated budget to periodicals at the expense of other | 3 | 2.4 |
| 20 | Other actions taken | 9 | 7.1 |
| | Total | 127 | 100.0% |

Source:   Machlup, Leeson, and Associates.

"solicited gift subscriptions," "donations," "annual review of periodical subscriptions," "purchased older titles through used-book dealers," "more judicious selection of books," "used more interlibrary loans," "reduced library staff," and, in a variety of formulations, "cancelled serials" and "bought fewer books." For the last two actions some of our suggested answers could have been used, but the librarians probably preferred using more direct language. One answer, which implied reduced purchases of books, specified "maintain file of items wanted but deferred until funds permit." (our fear is that this time may never come if the backlog of deferments grows too large.)

Since each of the 210 responding libraries had a choice of circling the code numbers designating 21 possible actions taken, there could have been 4,410 encirclings. In actual fact, there were 885 such circles, which means 20.1 per cent of the potential, or an average frequency of about one-fifth per action. Table 6.5.7 shows nine lines above this average, and 12 lines below it. To repeat, the actions taken most frequently were reductions in subscriptions to periodicals and reductions in acquisitions of books.

An economy measure adopted most frequently is not necessarily regarded as the most effective one. There may be economy measures that hurt least, but they need not be the ones that save the largest amount of money. For this reason a separate question had to be put to the libraries.

*The Most Effective Cost-Reduction*

Which of the 21 listed actions proved to be most effective in reducing budget pressures experienced in 1976? This question was asked in our questionnaire and answered by 127 of the 154 libraries that had reported some actions. Table 6.5.8 records the answers.

Three cost-reducing actions were far ahead of the rest, and it happens that they were among the actions most frequently taken. Top honors go to "dropping the only subscription to periodicals"; this action was regarded as the most effective by 37 libraries, or 29.1 per cent of the 127 respondents. In second place was "reallocated budget to periodicals at the expense of books," which was reported as the most effective action by 26 libraries, or 20.5 per cent of the group. In third place was "added fewer new subscriptions to periodicals," the measure named as most effective in cost reduction by 20 libraries, or 15.7 per cent of the group. No other action came close to these three, though 13 other actions from our list received some votes for first place and the "write-in"

specifics received votes from 9 libraries as the most effective cost-reducers.

Perhaps it would be interesting to state the write-ins
specifying the most effective actions: "strict justification
of serial subscriptions," "restricted purchases of selected
books," "eliminated staff positions," "gift subscriptions
solicited," "more judicious book selection," "book-acquisi-
tion budget limited," "closed undergraduate library," and
"cooperative subscriptions with other libraries."

We wanted to get an idea of whether all types of libraries
had similar experiences. As the sample of 127 libraries
participating in this rating-exercise included 26 public libraries, 5 special libraries, and 2 Federal libraries, besides
94 academic libraries, we can make a few observations. One of
the Federal libraries named "adding fewer new subscriptions
to periodicals" as its most effective economy measure and thus
shared this appraisal with many of the other libraries. The
other Federal library saved most money by dropping newspaper
subscriptions. Of the five special libraries, one joined the
majority of libraries in choosing the dropping of some single
subscriptions to periodicals as the most effective cost-reducing action; another gave top place to "adding fewer new subscriptions of periodicals;" a third saved most by "purchasing
microforms of periodicals in lieu of binding;" and the remaining two rated their own techniques of cutting costs above any
of the alternatives listed in our questionnaire.

The 26 public libraries were not much different from the
majority. Indeed their most frequent choices as most effective economy measures were identical with those of the other
academic libraries: dropping single subscriptions to periodicals and switching funds from books to periodicals. However,
dropping duplicate subscriptions to periodicals was tied in
second place. The only nonconformance with majority choices
was by some public libraries naming as most efficient economies the purchase of microform of periodicals in lieu of original issues and in refusals to add new subscriptions to indexing and/or abstracting services.

The judgments of the 94 academic libraries on the effec-
tiveness of cost-reducing actions were, of course, fully re-
flected in the data reported in Table 6.5.8. The three most
effective economy measures according to that table achieved
these top ratings because of the overwhelming participation of
academic libraries in reporting their experiences. Thus we
find the dropping of single subscriptions to periodicals given
top place, buying fewer books, second place, and adding fewer
new subscriptions to periodicals, third place in the ratings
by academic libraries. The numerical scores are the following: of the 94 academic libraries in this group, 31 found buy-

ing fewer periodicals, 22 buying fewer books, and 16 adding fewer periodicals to be the most effective economy measure.

Although this particular survey is of the impressionistic type, it is consistent with the numerical data for journals and books — the publishers sold less, and the libraries acquired less. The reduction in books acquired, however, was much more drastic than in journals.

## SOME CHARACTERISTICS OF HOLDINGS AND ACQUISITIONS

The chapter before this dealt with *library expenditures*. Acquisitions of books and serials were of course a major part of library expenditures, indeed the part most pertinent to our research; but there are aspects of acquisitions that are more reasonably discussed separately from considerations of budgets and budget allocations. The chapter after this will be concerned with *acquisitions of library materials classified by field*. A discussion of characteristics of acquisitions not related to a field breakdown would not fit into that chapter. The present chapter accommodates discussions of aspects of holdings and acquisitions that fit neither into the previous nor into the next chapter. It will deal with library statistics of books and periodicals not classified by field, with acquisitions that are designed to fill gaps in the collections, acquisitions of imported materials, acquisitions classified by type of publisher, acquisitions classified by type of distributor, and the librarians' assessments of their collections for different subjects in terms of approximation to or distance from completeness.

### REPORTS ON HOLDINGS, ACQUISITIONS, AND SUBSCRIPTIONS

In our questionnaire we had requested from the libraries their data on acquisitions and holdings of books and on subscriptions to periodicals, from 1970 to 1976. (These were the first questions in the sections on "Book Purchases" and on "Periodical Purchases.") These data did not have to be broken down by subject or field. With regard to books we provided separate columns for volumes and for titles, and regarding periodicals we had separate columns for subscriptions and for titles. It is understood that the number of volumes ordinarily exceeds the number of book titles, partly because of titles that come in two or more volumes and partly because of duplicate volumes of the same title.  Likewise, the number of subscriptions to periodicals will exceed the number of periodicals (titles) subscribed to by the number of duplicate subscriptions.


## The Responses

The response rates to these questions were most disappointing.  Of the 223 libraries that had returned (fully or partly completed) questionnaires, only 48 libraries furnished data on books (volumes and/or titles) acquired and held; and only 16 libraries furnished data on periodicals (subscriptions and/or titles) received.  We processed the data despite the small number of responding libraries.

We have decided not to present the resulting tabulations, for we discovered exorbitant inconsistencies between the numbers of reported volumes added (or titles added), on the one hand, and the increments in volumes held (or titles held), on the other.  Small differences could be attributed to losses through theft or withdrawal from the collection, but the discrepancies went far beyond tolerable limits.  For 1975, for example, the 48 libraries reported that they had added 2,165,000 volumes to their collections, but the accretions to their reported holdings amounted to only 1,328,000 volumes — a discrepancy of 38.7 per cent.  Similar inconsistencies vitiated the statistics of book titles.  Even the data on periodical subscriptions were inconsistent although the questionnaire forms had provided columns for subscriptions cancelled as well as for subscriptions added.


## The Findings

We may nevertheless report some of our findings.

1.  In none of the years 1972 to 1976 was the number of volumes of books reported as added to the collection as high as in 1970 or 1971.  The number reported for 1976 was 15 per cent below that of 1971.

2.  The annual increments to the number of volumes held in the collections showed similar reductions.  The increment in 1975 was 29.4 per cent below that of 1970.

3.  The ratio of volumes added to the book collection declined from 7.7 per cent in 1970 to 5.9 per cent in 1973, and to 5.2 per cent in 1976.

4. The ratio of titles added to total holdings declined from 6.7 per cent in 1970 to 5.5 per cent in 1973, and to 4.6 per cent in 1976.

5. The absolute number of subscriptions to periodicals increased from 1970 to 1972, but then stayed approximately at that level. Still, the number of subscriptions in 1976 exceeded that of 1970 by 4.0 per cent and that of 1972 by 1.0 per cent.

6. The number of periodical titles subscribed to increased from 1970 to 1976 by 5.0 per cent.

These findings seem warranted despite the small number of libraries in the sample and the poor data received.

## HOLDINGS AND ACQUISITIONS BY ALL ACADEMIC LIBRARIES

In Chapter 6.2 we referred to the *Library Statistics of Colleges and Universities* published by the National Center for Education Statistics (NECS) for selected years since 1960, and to the annual compilations by the Association of Research Libraries (ARL) published since 1963 in *Academic Library Statistics* and now under the title *ARL Statistics*. These statistics are not broken down by subject or field, for the very sound reason that the data would not be obtainable. They have, however, the great merit of covering the entire population of academic libraries and, respectively, of the population of academic research libraries. The response rates to the questionnaires of the Library Survey Branch of the NCES were between 95 and 99 per cent, and for the small number of nonresponding libraries the figures were estimated, so that a complete enumeration was achieved. (The statistics omit only a few joint libraries.) The ARL statistics, likewise, contain complete enumerations of volumes held and volumes added, the latter divided into gross and net.

### The Data

The NCES statistics are broken down by "control" — public versus private institutions — and by "type" of institution — (a) universities with graduate programs and with at least two professional schools; (b) other 4-year institutions with graduate programs; (c) other 4-year institutions without graduate students; and (d) 2-year institutions (including community colleges, trade schools and business schools with less-than-four-year programs).

77

In addition to data on expenditures (on which we reported in Chapter 6.5) and on library staff, the following data on acquisitions and holdings were compiled, some for all reports; some only for the most recent ones:

Volumes of books: added during year, and held at end of year;
Linear feet of government documents: held at end of year;

Volume-equivalent contained on microforms: added during year, and held at end of year;
Physical units of microform not reported above: added during year, and held at end of year;
Current periodicals (at year end): titles, and copies.

As we are interested chiefly in books and journals, we show the data for only these two kinds of library materials in Table 6.6.1. In the absence of uninterrupted time series we cannot check the consistency of "volumes added" with the increase in holdings. Only in one instance can we make such a test, namely, for the increment in year-end holdings of 1969 over those of the preceding year, 1968. Unfortunately, the statistics do not pass this test with flying colors: the year-end holdings of 1968 plus volumes added in 1969 would yield holdings in 1969 exceeding the reported holdings by 1,844,000 volumes. Since the difference, however, is only 0.6 per cent of the 1968 holdings, one may explain it as the loss of volumes through theft or withdrawals from the collection.

We would have been interested also in a time series on microform holdings. Alas, NCES reported these figures only for 1973. We would have expected to see substantial growth rates in this novel form of library material. We are told that statistical information is difficult to obtain because it has been impossible up to now to formulate an operational definition of a physical unit of microform materials. Yet the

Association of Research Libraries has in fact provided a set of useful definitions, distinguishing the following units of microform materials: reels of microfilm, number of micro-cards, number of microprint sheets, and number of microfiches. Admittedly, these "units," operationally defined, may not give us a fair notion of the amount of information contained. (One reel, for example, may comprise the contents of several books or journals.) Still, counting of physical units has its place, particularly in studies of annual increments or secular growth. Thus, according to *ARL Statistics 1975-1976*, the median number of total microform units held by the participating university libraries increased from 355,490 in 1968-1969 to 924,610 in 1975-1976, that is, by 160.1 per cent. Over the same period, the median number of volumes (books and journals) in the collections of the participating university libraries

TABLE 6.6.1  Volumes of Books Added and Held, and
Periodical Titles Received, by All College and University
Libraries of the United States, in Selected Years 1960-1975

| Year | Number of libraries | Volumes of Books* | | | | Periodicals | |
| | | Added during year | Held at end of year | Per cent of annual growth | Titles currently received | Copies currently received |
|---|---|---|---|---|---|---|
| 1960 | 1,951 | 8,400,000 | 177,000,000 | 5.0 | 1,270,000 | n.a. |
| 1964 | 2,140 | 13,600,000 | 227,000,000 | 6.4 | 1,760,000 | n.a. |
| 1968 | 2,370 | 25,153,000 | 304,652,000 | 9.0 | 2,505,000 | n.a. |
| 1969 | 2,431 | 25,756,000 | 328,564,000 | 8.5 | 2,632,000 | n.a. |
| 1971 | 2,535 | 26,374,000 | 371,389,000 | 7.6 | 3,677,000 | n.a. |
| 1973 | 2,887 | 25,095,000 | 406,790,000 | 6.6 | 3,836,000 | 4,474,700 |
| 1975 | 2,972 | 23,242,000 | 447,059,000 | 5.5 | 4,434,000 | n.a. |
| Per cent changes | | | | | | |
| 1960-1975 | +52.3% | +176.7% | +152.6% | | +249.1% | |
| 1969-1975 | +22.2% | -9.8% | +36.1% | | +68.5% | |

Source:  NCES, Library Statistics of Colleges and Universities

*Note:  Although the Summary Report of 1973 specifically speaks of "volumes
of books," Section A of the NCES questionnaire requested the "number of
volumes in book stock and in bound periodicals collections," and the instructions defined "volume" as "any physical unit" of "work contained in one
binding or portfolio" and, hence, failed to separate periodicals from books.

increased from 1,268,159 to 1,592,582, that is, by only 25.6 per cent.


*Observations*

As to the statistics of books and periodicals, we should call attention to the declining rates of additions to the total collections. We must warn, however, that, although the caption in Table 6.6.1 reads "volumes of books," we learned from the questionnaire forms and instructions to the libraries that "volumes" in this instance refers to both books and periodicals. (This conceals some rather important information. It should be possible, we submit, for librarians to distinguish volumes of books and volumes of periodicals, and we hope that NCES will in future surveys provide for separate counts. The American Library Association in its official definition of books, has declared that "bound volumes of periodicals . . . are not considered books.")

The ratio of "volumes added" to volumes held at the beginning of the year[1] declined continuously from 9.0 per cent in 1968 to 5.5 per cent in 1975. The annual additions to total holdings declined in absolute numbers from 1971 to 1975; an *increased* number of libraries acquired a *reduced* total of volumes (reduced by 2,132,000 volumes). Acquisitions, as an average per library, fell from 10,404 volumes in 1971 to 7,820 volumes in 1975, a decline by 24.8 per cent.

In the same period of five years, the number of periodicals subscribed to increased from 1,450 (as an average per library) in 1971 to 1,491 in 1975, an increase by 2.9 per cent. From 1969 to 1975 total subscriptions to periodicals increased by 68.5 per cent, while acquisitions of volumes — chiefly books, undoubtedly — decreased by 9.8 per cent. An increase in periodical *titles* need not imply an increase in periodical *subscriptions*, owing to the fact that a library may subscribe to more journals but cancel some duplicate subscriptions. That there are many duplicate subscriptions can be clearly seen from the 1973 statistic in Table 6.6.1, which shows that the number of *copies* received by the libraries ex-

---

[1]Since annual "growth rates" are, as a rule, expressed in per cent of the stock at the beginning of the year, we deducted the additions during the year from the year-end holdings and used the resulting numbers as the basis for calculating the percentages.

ceeded the number of *titles* of periodicals they subscribed to
by as much as 16.7 per cent. (What a pity that this information is not available for other years. A time series of
copies of periodicals received besides that of titles, would
be most informative.)

The regrets we have expressed regarding statistics not
supplied should not be interpreted as a lack of appreciation
for the statistics that have been supplied. The NCES reports
are important contributions to our knowledge about the holdings and acquisitions of our academic libraries.

The same statements may be made about ARL statistics. We
hope to be able in the near future to present a comparative
analysis of their data on holdings and acquisitions. Such an
analysis could provide insights into possible differences between the set of academic libraries and the sub set of academic research libraries; and provide also some check of the
representativeness of our own findings regarding academic
libraries.


FILLING GAPS

Acquisitions designed to fill gaps in the collection may
relate to books or serials. A library acquires books published in earlier years, the purchase of which had been
missed or deferred, or books that have been lost and have to
be replaced. There may also be instances where duplicates of
books are needed for teaching purposes or books the need for
which had not been apparent in the past. As to serials, back
issues are acquired most frequently because the library began
subscribing only sometime after the serial publication was
started and it is found desirable to have a complete set; in
some instances a library had long been trying to acquire the
earlier issues which it now found available; or back issues
are purchased to replace volumes that were lost.

We were interested in the proportion of expenditures for books that was devoted to the acquisition of books published in the past. Thus we asked in our questionnaire for "the per cent of 1976 book expenditures that was for books published prior to 1970."

The question was answered by 152 libraries, including 91 academic libraries, 36 public libraries, 12 special libraries, and 13 Federal libraries. We took an unweighted arithmetic average of all reported percentages — which means that each library was given equal weight regardless of the size of its expenditures — and we found that this average was 9.4 per cent. We also found "interesting" variations of the average percentages spent for books of old vintage by the different types of libraries. We realized, however, that it made little sense to calculate unweighted averages. If one library used 10 per cent of its book budget for old backlist books, while another used only 5 per cent, the unweighted average of 7.5 per cent means nothing; perhaps one library spent ten times as much as the other. Thus, we had to calculate average percentages weighted by total expenditures for books.

Unfortunately, these weights were available only for those libraries that had given us their book expenditures for 1976. As a result, our sample was drastically reduced. Of the 91 academic libraries only 75 had reported their expenditures; of the 36 public libraries only 31 had done so; of the 12 special libraries, only 6; and of the 13 Federal libraries, only 11. Thus, the usable sample shrank from 152 libraries to 123. Table 6.6.2 presents the duly weighted averages, separate for the four types of libraries, and for academic libraries also by expenditure strata.

For the entire sample the weighted average of spending for books of old vintage was 10.9 per cent of the combined book budgets. The separate figures for the four types of libraries reveal no longer the "interesting differences" we had "observed" before we started to weight the reported percentages. (We even had "good explanations" for the supposed variances which turned out to be nonexistent.) The weighted averages show a somewhat higher percentage for Federal libraries, but we shall not attempt to explain it; after all, the variance might disappear if we had a larger number of Federal libraries reporting.

As far as the breakdown of academic libraries by the size of their budgets is concerned, we find the first three rows in Table 6.6.2 quite understandable, with the largest libraries using larger percentages of their book expenditures for books published years ago. Some members of the faculty may have "just discovered" that they needed these old books for their

*TABLE 6.6.2 Purchases of Backlist Books: Estimated Part of Total Book Expenditures by 123 Libraries in 1976 for Books Published Before 1970, in Per Cent of Total (Reported Averages Weighted by Each Library's Expenditures for Books)*

| Number of reporting libraries | Type of library | Range of total expenditures of reporting libraries in 1976 | Per cent of expenditures for books in 1976 used for purchases of books published before 1970 |
|---|---|---|---|
| 13 | academic | $4,000,000 or more | 12.4 |
| 21 | academic | $2,000,000 to $3,999,999 | 9.6 |
| 14 | academic | $1,000,000 to $1,999,999 | 8.2 |
| 27 | academic | Less than $1,000,000 | 12.8 |
| 75 | academic | all sizes | 10.8 |
| 31 | public | all sizes | 11.1 |
| 6 | special | all sizes | 10.8 |
| 11 | federal | all sizes | 12.3 |
| 123 | all types | all sizes | 10.9 |

*Source: Machlup, Leeson, and Associates.*

83

research but that the library had missed ordering them when
they were published.  Smaller libraries are usually attached
to institutions with less research-minded professors, or they
have not enough funds for filling these gaps.  Hence, we are
puzzled to find the largest ratio, 12.8 per cent, reported by
the 27 academic libraries with the smallest book budgets.  A
possible explanation might be that several of the small libraries are relatively new and find it necessary to build up
their collections with basic books of old vintage in the
fields of their strongest interest.


## Back Issues of Periodicals

We asked in our questionnaire what per cent of the 1976
expenditures for periodicals was used for back issues published prior to 1976; we received answers from 167 libraries,
including 97 academic, 46 public, 12 special, and 14 Federal.
Again we faced the problem of unweighted versus weighted
averages.  In order to obtain appropriate weights for the percentages reported by the libraries we had to eliminate from
the sample all those that failed to give us their expenditures for serials.  This left us with a sample of 78 academic,
35 public, 4 special and 8 Federal libraries, together 125.
Table 6.6.3 summarizes the results.

The percentage figures shown in this table are much smaller than those seen in the table giving the ratios applying to
books of old vintage.  There is far less buying of back issues
of periodicals than there is of books from the publishers' old
backlists.  The weighted average of the percentages reported
by the 125 libraries is 4.4 per cent.  (Incidentally, the unweighted average of the percentages reported by the larger
group of 167 libraries was calculated to be 3.8.)  A reserva-
tion of uncertain significance seems called for:  We cannot
know whether only periodicals or perhaps all serials were used
as the basis of the comparison.  We should recall that many
libraries were unable to provide separate data for acquisitions of periodicals and other serials.

In the case of books, academic libraries were the largest
buyers of old titles; in the case of periodicals, special libraries used the largest percentage, 13 per cent, of their expenditures for periodicals for the acquisition of back issues.
Since the sample, however, includes only four special libraries, we surely must not generalize this result.  As a matter
of fact, we checked the returns from these four libraries and
found that two of them had reported zero purchases of back issues, the third had reported only 2 per cent, but the fourth
20 per cent of total expenditures for periodicals.  Since this

TABLE 6.6.3 *Purchases of Back-Issues of Periodicals: Part of Total Expenditures for Periodicals by 125 Libraries in 1976 for Issues of Periodicals Published Before 1976, in Per Cent of Total (Reported Averages Weighted by Each Library's Expenditures for Periodicals)*

| Number of reporting libraries | Type of library | Range of total expenditures of reporting libraries in 1976 | Per cent of expenditures for serials in 1976 used for purchases of issues published before 1976 |
|---|---|---|---|
| 13 | academic | $4,000,000 or more | 4.8 |
| 25 | academic | $2,000,000 to $3,999,999 | 4.3 |
| 15 | academic | $1,000,000 to $1,999,999 | 4.9 |
| 25 | academic | Less than $1,000,000 | 5.5 |
| 78 | academic | all sizes | 4.6 |
| 35 | public | all sizes | 2.4 |
| 4 | special | all sizes | 13.0 |
| 8 | Federal | all sizes | 2.2 |
| 125 | all types | all sizes | 4.4 |

Source: Machlup, Leeson, and Associates.

85

library received the heaviest weight because it had very large expenditures for serials, the weighted average of the group of four was 13 per cent. The reason for its large purchases of back issues becomes clear as soon as one notes that this very special special library is less than ten years old. If we disregard the special libraries, we find again that the percentage of expenditures used for the acquisition of back issues of periodicals was higher for academic libraries than for the other two types. This is understandable, since academic libraries are more interested in learned journals and in keeping their sets of scientific and scholarly periodicals complete. Some university libraries are always on the lookout for opportunities for filling gaps in their sets of journals.

The percentages of back-issue purchases broken down by size-brackets of the reporting academic libraries show no systematic pattern. The 25 smallest academic libraries — evidently much the same group that spent the largest percentage of the book budget for books more than seven years old — spent again the largest percentage of its budget for serials, 5.5 per cent, for issues more than one year old. Strangely enough, the libraries in the adjacent size bracket, with still rather small budgets, spent the second largest percentage, 4.9 per cent, for back issues of periodicals. It may be a mere accident of composition.


IMPORTED MATERIALS

There are several objectives to our inquiry into holdings and acquisitons of American libraries as essential intermediaries in the dissemination of knowledge through the printed word. One of these is the role of libraries as purchasers of the output of the American publishing industry. The books and journals bought by American libraries are not exclusively American publications. What portion of the acquisitions of the libraries are imports from abroad? To get answers, four questions were included in our questionnaire, two regarding books and two regarding periodicals, two in terms of dollar outlays and two in terms of physical volumes.


*Imported Books*

Our questions regarding imported books were answered by 170 libraries, of which 104 were academic, 41 public, 12 special, 13 Federal. We had to eliminate those that did not report their total expenditures for books, a figure required

for calculating weighted averages. The sample was thus reduced to 87 academic, 31 public, 7 special, and 12 Federal libraries, together 137. The importance of calculating weighted
averages is clearly shown by the fact that an unweighted average of the percentages reported by the 170 libraries gave us a
figure of 14.8 per cent, while the weighted average of the
figures reported by the 137 libraries was nearly twice as
high, namely, 25.3 per cent.

A breakdown of the academic libraries into four strata
according to the size of their total expenditures shows, in
Table 6.6.4, that the percentages decrease drastically with
the size of the library. In 1976 the largest academic libraries spent 38.9 per cent of their total book budgets for imported books, while the smallest spent only 6.5 per cent.
This seems to be perfectly in accordance with common-sense
expectations. Table 6.6.4 shows also the drastic difference
between academic and public libraries. While imports of books
absorbed 29.8 per cent of the book budgets of the 87 academic
libraries, they absorbed only 4.5 per cent of the book allocations of the 31 public libraries.

These findings in terms of dollar outlays are fully cor-
roborated by the findings in terms of physical volumes of
books imported. The sample of libraries with usable data for
these comparisons is almost the same: 76 academic, 32 public,
7 special, and 12 Federal libraries, together 127. Their reported estimates are summarized in Table 6.6.5, which shows
the percentages of the total number of volumes of books added
to the collections of the libraries in 1976 that were published outside the United States. We see again that for the
academic libraries, stratified by the size of their budgets,
the percentages of imported volumes vary with their size. The
differences are even more conspicuous. The largest academic
libraries imported 43.4 per cent of all the books that they
added to their collections, while the smallest academic libraries imported only 7.0 per cent. Comparing libraries of
all types and sizes, we find that the percentages in terms of
dollar outlays and in terms of numbers of volumes are almost
the same. We may assume that a good many of the responding
librarians have made their estimates of dollars spent and
volumes acquired by the same internally consistent procedure.
Since imported books, however, are often more expensive than
those published in the United States, we would have expected
the percentages in terms of volumes to be lower than those in
terms of dollars. Perhaps our assumption about cost differences is false; on the other hand, it is not impossible that
many of the estimates are off the mark. In any case, what
matters chiefly are the differences between libraries of different type and size, and not the exact magnitude of the
estimated figures.

TABLE 6.6.4  Purchases of Imported Books: Estimated Parts of Total Book Expenditures by 137 Libraries in 1976 for Books Published Outside the United States, in Per Cent of Total (Reported Averages Weighted by Each Library's Expenditures for Books)

| Number of reporting libraries | Type of library | Range of total expenditures of reporting libraries in 1976 | Per cent of Expenditures for books in 1976 used for purchases of imported books |
|---|---|---|---|
| 20 | academic | $4,000,000 or more | 38.9 |
| 25 | academic | $2,000,000 to $3,999,999 | 23.7 |
| 16 | academic | $1,000,000 to $1,999,999 | 18.1 |
| 26 | academic | Less than $1,000,000 | 6.5 |
| 87 | academic | all sizes | 29.8 |
| 31 | public | all sizes | 4.5 |
| 7 | special | all sizes | 0.8 |
| 12 | Federal | all sizes | 23.5 |
| 137 | All types | all sizes | 25.3 |

Source: Machlup, Leeson, and Associates.

88

TABLE 6.6.5 Purchases of Imported Books: Estimated Parts of Total Number of Volumes of Books Added to the Collection of 127 Libraries in 1976 that were Published Outside the United States, in Per Cent of Total (Reported Averages Weighted by Each Library's Expenditures for Books)

| Number of reporting libraries | Type of library | Range of total expenditures of reporting libraries in 1976 | Per cent of total volumes added to collection in 1976 that were imported |
|---|---|---|---|
| 18 | academic | $4,000,000 or more | 43.4 |
| 17 | academic | $2,000,000 to $3,999,999 | 20.7 |
| 16 | academic | $1,000,000 to $1,999,999 | 16.6 |
| 25 | academic | Less than $1,000,000 | 7.0 |
| 76 | academic | all sizes | 31.3 |
| 32 | public | all sizes | 4.6 |
| 7 | special | all sizes | 1.4 |
| 12 | Federal | all sizes | 26.7 |
| 127 | All types | all sizes | 25.8 |

Source: Machlup, Leeson, and Associates.

*Imported Periodicals*

The share of foreign periodicals acquired by our responding libraries is even higher than the share of their imports
of books.  This is clearly shown by Tables 6.6.6 and 6.6.7,
the former showing the percentages of total expenditures for
periodicals that went for the purchase of foreign periodicals,
the latter showing the percentages of subscriptions to periodicals published abroad.  Most of the libraries that furnished us their estimates of relative dollar expenditures are
evidently included among the libraries that reported their
estimates of the relative number of subscriptions.  Our questions about expenditures were answered by 152 libraries — 89
academic, 41 public, 10 special, and 12 Federal — and the
questions about the number of subscriptions were answered by
155 libraries — 90 academic, 44 public, 10 special and 11
Federal.  The need for proper weights for the calculation of
weighted averages called for supplementary information, the
libraries' total expenditures for periodicals and their total
number of subscriptions.  This excluded several libraries for
usable samples.  There remained 111 libraries — 71 academic,
30 public, 3 special, and 7 Federal — for the expenditures
sample, and 115 libraries — 72 academic, 33 public, 3 special,
and 7 Federal — for the subscriptions sample.  The data are
summarized in Tables 6.6.6 and 6.6.7.

The most important figures are surely those shown in the
first row of each of the two tables, namely, the percentages
for the academic libraries with annual budgets above
$4,000,000.  They spent for foreign periodicals 39.8 per cent
of their total expenditures for periodicals.  Likewise, 43.7
per cent of all their subscriptions were for periodicals published abroad.

In all rows of both tables — for academic libraries of
various sizes as well as for different types of libraries —
the reported percentages for imports were higher for periodicals than for books.  Not all of the estimates, however, seem
to be consistent.  The percentages of dollar outlays and of
numbers of subscriptions can, of course, differ because of
different subscription prices, so that a group of libraries
subscribing to more expensive foreign journals will spend a
larger share of its periodical budget but have a smaller share
of its periodical subscriptions for foreign journals than a
group of libraries subscribing to relatively less expensive
foreign journals.  Thus, we need not be baffled when we see
that the estimates in terms of dollars and in terms of subscriptions are not always parallel; for example, 39.8 against
43.7 per cent for the largest academic libraries, but 30.6
against 28.6 per cent for the second-largest.

90

*TABLE 6.6.6  Purchases of Imported Periodicals: Estimated Parts*
*of Total Expenditures for Periodical Subscriptions by 111 Libraries*
*in 1976 that were for Periodicals Published Outside the United States,*
*in Per Cent of Total (Reported Averages Weighted*
*by Each Library's Expenditures for Periodicals)*

| Number of reporting libraries | Type of library | Range of total expenditures of reporting libraries in 1976 | Per cent of total expenditures for periodicals in 1976 that were imported |
|---|---|---|---|
| 17 | academic | $4,000,000 or more | 39.8 |
| 20 | academic | $2,000,000 to $3,999,999 | 30.6 |
| 13 | academic | $1,000,000 to $1,999,999 | 25.3 |
| 21 | academic | Less than $1,000,000 | 16.7 |
| 71 | academic | all sizes | 34.0 |
| 30 | public | all sizes | 18.7 |
| 3 | special | all sizes | 27.5 |
| 7 | Federal | all sizes | 41.8 |
| 111 | All types | all sizes | 33.4 |

*Source: Machlup, Leeson, and Associates.*

TABLE 6.6.7  Purchases of Imported Periodicals: Estimated Parts of Total
Periodicals Subscriptions Held by 115 Libraries in 1976 that were for Periodicals
Published Outside the United States  (Reported Averages Weighted
by Each Library's Expenditures for Periodicals)

| Number of reporting libraries | Type of library | Range of total expenditures of reporting libraries in 1976 | Per cent of total periodicals subscriptions held in 1976 that were imported |
|---|---|---|---|
| 16 | academic | $4,000,000 or more | 43.7 |
| 19 | academic | $2,000,000 to $3,999,999 | 28.6 |
| 16 | academic | $1,000,000 to $1,999,999 | 21.4 |
| 21 | academic | Less than $1,000,000 | 15.2 |
| 72 | academic | all sizes | 34.3 |
| 33 | public | all sizes | 17.8 |
| 3 | special | all sizes | 20.5 |
| 7 | Federal | all sizes | 53.1 |
| 115 | All types | all sizes | 34.0 |

Source:  Machlup, Leeson, and Associates.

On the other hand, the general tendency for the percentages of expenditures for and subscriptions to foreign periodicals to vary with the size of the library prevails. The figures for the four budget strata of the samples of academic libraries run down very fast, from 39.8 to 16.7 per cent in Table 6.6.6, and from 43.7 to 15.2 per cent in Table 6.6.7. Although one would expect this, one cannot help being impressed with the statistical confirmation.


TYPE OF PUBLISHER

In Part Two, on Book Publishing, we had a discussion in Chapter 2.1 of the market outlets for different types of books. We were interested in knowing what portions of the publishers' sales of various types of books were going to libraries. Now we want to look at the other side of the coin and ask how the book purchases of libraries are divided among books brought out by different types of publishers. The same question is asked for periodicals acquired by libraries. Having just dealt with foreign publishers, we can now confine our discussion to books and journals published in the United States.


*Domestic Books Classified by Type of Publisher*

In Table 6.6.8 we show the average percentages of library acquisitions in 1976 of books published in the United States by (A) Commercial publishers, (B) University presses, (C) Societies and Associations, (D) Federal and State governments and (E) Other publishers. The statistic is not in terms of dollar expenditures but in terms of physical volumes, expressed in per cent of the total number of book volumes added to the collection in 1976. The requested percentage distributions were furnished by 166 libraries, including 90 academic, 49 public, 12 special, and 15 Federal. In order to obtain weights for averaging the reported percentages we again had to eliminate the libraries which did not furnish their data for their total expenditures for books. The sample was then reduced to 131 libraries, of which 75 were academic, 38 public, 6 special, and 12 Federal. (Total book volumes acquired would have been a more appropriate weight, but many more libraries reported their expenditures in dollars, and thus we accepted for purposes of weighting the expenditures for books as proxies for physical volumes of books acquired.)

93

TABLE 6.6.8 Purchases of Books Classified by Type of Publisher: Estimated Shares of Volumes of Domestic Books, by Type of Publisher, Acquired for 131 Libraries, in Per Cent of Total Number of Volumes Added to Collections in 1976 (Averages Weighted by Total Expenditures for Books)

| Number of reporting libraries | Type of library | Range of total expenditures of reporting libraries in 1976 | Per cent of volumes of books published by | | | | | |
|---|---|---|---|---|---|---|---|---|
| | | | Commercial publishers | University presses | Societies and associations | Federal & state governments | Other publishers | Total |
| 17 | academic | $4,000,000 or more | 49.6 | 21.1 | 13.0 | 11.7 | 4.6 | 100 |
| 21 | academic | $2,000,000 to $3,999,999 | 52.2 | 22.4 | 14.3 | 7.7 | 3.4 | 100 |
| 14 | academic | $1,000,000 to $1,999,999 | 56.9 | 17.5 | 9.5 | 5.6 | 10.5 | 100 |
| 23 | academic | Less than $1,000,000 | 53.8 | 24.7 | 10.3 | 8.1 | 3.1 | 100 |
| 75 | academic | all sizes | 51.5 | 21.3 | 12.9 | 9.5 | 4.8 | 100 |
| 38 | public | all sizes | 79.8 | 8.1 | 4.6 | 4.7 | 2.8 | 100 |
| 6 | special | all sizes | 88.7 | 3.2 | 5.9 | 2.2 | 0.0 | 100 |
| 12 | Federal | all sizes | 54.6 | 21.6 | 9.8 | 10.9 | 3.1 | 100 |
| 131 | All types | all sizes | 57.4 | 18.6 | 11.1 | 8.6 | 4.3 | 100 |

Source: Machlup, Leeson, and Associates.

The reported data reveal a surprising fact, to some readers with special interests perhaps an appalling fact: public libraries seem to be not interested in books published by university presses, societies and associations, and government. They acquired in 1976 no less than 79.8 per cent of all the volumes added to their collections from commercial publishers; of books published by university presses they acquired only 8.1 per cent; of publications by societies and government presses, only 4.6 and 4.7 per cent, respectively. By contrast, academic libraries acquired only 51.5 per cent of books published by commercial publishers, 21.3 per cent by university presses, 12.9 per cent by societies and associations, and 9.5 per cent by government agencies. The acquisition pattern of Federal libraries is similar to that of academic libraries. The explanation for the apparent "bias" of public libraries is probably quite simple: they cater not to teachers of researchers but to the general reader, whose interest is mainly in fiction and general, adult and juvenile, books published almost exclusively by commercial publishers. On the other hand, it is also possible that the promotion and marketing efforts of commercial publishers — mainly advertising — have something to do with their success with the staffs of public libraries.

## Domestic Periodicals Classified by Type of Publisher

The situation is similar with regard to periodicals, as we see in Table 6.6.9. Perhaps we had better speak of serials rather than periodicals, because many of the responding libraries were unable to separate periodicals from the rest of their serials subscriptions. This is especially true for public libraries and it may be a partial explanation for the exceptionally high percentage share that subscriptions for serial publications of commercial publishers command in their total subscription program. While libraries of other types estimate the share of subscriptions to periodicals published by commercial publishers at between 35.5 and 48.0 per cent, public libraries estimate it to be 74.7 per cent on the average.

Many scholarly and scientific periodicals are published by university presses or professional associations. This explains why the combined percentages of subscriptions placed with university presses and associations are, on the average, 38.0 per cent for academic libraries, 43.7 per cent for special libraries, and 30.9 per cent for Federal libraries. The average for public libraries is only 19.1 per cent. We may conclude that public libraries are not much interested in learned journals. They probably subscribe to the serials which the general public wants to read, and no one can blame them for it.

95

TABLE 6.6.9 Purchases of Periodicals, Classified by Type of Publisher: Estimated Shares of Subscriptions to Domestic Periodicals, by Type of Publisher, Subscribed for 113 Libraries, in Per Cent of Total Subscriptions to Periodicals (or Serials) in 1976

(Averages Weighted by Total Expenditures for Serials)

| Number of reporting libraries | Type of library | Range of total expenditures of reporting libraries in 1976 | Per Cent of Subscriptions to Periodicals Published by | | | | | |
|---|---|---|---|---|---|---|---|---|
| | | | Commercial publishers | University presses | Societies and associations | Federal & state governments | Other publishers | Total |
| 13 | academic | $4,000,000 or more | 50.0 | 14.4 | 21.6 | 9.3 | 4.7 | 100 |
| 20 | academic | $2,000,000 to $3,999,999 | 48.0 | 15.7 | 21.7 | 10.1 | 4.5 | 100 |
| 15 | academic | $1,000,000 to $1,999,999 | 44.1 | 16.1 | 26.6 | 6.6 | 6.6 | 100 |
| 23 | academic | Less than $1,000,000 | 42.1 | 30.3 | 17.2 | 7.5 | 2.9 | 100 |
| 71 | academic | all sizes | 48.0 | 16.1 | 21.9 | 9.2 | 4.8 | 100 |
| 31 | public | all sizes | 74.7 | 6.9 | 12.2 | 3.8 | 2.4 | 100 |
| 4 | special | all sizes | 35.5 | 17.1 | 26.6 | 20.1 | 0.7 | 100 |
| 7 | Federal | all sizes | 37.3 | 15.5 | 15.4 | 26.7 | 5.1 | 100 |
| 113 | All types | all sizes | 49.1 | 15.6 | 21.1 | 9.6 | 4.6 | 100 |

Source: Machlup, Leeson, and Associates.

When we examined the statistical information obtained from publishers, we found that they could not tell who bought their books and who subscribed to their journals.  The reason for this information gap was that a substantial part of publishers' sales went to wholesalers.  We lacked wholesalers' data, and knew only that libraries were their largest customers. Thus we were anxious to learn from libraries how many books and journals they bought through wholesalers and jobbers. With detailed numerical records unavailable from libraries as well, we asked for their estimates of the percentages of their purchases of books and periodicals they bought from various sources, including wholesalers.

## Domestic Books Classified by Distributors

We requested librarians to estimate what per cent of the total number of book volumes, published in the United States, which they added to their collections in 1976 was purchased directly from (a) commercial and university presses, (b) societies and associations, (c) Federal and State governments, or through intermediaries such as (d) wholesalers and jobbers, (e) bookstores, (f) special dealers (second hand, out of print), and (g) other publishers (distributing books not originally published by them).  Answers were received from 180 libraries, including 101 academic, 51 public, 13 special, and 15 Federal libraries.  In order to calculate weighted averages of the reported percentage distributions, we needed the weights to be attached to each estimate and, hence, the respondents' total acquisitions of book volumes or, as an alternative, their total expenditures for books.  The resulting reduction in the size of the sample left us with 82 academic libraries, 40 public, 7 special, and 12 Federal, together 141.

The results for the reduced sample are shown in Table 6.6.10.  The most conspicuous piece of information conveyed by the data for the 141 libraries is that the largest portion of book purchases is made from wholesalers, though this holds only for three types of libraries, not for special libraries. The academic libraries in our sample bought in 1976 from wholesalers 63.8 per cent of all the books they acquired; public libraries, 78.2 per cent; special libraries 4.2 per cent; and Federal libraries 63.4 per cent.  Direct purchases from commercial and academic publishers were  only 10.3 per cent for academic libraries, 8.7 per cent for public libraries, and 18.4 per cent for Federal libraries, but a whopping 88.1 per cent for special libraries.  The paramount importance of

97

TABLE 6.6.10  Purchases of Books, Classified by Distribution Channel:  Estimated Shares of Volumes
of Domestic Books, by Type of Distributor, Acquired by 141 Libraries, in Per Cent of Total Number of Volumes Added to Collections in 1976

(Averages Weighted by Total Expenditures for Books)

| Number of reporting libraries | Type of library | Range of total expenditures of reporting libraries in 1976 | Per cent of volumes of books purchased from | | | | | | | |
|---|---|---|---|---|---|---|---|---|---|---|
| | | | Commercial and University presses | Societies and associations | Federal and state governments | Wholesalers | Book-stores | Special dealers | Other publishers | Total |
| 18 | academic | $4,000,000 or more | 8.5 | 8.8 | 6.4 | 62.2 | 3.2 | 5.5 | 5.4 | 100 |
| 23 | academic | $2,000,000 to $3,999,999 | 11.6 | 6.9 | 7.2 | 64.5 | 1.5 | 6.0 | 2.3 | 100 |
| 19 | academic | $1,000,000 to $1,999,999 | 13.0 | 6.7 | 3.4 | 66.4 | 3.8 | 2.7 | 4.0 | 100 |
| 22 | academic | Less than $1,000,000 | 13.8 | 9.1 | 4.7 | 67.7 | 1.3 | 3.6 | 2.8 | 100 |
| 82 | academic | all sizes | 10.3 | 7.8 | 6.2 | 63.8 | 2.6 | 5.3 | 4.0 | 100 |
| 40 | public | all sizes | 8.7 | 3.3 | 4.4 | 78.2 | 0.8 | 1.2 | 3.4 | 100 |
| 7 | special | all sizes | 88.1 | 3.0 | 1.6 | 4.2 | 1.8 | 1.3 | 0.0 | 100 |
| 12 | Federal | all sizes | 18.4 | 5.0 | 4.2 | 63.4 | 3.3 | 2.2 | 3.5 | 100 |
| 141 | all types | all sizes | 10.5 | 6.9 | 5.8 | 66.2 | 2.3 | 4.4 | 3.9 | 100 |

Addendum:  The exclusion of one particularly "unusual" but relatively large special library from the sample above results in the following changes
in the rows for special libraries and for all types of libraries:

| 6 | special | all sizes | 49.9 | 12.8 | 6.6 | 17.6 | 7.5 | 5.5 | 0.1 | 100 |
| 140 | all types | all sizes | 10.3 | 6.9 | 5.8 | 66.4 | 2.3 | 4.4 | 3.9 | 100 |

Source:  Machlup, Leeson, and Associates.

wholesalers in the distribution of books, and particularly as
intermediaries between publishers and libraries (except special libraries), is of course well known to both publishers
and librarians, but may be surprising to outsiders.  The explanation for the practice lies in economies of scale; it
would be much more costly for libraries to deal with hundreds
of different publishers in ordering books, receiving invoices,
keeping accounts, sending checks, and so forth.  Some wholesalers, moreover, render a variety of supplementary services
to libraries, for example, through approval plans tailored to
the libraries' particular needs.

If we examine the first four rows of Table 6.6.10, showing
the distributions for each of the size strata of academic libraries separately, we find an unexpected regularity:  the
relative shares *both* of the direct purchases from publishers
and of purchases through wholesalers increase as we go down
from the largest to the smaller libraries.  One wonders what
may be the compensating reductions in relative shares, and
finds on inspection that they are of purchases from societies
and associations, and, though less regularly, from governments
and special dealers.  On second thought, all this does not
seem to be so very peculiar, since most smaller libraries cannot concern themselves with the more special, sometimes even
recondite, titles published by societies or governments or
titles obtainable only through "special dealers," that is,
dealers of books out of print, which can only be bought
second-hand.

Now we have to attend to our exception, the special libraries.  Their percentage shares of books acquired through
wholesalers, on the one hand, and directly from publishers, on
the other, looked so much out of line with the rest of the
sample that we suspected an error, possibly in key-punching.
We went back to check against the returned questionnaires and
ascertained that there was no error.  Instead, we found that
several special libraries were very special in their buying
practices; by eliminating the most special one, which did most
of its ordering directly from the publishers and, moreover,
was much larger than the rest, we reduced the average percentage from 88.1 to 49.9.  This is still much larger than for
all other types of libraries and, hence, calls for an explanation.  It is not difficult to find a plausible explanation.
If a library is specialized in a particular field, say, Law or
Medicine, and if publishers are specialized too, so that the
library would have to order books from only five or six publishers, there would not be any economies involved in purchasing through wholesalers.  This distinguishes the special library from one that has to build its collection in many different fields, served by dozens or even scores of publishers.

Before we look into the distribution channels used for domestic periodicals subscribed to by libraries, we should repeat our warning about the inadequate separation of periodicals from other serials. Libraries without separate subscription records cannot easily make estimates applying to periodicals only.

Our request for estimates of the percentages of subscriptions placed directly with the various types of journal publishers and indirectly with subscription agents yielded responses from 168 libraries, including 96 academic, 47 public, 11 special, and 14 Federal. The need for complementary data on total expenditures for periodicals (or serials), to be used as weights in the calculation of averages, forced us to eliminate a good many of the respondents from this sample. The reduced sample consists of 82 academic, 33 public, 5 special, and 8 Federal libraries, a total of 128.

Table 6.6.11 shows for periodicals what the previous table showed for books, that most of them are not purchased directly from the publishers but, instead, from serial subscription agents. For some types of libraries the relative shares of purchases through intermediaries were even above those shown for books. No doubt, it is more convenient and less expensive for libraries to place hundreds, or thousands, of subscriptions through one or a few agents than to deal with each publisher of serials separately. Thus, it is easy to understand that the percentages of periodicals (or all serials) libraries purchased through subscription agents were between 54.7 and 77.6 per cent of the total numbers of their subscriptions. The low figure was reported by special libraries; they had placed relatively more subscriptions directly with the publishers of the journals.

The breakdown of the percentage distributions by the size of academic libraries yields no systematic pattern, except that the largest libraries place relatively more subscriptions with the publishers, especially for periodicals published by societies and associations and by Federal and State governments. This reduces the relative share of subscriptions they purchase through agents.

ASSESSMENT OF COLLECTION LEVEL

A separate section of our questionnaire was devoted to the librarians' assessments of the "collection level and subject emphasis" of their libraries. This part of our survey was based on a preliminary edition of *Guidelines for the Formula-*

TABLE 6.6.11 Purchases of Periodicals, Classified by Distribution Channel:
Estimated Shares of Subscriptions to Domestic Periodicals, by Type of Distributor, Acquired by 128 Libraries,
in Per Cent of Total Expenditures for Periodicals (or Serials) in 1976
(Averages Weighted by Total Expenditures for Serials)

| Number of reporting libraries | Type of library | Range of total expenditures of reporting libraries in 1976 | Per Cent of Subscriptions Purchased from | | | | |
|---|---|---|---|---|---|---|---|
| | | | Commercial and university presses | Societies and associations | Federal and state governments | Serial subscriptions agents | Total |
| 14 | academic | $4,000,000 or more | 18.8 | 13.5 | 12.8 | 54.9 | 100 |
| 24 | academic | $2,000,000 to $3,999,999 | 16.5 | 10.5 | 7.5 | 65.5 | 100 |
| 19 | academic | $1,000,000 to $1,999,999 | 15.0 | 9.4 | 3.6 | 72.0 | 100 |
| 25 | academic | Less than $1,000,000 | 24.1 | 9.2 | 5.8 | 60.9 | 100 |
| 82 | academic | all sizes | 17.6 | 11.5 | 9.0 | 61.9 | 100 |
| 33 | public | all sizes | 18.8 | 7.1 | 2.3 | 71.8 | 100 |
| 5 | special | all sizes | 23.9 | 13.9 | 7.5 | 54.7 | 100 |
| 8 | Federal | all sizes | 10.2 | 6.7 | 5.5 | 77.6 | 100 |
| 128 | all types | all sizes | 17.4 | 11.1 | 8.5 | 63.0 | 100 |

Source: Machlup, Leeson, and Associate.

*tion of Collection Development Policies*, prepared by the Collection Development Committee, Resources Section, RTSD, of the American Library Association, March 1976.


## Definitions

Five levels were distinguished to judge the strength or weakness of the library's collection, or rather the degress to which it can satisfy the needs of researchers, students, or general readers in various subjects. The following devinitions were supplied:

(a) Comprehensive level: Collecting all significant works of recorded knowledge; the aim, if not the achievement, is exhaustiveness.

(b) Research level: Collecting the major source materials required for pure and applied research; the aim is to include all important reference works and abstracting and indexing services, a wide selection of specialized monographs and extensive journal collections.

(c) Study level: Collecting a wide range of basic monographs (with complete collections of important writers and selections from secondary writers), a selection of representative journals and basic subject-related reference and bibliographical tools; the aim is to support the collection at the equivalent of undergraduate or graduate coursework, but at less intensity than the research level.

(d) Basic level: Collecting highly selective introductory materials, including major dictionaries and encyclopedias, selected important works and surveys, a few major periodicals and bibliographies; the aim is to define the subject and to indicate the varieties of information available elsewhere.

(e) Minimal level: Collecting only a few primary materials and the basic reference tools; the subject is out of scope of the collection.

To help respondents in interpreting these definitions we inserted the following warning: "It is quite likely that very few libraries will hold comprehensive-level collections in any area. Similarly, public, undergraduate and community-college libraries which are not oriented toward specialized research may not have any research-level collections."

Since some libraries may have excluded some subjects from their collections, we added a sixth possibility: "Not applicable." Every one of the 206 libraries that complied with our request for an assessment found *some* subjects not applicable. "Juvenile Fiction and Nonfiction" scored highest in nonapplicability, with 77 libraries circling this code. That

an even higher score — 94 — in nonapplicability was given to
"Interdisciplinary subjects" is partly due to our poor formulation — we should have called it "Interdisciplinary publications" — but chiefly to the fact that we failed to make it
clear that this space could be used for dictionaries, encyclo-
paedias, and any works encompassing more than one of the
listed subjects.

## The Subjects Listed

Altogether 34 subjects were listed in our questionnaire
and two extra lines were provided for "interdisciplinary" and
"other" publications. A few librarians complained about the
inclusion of new subjects for which the customary classification systems had no catalog code, for example, "Environmental
Sciences" and "Urban Studies." Yet, most of the respondents
seem to have had no difficulty in assessing the strength or
weakness of their collections in these subjects. Only 18 of
the 206 libraries found Environmental Sciences not applicable,
and only 32 libraries did so with regard to Urban Studies.
The response rate to the request for an assessment of the collection levels for different subjects was far higher than that
for such matters as budgets, expenditure, numbers of volumes,
and others that required quantitative information.

Table 6.6.12 is a score card showing the librarians' ratings of their collections in the various subjects. Assessments of the collection of 206 libraries in 36 subjects (34
plus "Interdisciplinary" and "Other") would make for 7,416
scores. Of these markings, however, 1,280 merely signified
that certain subjects were not relevant ("not applicable") to
the reporting libraries. The actual 6,136 assessments of the
collections in applicable subjects yielded only 72 ratings as
"comprehensive." These ratings were given to six collections
each in Mathematics, Education, and Interdisciplinary publications, to four collections in Agriculture and to three in
Physics. For all other subjects only one or two libraries
rated their collections as comprehensive. The 72 top ratings
were given to only 1.2 per cent of the collections judged by
the 6,136 assessments.

Ratings of collections as of "research level" were much
more frequent: 1,678 subject collections, or 27.3 per cent,
were so rated. This is a relatively large number and one
might suspect something like "grade inflation" unless one
realized that most of our most cooperative respondents were
the directors of research libraries — so that it is hardly
surprising that the collections in many subjects are actually
found to be of true research level. The subject that received

TABLE 6.6.12  Assessments of the Collection Level, or the Strength or Weakness of the Collection for Purposes of Research and Study in 36 Subjects, by 206 Libraries

| Subjects | Comprehensive (virtually exhaustive) | Research level | Study level | Basic level | Minimal level | Not applicable | Total |
|---|---|---|---|---|---|---|---|
| Astronomy | 2 | 36 | 32 | 57 | 41 | 38 | 206 |
| Biology | 2 | 81 | 37 | 44 | 28 | 14 | 206 |
| Chemistry | 2 | 79 | 41 | 38 | 30 | 16 | 206 |
| Environmental sciences | - | 51 | 60 | 46 | 31 | 18 | 206 |
| Geology | 2 | 59 | 41 | 31 | 42 | 31 | 206 |
| Mathematics | 6 | 70 | 43 | 43 | 28 | 16 | 206 |
| Physics | 3 | 68 | 43 | 39 | 30 | 23 | 206 |
| Zoology | 2 | 64 | 41 | 39 | 28 | 32 | 206 |
| Engineering & technology | 2 | 56 | 35 | 41 | 49 | 23 | 206 |
| Agriculture | 4 | 27 | 12 | 45 | 58 | 60 | 206 |
| Anthropology | - | 42 | 51 | 49 | 37 | 27 | 206 |
| Economics | 1 | 68 | 50 | 49 | 23 | 15 | 206 |
| Geography | - | 36 | 51 | 59 | 33 | 27 | 206 |
| History | - | 69 | 67 | 38 | 10 | 22 | 206 |
| Political science | - | 61 | 69 | 38 | 16 | 22 | 206 |
| Psychology | 1 | 69 | 65 | 43 | 13 | 15 | 206 |
| Sociology | 2 | 59 | 77 | 34 | 17 | 17 | 206 |
| Statistics | 2 | 52 | 58 | 39 | 39 | 16 | 206 |
| Urban studies | 1 | 34 | 58 | 44 | 37 | 32 | 206 |
| Architecture | 2 | 36 | 46 | 47 | 41 | 34 | 206 |
| Art | 1 | 51 | 77 | 37 | 14 | 26 | 206 |
| Archaeology | 2 | 27 | 41 | 53 | 43 | 40 | 206 |
| Classics | 1 | 32 | 54 | 51 | 28 | 40 | 206 |
| Language & literature (including linguistics) | - | 67 | 64 | 33 | 16 | 26 | 206 |
| Music | - | 49 | 60 | 43 | 16 | 38 | 206 |
| Philosophy | - | 52 | 59 | 41 | 27 | 27 | 206 |
| Religion | 1 | 24 | 64 | 61 | 23 | 33 | 206 |
| Health sciences | 3 | 43 | 49 | 47 | 43 | 21 | 206 |
| Law | 1 | 29 | 22 | 41 | 64 | 49 | 206 |
| Education | 6 | 64 | 48 | 37 | 33 | 18 | 206 |
| Bibliography and library science | 2 | 47 | 53 | 57 | 29 | 18 | 206 |
| Interdisciplinary subjects | 6 | 27 | 40 | 23 | 16 | 94 | 206 |
| Popular adult nonfiction (e.g., recreation, travel, hobbies, etc.) | 2 | 6 | 35 | 58 | 49 | 56 | 206 |
| Adult fiction | 2 | 19 | 48 | 45 | 34 | 58 | 206 |
| Juvenile fiction & nonfiction | 2 | 11 | 42 | 44 | 30 | 77 | 206 |
| Other | 9 | 13 | 13 | 8 | 2 | 161 | 206 |
| Total | 72 | 1,678 | 1,746 | 1,542 | 1,098 | 1,280 | 7,416 |
| Per cent of 6,136 applicable ratings | 1.2% | 27.3% | 28.5% | 25.1% | 17.9% | | |

Source: Machlup, Leeson, and Associates.

the largest number of this rating is Biology: no less than 81 libraries have their biology collections at research level. Chemistry comes next with 79 collections on that level. For the following subjects between 60 and 76 libraries reported that their collections are of research level or better (that is, comprehensive): Geology, Mathematics, Physics, Zoology, Economics, History, Political Science, Psychology, Sociology, Language and Literature, and Education.

Collections at "study level" can be found for many subjects, with 28.5 per cent of all ratings. Since any collections judged to be comprehensive or at research level are *a fortiori* adequate for purposes of study, one can reasonably cumulate the percentages given for the three top levels. Thus, 57 per cent of all subject collections assessed by the 206 libraries are of study level or better. The other 43 per cent are "basic" or "minimal."

We mentioned six collections of Interdisciplinary publications that were rated as comprehensive. Most of them were in regional studies. Regional studies are also prevalent in the research-level collections of Interdisciplinary works. Latin-American, African and Asian studies were most frequently mentioned. The same type of collections were specified also in the blank lines for "other" subjects. But among the nine collections in "other" subjects were such specialties as Veterinary Medicine, Ornithology, Microbiology, Soil Sciences, and Water Resources.

If we look once more at the first two columns of ratings in Table 6.6.12 and count the numbers of collections assessed to be of "research level or better," we find the three leading subjects to be Biology (83), Chemistry (81) and Mathematics (76). This suggests to us two possibilities: the librarians' interests in these fields are more intensive or it is easier to assemble and maintain a high-level collection in these fields. We are inclined to place more emphasis on the second alternative. These are fields in which fewer books are published and in which the flow of new knowledge is embodied chiefly in journals. A new library can probably build a research collection in Biology or Chemistry much more easily than in English Literature or French Literature, let alone in "Literature, English and Foreign." Not a single library in our sample of 206 assessed its collection in Language and Literature to be of comprehensive level; but six libraries gave such a rating to their collections in Mathematics.

CHAPTER 6.7

LIBRARY ACQUISITIONS CLASSIFIED BY FIELD

In this chapter we come back to the main task of our research:  the distribution of books and journals classified
by subject or field.  At this juncture we shall report what
we have found out about American libraries as buyers of such
publications.  Before that, however, it may be well to remind
ourselves of the circumstances that led to the inquiry.

## LIBRARY INFORMATION ON PURCHASES BY FIELD

For a number of years, publishers of scientific-scholarly
books had noticed that they were selling fewer copies per
title.  Since such complaints had come largely from university
presses, and since university presses sell primarily to libraries, the suggestion was strong that library purchases of
scholarly books were declining.  Did commercial publishers
of books in the natural and social sciences and in the humanities have similar experiences?  This question could not be con-
clusively answered, because many publishers had substantial
portions of their total sales to wholesalers and no information was available on just what the wholesalers were selling
to libraries.
Thus it seemed to be of primary importance to find out
from libraries how their acquisitions of books and periodicals
have changed, and especially whether they have been buying
fewer books in particular fields.  Have their purchases of
books in the natural sciences been kept up, or perhaps increased, at the expense of books in the humanities?  How did
the libraries, during the last six or seven years, allocate
their budgets among different fields?  How many books — titles
and volumes — did they acquire in the various subjects?  If
their expenditures for periodicals increased at the expense of
purchases of books, were some fields favored and others ne-

glected? These were some of the questions for which we hoped to get answers from the librarians.


## Unanswerable Questions

Unfortunately, the librarians did not have the answers to our questions. Their records were not designed to yield information sufficiently detailed for our purposes. In our naïveté we had thought that research libraries would be able to cull the answers from a variety of records. Were not their budgets allocated according to the departmental organization of academic institutions? Would not orders of books and periodicals be recorded either according to the department for which they were ordered or according to the subject classification used by the library? Were not invoices and bills from publishers or wholesalers charged against departmental allocations or, alternatively, recorded according to the subject classification used for cataloguing? Were not the books and journals received and catalogued entered into some sort of "additions to the shelflist?" Thus, we thought, our questions could be answered not only from one but from several different records which we thought were regularly kept by libraries.


## A Questionnaire to Help Design Another Questionnaire

Our first inquiries with librarians sufficed to shock us out of our innocence. We were told that such detailed record-keeping was not generally practiced, and that only in highly exceptional cases would we be able to obtain the needed data. This led to our first questionnaire survey, for which we had the helpful support and advice from the officers and staff of the Association of Research Libraries. This questionnaire did not request any quantitative data but, instead, asked only whether our respondents would be able to furnish answers to a variety of specified questions at a reasonable cost, high cost, excessive cost, or not at all. A copy of this questionnaire can be found in Appendix A of Part Six.

The answers from the respondents disabused us of any optimistic expectations. Now we had learned that most libraries could not tell us for any of the past six years how many books in each field they had acquired, and/or how much money they had spent on books in each field. We decided that we must not mail the questionnaires which we had designed to obtain answers to these questions, and we resigned ourselves to the fact that we could at best ask for "impressionistic answers."

*Impressions versus Records*

Our quest for expressions of impressions where there were no records yielding objective numerical data was perhaps an "unscientific" way to obtain answers.  However, our desire to learn  more about the libraries' purchases broken down by field (subject or department) was so great that we believed we should not disdain non-numerical assessments of the accretions to their collections in the various fields.  From their dealings with library users — teachers, students, researchers and other readers — and from their considerations of complaints and pressures of various sorts, including those evolved within the library staff, librarians may have formed impressions of "how they were doing" in various parts of their colleciton. Reports on these impressions should serve as substitutes, however imperfect, for quantitative data.

An example of a question calling for impressionistic answers was one about "Changes in Book-Buying Patterns by Subject."  We requested the respondent simply to mark a symbol telling us whether in any of the special subjects they were buying "significantly more," "slightly more," "unchanged numbers," "slightly less," or "significantly less" of books (volumes) than they had in the past.  This question was answered by 179 libraries.  A compilation of the replies, subject by subject, will be presented later on, in this chapter. At this point, we will show the tallies for only five fields, comment on the whole exercise, and undertake a brief consistency test.

| | Buying signif- icantly more | Buying slight- ly more | No change | Buying slightly less | Buying signif- icantly less | Not appli- cable |
|---|---|---|---|---|---|---|
| Physics | 4 | 28 | 68 | 32 | 26 | 21 |
| Psychology | 30 | 45 | 62 | 15 | 16 | 11 |
| Sociology | 31 | 36 | 64 | 21 | 12 | 15 |
| Anthropology | 16 | 35 | 61 | 26 | 9 | 32 |
| Language and literature | 20 | 27 | 54 | 28 | 26 | 24 |

According to these answers we find that 100 libraries said they were buying more or unchanged numbers of books in Physics while only 58 libraries reported buying less in 1976 than in 1970.  In Psychology, 137 libraries told of buying more or unchanged numbers of books while only 31 told of buying fewer books.  In Sociology, 131 libraries reported buying more or unchanged numbers of books in 1976 while only 33 libraries said they bought fewer books. In Anthropology, 112 libraries believed they bought more or unchanged numbers of books in 1976 while only 35 libraries thought they were buying less than in 1970. In Language and Literature 101 libraries reported buying more and only 54 buying less. Making the same kind of comparison for other scientific and scholarly fields, we find that it has been the impression of librarians that they had *increased* the acquisition of books.

In a different part of the questionnaire we had asked a question to which 119 librarians had numerical answers, namely, regarding their expenditures for book purchases, not broken down by field. We learned that these 119 libraries had spent in 1970 a total of $28,012,600 for books, and in 1976 a total of $29,226,400. This was an increase of about 4 per cent. However, from 1970 to 1976 the average net price of books had increased from $4.01 to $6.02, or by 50 per cent.[1] Using these figures of total expenditures and average prices, we calculate that the group of 119 libraries was able to buy 6,985,700 books in 1970 but only 4,854,900 books in 1976 — a *reduction* by 31 per cent.

Now, what should we say about the consistency between the numerical data on expenditures for books and the impressionistic replies on changes in book-buying patterns? Obviously, the "impressions" conflict flagrantly with the results of the expenditures records. These records show a decline of 31 per cent in the number of books purchased, while the librarians' impressions were that they bought more, not fewer, books in 1976. We can think of several ways to reconcile the conflicting reports. (1) The answers to the two questions may have been supplied by libraries of totally different institutions, that is, the group of 119 libraries reporting their expenditures and the group of 179 libraries reporting on their book-buying patterns may have been quite dissimilar. (2) Those among the 179 libraries that reported their impressions of having bought more rather than fewer books in most subjects may have had smaller budgets than those that reported reduc-

---

[1]These prices are derived from Table 2.3.2 (A) of Chapter 2.3. The average net price for 1976 is an estimated figure based on the assumption of an increase of 7 per cent over the previous year. This is the average percentage increase for the previous five years. By comparison, the average percentage increase in the list prices of *new hardbound* books over the same period as reported by Bowker was more than 9 per cent, although the increase from 1975 to 1976 had been less than one per cent.

tions in book-buying, with the result that *total* expenditures suffered a decline in book-purchasing power that would still be compatible with increased purchases of books by a larger number of smaller libraries. (3) Some respondents to the question on book-buying patterns may have misunderstood it and checked "buying more" when the dollar volume of their purchases in 1976 was above that of 1970 (although we had mentioned "book volumes" in an example given to make the instructions clear). (4) Impressions are less reliable than numerical records; thus it may be that many of the responding librarians had not been fully aware of the serious decline in their acquisition of books.

The four possible causes for the conflicts in reports are not mutually exclusive; all four of them could be valid. In any case the numerical reports speak louder than the merely impressionistic ones.


CHANGES IN BOOK-BUYING PATTERNS

Although we may now have discredited the reports on how, between 1970 and 1976, libraries changed their book-buying patterns by subject, we shall nevertheless present a summary of the replies and examine what they seem to indicate.


*A Sample of 179*

The response to our request for indications of changes in book-buying patterns was relatively good: 179 libraries went down the list of 36 subjects and marked one of the code numbers indicating that significantly more, slightly more, unchanged numbers, slightly fewer, or significantly fewer "book volumes" were bought in 1976 compared with 1970. (A sixth code number stood for "not applicable," that is, for subjects not relevant to the library's collection.) With 179 respondents marking code numbers in 36 subjects, a total of 6,444 marks were received and fed into the computer. Table 6.7.1 presents the results.

The bottom line of the table shows that, of the 6,444 answers, 1,333 were to the effect that the particular subject was not relevant to the library's collection. Of the 5,111 answers regarding relevant subjects, 2,085, or about 41 per cent, signified that there was no change, hence, that approximately the same number of volumes were bought in 1976 as in 1970. Significantly more volumes were bought for 577 subject collections, or 11 per cent, and slightly more for 1,109

TABLE 6.7.1  Changes in Book-Buying Patterns by Subject,
1976 Compared with 1970, Reported by 179 Libraries

| Subjects | Number of libraries reporting that they were buying | | | | | Subject not relevant to library | Total reports |
|---|---|---|---|---|---|---|---|
| | Significantly more | Slightly more | Unchanged quantities | Slightly less | Significantly less | | |
| Astronomy | 6 | 21 | 68 | 18 | 22 | 44 | 179 |
| Biology | 16 | 46 | 58 | 23 | 21 | 15 | 179 |
| Chemistry | 11 | 34 | 67 | 24 | 24 | 19 | 179 |
| Environmental sciences | 53 | 59 | 30 | 11 | 9 | 17 | 179 |
| Geology | 6 | 25 | 67 | 28 | 21 | 32 | 179 |
| Mathematics | 13 | 28 | 76 | 25 | 20 | 17 | 179 |
| Physics | 4 | 28 | 68 | 32 | 26 | 21 | 179 |
| Zoology | 8 | 39 | 64 | 22 | 14 | 32 | 179 |
| Engineering & technology | 15 | 35 | 52 | 21 | 22 | 34 | 179 |
| Agriculture | 9 | 20 | 55 | 11 | 11 | 73 | 179 |
| Anthropology | 16 | 35 | 61 | 26 | 9 | 32 | 179 |
| Economics | 24 | 38 | 68 | 23 | 10 | 16 | 179 |
| Geography | 8 | 24 | 70 | 27 | 11 | 39 | 179 |
| History | 19 | 34 | 58 | 24 | 22 | 22 | 179 |
| Political science | 19 | 31 | 63 | 24 | 17 | 25 | 179 |
| Psychology | 30 | 45 | 62 | 15 | 16 | 11 | 179 |
| Sociology | 31 | 36 | 64 | 21 | 12 | 15 | 179 |
| Statistics | 9 | 25 | 90 | 26 | 8 | 21 | 179 |
| Urban studies | 23 | 49 | 49 | 19 | 7 | 32 | 179 |
| Architecture | 14 | 22 | 65 | 22 | 15 | 41 | 179 |
| Art | 24 | 29 | 54 | 26 | 18 | 28 | 179 |
| Archaeology | 7 | 29 | 62 | 22 | 10 | 49 | 179 |
| Classics | 7 | 19 | 57 | 30 | 21 | 45 | 179 |
| Language & literature (including linguistics) | 20 | 27 | 54 | 28 | 26 | 24 | 179 |
| Music | 21 | 38 | 45 | 28 | 12 | 35 | 179 |
| Philosophy | 9 | 25 | 69 | 30 | 17 | 29 | 179 |
| Religion | 17 | 25 | 54 | 28 | 19 | 36 | 179 |
| Health sciences | 32 | 52 | 46 | 12 | 7 | 30 | 179 |
| Law | 15 | 29 | 54 | 18 | 9 | 54 | 179 |
| Education | 15 | 27 | 65 | 30 | 19 | 23 | 179 |
| Bibliography and library science | 13 | 39 | 80 | 21 | 12 | 14 | 179 |
| Interdisciplinary subjects | 18 | 32 | 39 | 12 | 6 | 72 | 179 |
| Popular adult nonfiction (e.g., recreation, travel, hobbies, etc.) | 12 | 21 | 51 | 18 | 18 | 59 | 179 |
| Adult fiction | 11 | 21 | 50 | 23 | 20 | 54 | 179 |
| Juvenile fiction & nonfiction | 13 | 17 | 43 | 21 | 11 | 74 | 179 |
| Other | 9 | 5 | 7 | 5 | 4 | 149 | 179 |
| Total | 577 | 1,109 | 2,085 | 794 | 546 | 1,333 | 6,444 |

Source:  Machlup, Leeson, and Associates.

subject collections, or 22 per cent. Slightly less was bought for 794 subject collections, or 15 per cent, and significantly less for 546 subject collections, or 11 per cent. Thus, increased purchases were reported in 33 per cent of the answers, reduced purchases in 26 per cent of the answers. We have pointed out that this prevalence of growth-reports cannot be easily reconciled with the aggregative statistics on library expenditures deflated by the index of book prices. Let us look, nevertheless, in what subjects the majority of our respondents believe that the additions to their collections were larger in 1976 than in 1970.

*Gainers and Losers in the Scramble for Books*

The largest increase in book-buying was reported in Environmental Sciences, a new field, for which 112 of the 179 libraries in the sample reported increased acquisitions, with only 20 reports of reduced buying. Health Sciences is the second-highest achiever, with a ratio of 84:19 of reported increases and reductions. In third place is Psychology with a ratio of 75:31. Urban Studies with 72:36 take fourth place, followed by Sociology with 67:33, Economics with 62:33 and Biology with 62:44. In altogether 20 of the 36 rows the number of libraries reporting increased buying exceeds the number of those reporting reductions.

Which are the subjects for which the number of libraries reporting reduced book-buying exceeds the number of reported increases? Strangely enough, Physics appears to be the biggest loser, with only 32 reports on increased buying against 58 reports of reduced buying. Next is Language and Literature with a ratio of 47:54, and Classics with a ratio of 26:51. We shall not continue with the "also rans" on the list, chiefly because the reported impressions of the librarians are probably not sufficiently accurate. Suffice it to say that Philosophy and Religion are among the losers, that is, among the subjects for which reports of reduced buying are more numerous than reports of increased buying. On the basis of the findings from our statistics on expenditures we are convinced that the scores in this assessment of changes in book-buying patterns would look much worse if they were based on quantitative records and not merely on impressions.

A good many libraries reported increases or decreases in "Interdisciplinary" books and in books on "other" subjects. Among the former they specified significant or slight increases in Latin-American Studies, Afro-American Studies, Asian Studies, Women's Studies, and books on Energy, though a few libraries reported decreases in some of the same subjects, for example, in Asian Studies and other Area Studies. Among the "other" subjects increases were reported in Latin Americana, Judaica, and Energy; decreases in Botany and Slavic Literature; and both increases and decreases in Business Administration.


## Ranking the Changes in Book-Buying Patterns

We went further in our inquiry into the librarians' impressions by asking them, after they completed tabulating the changes in their book-buying habits, to rank the subjects which they thought were most significantly affected by these changes. They were requested to rank the three subjects for which acquisitions were most significantly increased and the three subjects which suffered the most significant cuts in acquisition. While 179 libraries had furnished the subject-by-subject score of changes in book-buying patterns, much fewer cared to rank the subjects: 121 libraries gave us the ranking of the subjects for which more books were acquired and 94 libraries ranked the most disadvantaged subjects. The tallies are shown in Table 6.7.2.

In principle it would be possible that a subject is ranked among the top gainers and at the same time also among the top losers. It would mean that a large number of libraries decided to enlarge their collections in this subject while many other libraries preferred to build their collections in other directions and to go slow on the subject in question, which they had favored in the past. While such temporally inconsistent policies of collection development are quite common — as one can see from a closer examination of Table 6.7.1 — they were not sufficiently frequent to lead to top-ratings of the same subjects as simultaneously the most-favored and most-disfavored relative to the past, except in two cases: Engineering and Art. For the most part, different subjects emerged as top-gainers and top-losers according to the librarians' reports.

The three subjects most often mentioned for Rank 1 were Health Sciences (18 votes), Environmental Sciences (15 votes) and Interdisciplinary Works (11 votes) on the gaining side, and History (11 votes), Language and Literature (10 votes), and Adult Fiction (10 votes) on the losing side.

If we take Rank 1 and Rank 2 together and count the votes, the three most significant gainers were Environmental Sciences (30), Health Sciences (23), and Interdisciplinary Works (18); and the three most significant losers were — as in Rank 1 — History (18), Language and Literature (16), and Adult Fiction (15).

114

TABLE 6.7.2 Ranking the Changes in Book-Buying Patterns by Subject: Stating the Three Subjects for Which Acquisitions Most Significantly Increased or Most Significantly Decreased in 1976 Relative to 1970, Reported by 121 and 94 Libraries, Respectively

| Subjects | Most significant increases | | | Most significant decreases | | |
|---|---|---|---|---|---|---|
| | Rank 1 | Rank 2 | Rank 3 | Rank 1 | Rank 2 | Rank 3 |
| Astronomy | 1 | 1 | – | 4 | 3 | 2 |
| Biology | 6 | 3 | 2 | 3 | 5 | 3 |
| Chemistry | 3 | 3 | 2 | 8 | 3 | 5 |
| Environmental sciences | 15 | 15 | 11 | 2 | 3 | – |
| Geology | – | 1 | – | 2 | 3 | 2 |
| Mathematics | 1 | 3 | 1 | 2 | 2 | 5 |
| Physics | – | – | 1 | 4 | 9 | 3 |
| Zoology | 1 | 2 | 2 | – | 2 | – |
| Engineering & technology | 7 | 4 | 5 | 9 | 5 | 1 |
| Agriculture | 1 | 2 | 1 | 5 | 1 | – |
| Anthropology | 3 | – | 4 | 1 | 3 | – |
| Economics | 7 | 4 | 5 | 1 | – | 1 |
| Geography | – | 2 | – | 2 | 1 | 5 |
| History | 4 | 5 | 5 | 11 | 7 | – |
| Political science | 1 | 3 | 4 | 1 | 2 | 4 |
| Psychology | 7 | 6 | 3 | 3 | 2 | 1 |
| Sociology | 5 | 6 | 7 | – | 1 | 1 |
| Statistics | 1 | 1 | 2 | 1 | – | – |
| Urban studies | 4 | 2 | 4 | 1 | 1 | 3 |
| Architecture | 1 | 5 | – | 1 | 1 | 1 |
| Art | 7 | 6 | 4 | 5 | 4 | 4 |
| Archaeology | – | 1 | 2 | – | – | 1 |
| Classics | – | 1 | – | 7 | 1 | 3 |
| Language & literature (including linguistics) | 5 | 6 | 3 | 10 | 6 | 4 |
| Music | 4 | 6 | 1 | 1 | 2 | 2 |
| Philosophy | – | – | 2 | 1 | 3 | 3 |
| Religion | 2 | 5 | 5 | 2 | 2 | 3 |
| Health sciences | 18 | 5 | 8 | – | 4 | 2 |
| Law | 5 | 1 | 5 | 4 | 2 | 1 |
| Education | 2 | 2 | 3 | 4 | 5 | 1 |
| Bibliography and library science | 3 | 1 | 1 | – | 5 | 3 |
| Interdisciplinary subjects | 11 | 7 | 5 | 1 | – | 3 |
| Popular adult nonfiction (e.g., recreation, travel, hobbies, etc.) | 7 | 3 | – | 2 | 1 | 5 |
| Adult fiction | 3 | 4 | – | 10 | 5 | – |
| Juvenile fiction & nonfiction | 1 | 3 | 4 | 2 | 1 | 2 |
| Other | 1 | 3 | 2 | 2 | 1 | – |
| Total | 137 | 122 | 104 | 112 | 96 | 74 |
| Rank 1 | | 137 | | | 112 | |
| Ranks 1 and 2 | | 259 | 259 | | 208 | 208 |
| Ranks 1, 2, and 3 | | | 363 | | | 282 |
| Libraries responding | | | ÷3 = 121 | | | ÷3 = 121 |

Source: Machlup, Leeson, and Associates.

115

Taking now all three ranks together and expanding the lists of subjects nominated for these ranks to seven on each side, we see the subjects in the following order, where all gains and losses are in the acquisitions of 1976 compared with those of 1970:

| *In Ranks 1, 2, or 3 as most significant gainers* | *In Ranks 1, 2, or 3 as most significant losers* |
| --- | --- |
| Environmental Sciences (41 votes) | Language and Literature (20 votes) |
| Health Sciences (31 votes) | History (18 votes) |
| Interdisciplinary Studies (23 votes) | Chemistry (16 votes) |
| Sociology (18 votes) | Physics (16 votes) |
| Art (17 votes) | Engineering (15 votes) |
| Engineering (16 votes) | Adult Fiction (15 votes) |
| Economics (16 votes) | Art (13 votes) |

Engineering and Art appear on both sides, as both significant gainers and significant losers, only thanks to our expanding the list. If we had numerical data for book acquisitions, we might similarly see that some libraries increased and other libraries reduced the volumes of books acquired in the same fields by substantial quantities; but we could also see what changes occurred on balance. The mere ranking of increases and reductions cannot give us the net changes, and could not do so even if the rankings were perfectly accurate.


*Reasons for Changes in Book-Buying Patterns*

In response to our request for the libraries' rankings of the changes in their book-buying patterns, 121 libraries named the three subjects for which they bought in 1976 significantly more, and 94 libraries the three for which they bought significantly fewer volumes than in the past. These libraries obliged by answering our next question, about their reasons for the changes. Each library selected two subjects with the most significant increases and two with the most significant decreases in acquisitions, and marked for each of these four subjects the main reasons for the change. We had formulated twelve possible reasons but provided space for additional ones. The libraries were requested to mark as many of the reasons as they deemed relevant to their decisions. Here is the list of the twelve reasons formulated in our questionnaire: (1) Relative change in undergraduate student en-

116

rollment, (2) Relative change in graduate student enrollment, (3) Relative change in number of faculty, (4) Change in program emphasis, (5) Change in number of programs, (6) Increase in relative price of books, (7) Increase in relative price of serials, (8) Change in external private funding, (9) Change in external federal funding (10) Change in state or local funding, (11) Change in internal library funding priority, (12) Change in funding priority of supporting institution.

In Tables 6.7.3 and 6.7.4 the tallies are shown: in the former for the reasons for increased buying, in the latter for decreased buying of books in the subjects in which the most significant changes occurred. The figures in the column captioned "Number of Responses" add up to 238 and 188, respectively, or twice the number of libraries responding, because each library had two subjects for which it had to explain the change in book-buying. Horizontal additions of the figures bear no relation to the number of libraries responding, since the respondents could mark or state any number of reasons that may have influenced them.

The vertical additions show the numbers of times each of the reasons was mentioned by the librarians as having induced them to make the reported changes in their book-buying patterns. Below these sums the relative frequencies are given as percentages of the total number of marks. These totals, incidentally, came out to be about two and a half times the number of library responses to each of the two chosen subjects (605 ÷ 238, or 2.5, in Table 6.7.3, and 450 ÷ 188, or 2.4, in Table 6.7.4). That is to say, the librarians marked an average of 2.5 reasons for their decisions to increase, and likewise for their decisions to reduce, acquisitions of books in the subjects in which they changed their purchases most significantly. Comparing the relative frequencies in the two tables, we find that the reasons for increased buying are different from the reasons for decreased buying. The most frequently mentioned reason for buying *more* books on the most-favored subjects of 1976 was "change in program emphasis" (23.2 per cent). The most frequently mentioned reason for buying *fewer* books on the most disadvantaged subjects was "change in internal library funding priority" (14.9 per cent), with the second, third, and fourth of the most frequent reasons (of the twelve pre-formulated ones) "increase in the relative price of books" (14.4 per cent), "change in program emphasis" (12.7 per cent), and "increase in the relative price of serials" (9.6 per cent). These four reasons for reducing the number of books acquired in a particular subject may merge into one. The higher prices for both books and serials diminish the purchasing power of the library dollar; the higher prices for serials may reduce the relative size of the budget

TABLE 6.7.3  *Reasons for Increased Acquisitions of Books in the Two Relatively Most-Favored Subjects, 1976, by 119 Libraries*

Reasons for <u>significant increase</u> in book acquisitions

| Fields | Number of responses | Relative change in under-graduate student enrollment | Relative change in graduate student enrollment | Relative change in number of faculty | Change in program emphasis |
|---|---|---|---|---|---|
| Astronomy | 2 | | | | 1 |
| Biology | 9 | 3 | 5 | 3 | 6 |
| Chemistry | 4 | | 1 | 1 | 1 |
| Environmental sciences | 26 | 3 | 5 | 4 | 15 |
| Geology | 1 | 1 | | | |
| Mathematics | 4 | 1 | 1 | 2 | 1 |
| Physics | | | | | |
| Zoology | 2 | 1 | 1 | 1 | 2 |
| Engineering & technology | 9 | 3 | 3 | 1 | 5 |
| Agriculture | 4 | 3 | 2 | 2 | 3 |
| Anthropology | 3 | 1 | | 2 | 1 |
| Economics | 12 | 6 | 4 | 6 | 7 |
| Geography | 2 | | | | |
| History | 7 | 1 | 1 | 1 | 2 |
| Political science | 4 | 1 | | 2 | 3 |
| Psychology | 12 | 3 | 3 | 4 | 8 |
| Sociology | 12 | 4 | | 2 | 8 |
| Statistics | 2 | 1 | | | 1 |
| Urban studies | 7 | 4 | 4 | 3 | 6 |
| Architecture | 5 | 1 | 1 | 1 | 3 |
| Art | 11 | 3 | 1 | 3 | 9 |
| Archaeology | 1 | | 1 | 1 | 1 |
| Classics | 1 | | | | 1 |
| Language & literature | 9 | 1 | | 2 | 4 |
| Music | 11 | 3 | 3 | 3 | 8 |
| Philosophy | | | | | |
| Religion | 7 | 2 | 1 | | 2 |
| Health sciences | 21 | 9 | 4 | 8 | 11 |
| Law | 8 | | 1 | 1 | 5 |
| Education | 4 | | | 1 | 2 |
| Bibliography & library science | 5 | | 2 | 1 | 2 |
| Interdisciplinary subjects | 14 | 6 | 5 | 6 | 12 |
| Popular adult nonfiction | 9 | | | | 3 |
| Adult fiction | 3 | | | | 1 |
| Juvenile fiction & nonfiction | 3 | | | | 2 |
| Other | 4 | 1 | 1 | 1 | 3 |
| Total | 119 × 2 = 238 | 62 | 50 | 62 | 139 |
| Per cent of total | | 105% | 8.5% | 10.5% | 23.5% |

118

| Change in number of programs | Increase in relative price of books | Increase in relative price of serials | Change in external private funding | Change in external federal funding | Change in state or local funding | Change in internal library funding priority | Change in funding priority of supporting institution | Other |
|---|---|---|---|---|---|---|---|---|
|  |  |  |  |  |  | 1 |  | 1 |
| 3 | 1 | 1 |  |  | 1 | 2 | 1 | 2 |
|  | 2 | 2 |  |  |  | 1 | 4 | 1 |
| 9 |  |  |  | 1 | 3 | 5 | 1 | 10 |
| 1 |  |  |  |  |  | 1 |  |  |
| 1 |  |  |  |  |  | 1 |  | 2 |
| 1 |  |  |  |  |  |  |  |  |
| 2 | 2 |  |  | 1 |  | 1 |  | 3 |
| 1 |  |  |  |  |  |  |  |  |
| 2 |  |  |  |  |  |  |  |  |
| 1 |  |  |  | 1 | 2 | 3 |  | 2 |
|  |  |  |  |  |  | 1 |  | 1 |
| 1 | 3 | 1 | 1 | 3 | 3 | 1 |  | 1 |
| 1 |  |  |  | 2 | 1 | 2 |  | 5 |
| 4 |  |  |  | 1 | 1 | 1 | 1 | 4 |
|  |  |  |  |  |  | 1 |  | 1 |
| 2 |  |  | 1 | 1 | 1 |  |  |  |
| 2 | 1 |  | 1 |  | 2 | 1 | 1 | 5 |
| 2 | 2 | 1 | 2 | 1 | 1 | 1 |  | 3 |
| 1 |  | 1 |  | 1 | 1 | 4 | 1 | 5 |
| 3 | 1 |  |  | 1 | 2 | 7 | 1 |  |
| 4 | 1 |  | 1 |  | 1 | 1 | 1 | 1 |
| 10 | 2 | 1 | 1 | 4 | 2 | 3 | 2 | 5 |
|  | 1 | 1 |  | 1 | 1 | 2 | 2 | 2 |
| 1 |  |  | 1 |  |  |  | 1 | 2 |
|  |  |  |  |  |  | 3 |  | 2 |
| 4 |  |  | 2 |  | 1 | 2 | 1 | 1 |
|  | 1 |  |  | 1 | 3 | 2 |  | 7 |
|  |  |  |  |  |  | 2 |  | 2 |
|  |  |  |  | 1 |  | 3 |  | 1 |
| 1 | — | 1 | — | — | — | — | — | 1 |
| 57 | 17 | 9 | 10 | 20 | 26 | 52 | 17 | 70 |
| 9.6% | 2.9% | 1.5% | 1.7% | 3.4% | 4.4% | 8.8% | 2.9% | 11.8% |

Source: Machlup, Leeson, and Associates.

119

TABLE 6.7.4   Reasons for Reduced Acquisitions of Books in the Two Relatively Most Disadvantaged Subjects, 1976, by 94 Libraries

|  |  | Reasons for significant decrease in book acquisitions | | | |
|---|---|---|---|---|---|
| Fields | Number of responses | Relative change in under-graduate student enrollment | Relative change in graduate student enrollment | Relative change in number of faculty | Change in program emphasis |
| Astronomy | 5 | 2 | 3 | 2 | 4 |
| Biology | 7 | 2 | | | 1 |
| Chemistry | 12 | 2 | 3 | | 1 |
| Environmental sciences | 1 | | | | 1 |
| Geology | 5 | 1 | | | 3 |
| Mathematics | 4 | | 1 | | 2 |
| Physics | 9 | | | 1 | 1 |
| Zoology | 2 | 1 | | | 1 |
| Engineering & technology | 13 | 1 | 1 | | 3 |
| Agriculture | 5 | | | 1 | 5 |
| Anthropology | 3 | 2 | | 2 | 2 |
| Economics | | | | | |
| Geography | 4 | 3 | | 4 | 2 |
| History | 17 | 9 | 5 | 1 | 5 |
| Political science | 3 | | | | 1 |
| Psychology | 4 | | | | |
| Sociology | 1 | | | | 1 |
| Statistics | 1 | 1 | | | |
| Urban studies | 1 | | | | |
| Architecture | 2 | 1 | | 1 | 1 |
| Art | 10 | 2 | 2 | 2 | 3 |
| Archaeology | | | | | |
| Classics | 7 | 1 | 1 | 2 | 2 |
| Language & literature | 14 | 4 | 4 | 2 | 4 |
| Music | 4 | 1 | 1 | | 1 |
| Philosophy | 4 | 2 | 1 | 1 | 2 |
| Religion | 5 | 1 | | | 1 |
| Health sciences | 5 | 1 | | | |
| Law | 6 | | | | 1 |
| Education | 9 | 2 | 1 | 1 | 3 |
| Bibliography & library science | 3 | | | | 1 |
| Interdisciplinary subjects | 3 | 1 | 2 | | |
| Popular adult nonfiction | 5 | | | | |
| Adult fiction | 9 | | | | 1 |
| Juvenile fiction & nonfiction | 3 | | | | 1 |
| Other | 3 | 1 | 1 | 1 | 3 |
| Total | 94 × 2 = 188 | 41 | 26 | 21 | 57 |
| Per cent of total | | 9.1% | 5.8% | 4.7% | 12.7% |

120

Reasons for *significant decrease* in book Acquisitions

| Change in number of programs | Increase in relative price of books | Increase in relative price of serials | Change in external private funding | Change in external federal funding | Change in state or local funding | Change in internal library funding priority | Change in funding priority of supporting institution | Other |
|---|---|---|---|---|---|---|---|---|
|  |  |  |  |  |  | 2 | 1 | 1 |
|  | 5 | 3 | 1 | 1 | 1 | 2 |  | 2 |
| 1 | 7 | 9 |  |  | 3 | 6 | 1 |  |
| 1 |  |  |  |  |  |  |  |  |
|  | 2 | 3 |  |  | 1 | 1 |  | 1 |
| 1 | 1 | 1 |  |  | 1 | 1 | 1 |  |
|  | 6 | 4 |  | 1 | 2 | 3 |  | 3 |
|  |  |  |  |  | 3 | 2 |  | 1 |
| 2 | 7 | 8 |  | 1 |  | 2 | 1 | 2 |
| 2 | 1 | 1 |  |  |  | 1 |  |  |
| 1 | 1 |  |  |  |  | 1 |  |  |
| 2 |  |  |  |  |  |  |  |  |
| 1 | 7 | 4 | 2 | 4 | 5 | 5 |  | 5 |
|  |  |  |  |  |  |  |  | 2 |
|  | 2 | 1 |  |  |  | 2 |  | 3 |
|  |  |  |  |  |  | 1 |  |  |
|  |  |  |  |  |  |  |  | 1 |
|  | 1 |  |  |  |  |  |  | 2 |
|  | 5 |  | 1 | 2 | 1 | 3 |  |  |
|  | 1 | 1 |  |  | 1 | 1 |  | 5 |
|  | 4 | 4 | 1 | 2 | 3 | 7 | 1 | 5 |
|  | 2 |  | 1 |  |  | 3 |  |  |
| 1 |  |  |  |  |  | 1 |  | 3 |
| 1 |  |  |  |  |  | 1 |  | 3 |
|  | 2 | 1 |  |  |  | 2 | 3 | 1 |
| 1 | 2 | 2 |  |  |  |  |  | 4 |
| 1 | 1 |  |  | 1 | 1 | 1 |  | 6 |
|  |  |  |  |  |  | 3 |  |  |
| 2 | 1 |  |  |  |  | 2 | 1 |  |
|  | 2 | 1 |  | 2 |  | 4 |  |  |
| 1 | 3 |  |  | 1 | 2 | 6 |  | 4 |
|  | 1 |  |  |  | 1 | 3 |  | 2 |
| 1 | 1 | — | — | — | — | 1 | — | — |
| 19 | 65 | 43 | 6 | 15 | 25 | 67 | 9 | 56 |
| 4.2% | 14.4% | 9.6% | 1.3% | 3.3% | 5.6% | 14.9% | 2.0% | 12.4% |

Source: Machlup, Leeson, and Associates.

121

allocation for books and thus force the change in internal funding priority, which is closely associated with a change in program emphasis.

It would take too much of a busy administrator's time to differentiate these interrelated reasons for buying fewer books on any particular subject. If he is asked or urged to acquire more books than he did in the past on now most-favored subjects — say, Environmental Sciences and Health Sciences — this may well be a matter of a "change in program emphasis." The increase in purchases of these books, however, need not force him to reduce the number of volumes acquired on any other subject unless he is under budget pressure, and this budget pressure may be caused by increased prices of books and serials. Hence, the absolute *cut* in allocations for books in some subjects would not be forced by the change in program emphasis, but by a change in "internal library funding priorities" that is due to the reduced purchasing power of a limited budget, but not to a *reduced desirability* of getting the books which the library cannot now afford to buy. In other words, the change in priorities that is inherent in any change in buying patterns need not imply that the library's program has led it to de-emphasize certain subjects. It may, instead, be the price increases and the consequently worsened budget constraints that are the real causes of cuts in acquisitions.

Increased size of the student body and of the faculty were named as important reasons for increased book-buying in many subjects; the combined frequency of these reasons was 29.8 per cent. These reasons were most often mentioned for books on Health Sciences, Interdisciplinary Works, and Economics. In Table 6.7.4 one may be surprised to find changes — evidently reductions — in the number of students given as the most frequently mentioned reason for buying fewer books in History and in Language and Literature. We had not been aware of reduced enrollments in these subjects; to be sure, several other reasons were also mentioned (for example, increases in the prices of books and serials, and changes in internal library funding) to explain why these had become the most disadvantaged subjects as far as recent book acquisition is concerned.

A good many "other" reasons for significant increases in book acquisition in particular subjects were specified by our respondents. A frequently mentioned reason was increased supply, couched in such language as "more being published," "increase in number of items available," or "more new titles published." Another reason frequently appearing among the "write-ins" was increase in demand (also expressed as "borrowers' interest," "demand from students," and "demand from patrons"). A rather peculiar explanation for a significant increase in a library's purchase of books on Library Science was that in 1970 (the year with which the book acquisitions of 1976 were to be compared) "there was no librarian here."


## CHANGES IN PERIODICAL SUBSCRIPTIONS BY SUBJECT

There are reasons to expect the reports on changes in periodical subscriptions to be more accurate than those on book acquisitions; but other reasons to expect the opposite. Subscriptions to periodicals lend themselves to better record-keeping, and periodicals can be more easily classified by subject. On the other hand, periodicals are not easily distinguished from other serials and, where they are not distinguished, classification by subject is difficult. Thus we do not know the degree of confidence we may have in the reports which the libraries have furnished with considerable efforts. In any case we are grateful to them for the trouble they have taken and we have examined and analyzed their reports with great care.


*A Sample of 100*

The rate of response to our questions on periodicals was smaller than that to our questions on books, probably because many libraries in our random sample have no large serial departments. While 179 libraries reported on their changes in book acquisitions, only 100 reported on their changes in periodical subscriptions.

The librarians were asked to compare for each subject the number of subscriptions in 1976 with those in 1970, and to mark for each subject a symbol indicating whether they were now (1976) carrying significantly more, slightly more, unchanged numbers, slightly fewer, or significantly fewer subscriptions than in the past. A sixth symbol was to be marked if the subject was not within the scope of the library. With 100 libraries marking the appropriate symbol for each of 36 subjects, we obtained 3600 answers. As we see in Table 6.7.5, no less than 920 of these answers indicated that the subject was not relevant for the responding library; this left 2680 scores for changes in the numbers of subscriptions in the relevant subjects. "No change" in the number of subscriptions by the 100 libraries was marked 1219 times, or for 45 per cent of the possible answers for the 36 subjects. The remaining answers told of 247 instances (9 per cent) of significantly more subscriptions, 677 instances (25 per cent) of slightly more subscriptions, 398 instances (15 per cent) of slightly

123

TABLE 6.7.5  *Changes in Periodical Subscriptions by Subject,*
*1976 compared with 1970, reported by 100 Libraries*

| Subjects | Number of libraries reporting that they were subscribing to | | | | | | |
|---|---|---|---|---|---|---|---|
| | Significantly more | Slightly more | Unchanged numbers | Slightly less | Significantly less | Subject not relevant | Total reports |
| Astronomy | 3 | 15 | 34 | 14 | 5 | 29 | 100 |
| Biology | 9 | 22 | 34 | 14 | 5 | 16 | 100 |
| Chemistry | 7 | 18 | 32 | 15 | 9 | 19 | 100 |
| Environmental science | 22 | 36 | 21 | 7 | 2 | 12 | 100 |
| Geology | 4 | 15 | 31 | 16 | 4 | 30 | 100 |
| Mathematics | 6 | 20 | 33 | 15 | 6 | 20 | 100 |
| Physics | 4 | 12 | 40 | 17 | 7 | 20 | 100 |
| Zoology | 6 | 16 | 38 | 12 | 6 | 20 | 100 |
| Engineering & technology | 7 | 19 | 35 | 12 | 7 | 20 | 100 |
| Agriculture | 4 | 9 | 38 | 7 | 1 | 41 | 100 |
| Anthropology | 7 | 20 | 35 | 12 | 2 | 24 | 100 |
| Economics | 12 | 27 | 33 | 13 | 3 | 12 | 100 |
| Geography | 3 | 15 | 43 | 13 | 3 | 23 | 100 |
| History | 7 | 25 | 38 | 12 | 2 | 16 | 100 |
| Political science | 6 | 28 | 34 | 12 | 4 | 16 | 100 |
| Psychology | 13 | 29 | 35 | 12 | 4 | 7 | 100 |
| Sociology | 11 | 29 | 35 | 11 | 3 | 11 | 100 |

(Table continued)

| | | | | | | | |
|---|---|---|---|---|---|---|---|
| Statistics | 4 | 17 | 46 | 10 | 3 | 20 | 100 |
| Urban studies | 13 | 28 | 26 | 5 | 2 | 26 | 100 |
| Architecture | 6 | 14 | 42 | 10 | 3 | 25 | 100 |
| Art | 6 | 25 | 32 | 12 | 3 | 22 | 100 |
| Archaeology | 1 | 16 | 41 | 11 | 3 | 28 | 100 |
| Classics | 3 | 10 | 40 | 14 | 3 | 30 | 100 |
| Language & literature (including linguistics) | 10 | 18 | 33 | 16 | 3 | 20 | 100 |
| Music | 6 | 23 | 35 | 10 | 3 | 23 | 100 |
| Philosophy | 2 | 18 | 39 | 12 | 5 | 24 | 100 |
| Religion | 5 | 13 | 40 | 12 | 7 | 23 | 100 |
| Health sciences | 17 | 28 | 27 | 7 | 3 | 18 | 100 |
| Law | 7 | 17 | 30 | 7 | 2 | 38 | 100 |
| Education | 7 | 23 | 39 | 10 | 6 | 15 | 100 |
| Bibliography & library science | 7 | 28 | 41 | 13 | 3 | 8 | 100 |
| Interdisciplinary subjects | 11 | 16 | 29 | 9 | 3 | 32 | 100 |
| Popular adult nonfiction | 5 | 12 | 28 | 11 | 9 | 35 | 100 |
| Adult fiction | 2 | 5 | 27 | 7 | 3 | 56 | 100 |
| Juvenile fiction & nonfiction | 1 | 7 | 27 | 5 | 1 | 59 | 100 |
| Other | 3 | 4 | 8 | 3 | 2 | 80 | 100 |
| ALL 36 subjects | 247 | 677 | 1,219 | 398 | 139 | 920 | 3,600 |

Source: Machlup, Leeson, and Associates.

reduced and 139 instances (5 per cent) of significantly reduced numbers of subscriptions. Altogether, for the 100 reporting libraries, increases in subscriptions outweighed reductions at a ratio of 924:537 (or 1.7:1).

## Gainers and Losers in Subscriptions to Periodicals

This ratio referred to all 36 subjects combined. Now we want to see how the individual subjects fared in the reapportionment of subscriptions to periodicals. As a matter of fact, it was not a reapportionment of a given number of subscriptions but a generous net increase in the total. Indeed, 29 subjects were given additional subscriptions in our group of 100 libraries, while only 7 subjects lost subscriptions. Such losses implied that the number of libraries increasing the number of subscriptions to periodicals in the subject in question fell short of the number of libraries cutting down their subscriptions.

Perhaps we may spare our readers the effort of carefully scanning Table 6.7.5 if we enumerate the seven subjects which on balance lost subscriptions, and if we state the score by which they lost, or the ratio of the number of libraries increasing their subscriptions to that of libraries reducing subscriptions. In the order in which they are listed in the table, the losing subjects were Astronomy (18:19), Geology (19:20), Physics (16:24), Classics (13:17), Religion (18:19), Popular Adult Nonfiction (17:20), and Adult Fiction (7:10). The biggest loser was Physics — as also in book-buying — followed by Adult Fiction and Classics.

Which subjects were the biggest gainers in the periodical rooms of the responding libraries? The three subjects winning by the largest margins were Environmental Sciences (58:9, or 6.4:1), Urban Studies (41:7, or 5.9:1), and Health Sciences (45:10, or 4.5:1). We now understand and appreciate the decision of the subject classifiers in various divisions of the National Science Foundation to create separate lines for these "novel" subjects (novel as independent areas of specialization) — even if some librarians complain that the new subjects do not fit easily into the LC or Dewey systems of classification.

Of the remaining 26 subject in the list of gainers of subscriptions, nine gained by scores better than 2:1. In the order of their net gains these subjects were Sociology (40:14), Psychology (42:16), Economics (39:16), History (32:14), Interdisciplinary Studies (27:12), Music (29:13), Bibliography and Library Science (35:16), Political Science (34:16), and Art (31:15). The other 17 subjects gained by smaller ratios, but

126

gain they did, at least in the librarians' impressions, and we have reasons to believe — on the basis of small samples of libraries with numerical records — that these impressions are warranted.

We must bear in mind, however, that all the tallies of increases and decreases in subscriptions to periodicals related to comparisons of 1976 with 1970. If we had asked for comparisons with 1974 or 1975, the findings might have been quite different. We might possibly have seen a preponderance of reductions in subscriptions, but certainly not such large net increases as were achieved (largely at the expense of book-buying) relative to the year 1970. Unfortunately, no reliable counts are available and we had to be satisfied with the ordinal comparisons: "more" or "less." In order to learn a little more, we asked also for the type of "ratings" that seemed so helpful in judging the changes in the acquisition of books.

## Ranking the Changes in Periodical Subscriptions

When a library reports that it increased its subscriptions in some fields and reduced them in others, we neither know the magnitudes of these changes nor do we know in which subjects the changes were most substantial. The second of these gaps in our insights can be partially removed by having the libraries state and rank the three subjects for which subscriptions were increased most significantly, and the three for which subscriptions were decreased most significantly. In response to this request 86 libraries gave us their rankings of the subjects with the largest gains, and 57 libraries gave us their rankings of the subjects that suffered the severest decline in subscription. That fewer libraries supplied rankings of subjects that suffered reductions in subscriptions is easy to understand: they may not have cut the number of subscriptions in *any* subject even while they increased subscriptions in *several*.

Table 6.7.6 shows the rankings. The three top-gainers in Rank 1 were Environmental Sciences (15 votes), Economics (10 votes), and Biology (8 votes). As to the biggest losers, four subjects were tied in first place (6 votes each): Astronomy, Chemistry, Engineering and Technology, and Religion.

If we take Ranks 1 and 2 together and add up the votes, we find the three most substantial gainers to be the same as in Rank 1 and also in the same order: Environmental Sciences (22 votes), Economics (13 votes) and Biology (11 votes). On the side of the losing subjects we now have a clear first

TABLE 6.7.6  *Ranking the Changes in Periodical Subscriptions by Subject: Stating Those Subjects for Which Subscriptions Most Significantly Increased or Most Significantly Decreased in 1976 Relative to 1970, Reported by 86 and 57 Libraries, Respectively*

| Subjects | Most significant increases | | | Most significant decreases | | |
|---|---|---|---|---|---|---|
| | Rank 1 | Rank 2 | Rank 3 | Rank 1 | Rank 2 | Rank 3 |
| Astronomy | 1 | - | 2 | 6 | 2 | 1 |
| Biology | 8 | 3 | 2 | 4 | 2 | 2 |
| Chemistry | 2 | 2 | 3 | 6 | 5 | 3 |
| Environmental sciences | 15 | 7 | 10 | - | - | 1 |
| Geology | 2 | - | - | - | - | 2 |
| Mathematics | 1 | 3 | 1 | 4 | 2 | 2 |
| Physics | - | - | - | 4 | 3 | 4 |
| Zoology | 2 | 1 | - | 2 | 3 | - |
| Engineering & technology | 2 | 5 | 2 | 6 | 3 | 3 |
| Agriculture | 1 | - | 1 | 2 | 1 | 1 |
| Anthropology | 3 | 1 | - | 1 | 1 | - |
| Economics | 10 | 3 | 2 | - | - | 1 |
| Geography | - | - | 1 | 1 | - | 1 |
| History | 2 | 2 | 5 | - | 1 | - |
| Political science | 1 | 1 | 2 | 2 | 2 | - |
| Psychology | 4 | 6 | 6 | 2 | 2 | - |
| Sociology | 1 | 9 | 1 | 1 | 3 | - |
| Statistics | 1 | - | - | - | 1 | - |
| Urban studies | 4 | 5 | 1 | - | - | - |
| Architecture | 1 | 3 | 1 | - | 2 | - |
| Art | 3 | 1 | 1 | 4 | 1 | - |
| Archaeology | - | - | - | - | - | - |
| Classics | 1 | - | 1 | 2 | 2 | - |
| Language & literature (including linguistics) | 4 | 3 | 1 | 2 | 1 | 2 |
| Music | 1 | 4 | 4 | - | 1 | 1 |
| Philosophy | - | 1 | - | 1 | 1 | 2 |
| Religion | - | 2 | 1 | 6 | 4 | - |
| Health sciences | 1 | 9 | 6 | 2 | 4 | 2 |
| Law | 3 | 2 | 1 | 2 | - | - |
| Education | 3 | 3 | 2 | 4 | 3 | 1 |
| Bibliography and library science | 3 | 3 | 5 | 1 | 1 | 2 |
| Interdisciplinary subjects | 4 | 4 | 3 | - | - | 1 |
| Popular adult nonfiction (e.g., recreation, travel, hobbies, etc.) | 5 | 3 | 3 | 5 | 5 | 3 |
| Adult fiction | - | 1 | - | 4 | 1 | - |
| Juvenile fiction & nonfiction | - | 1 | 2 | 1 | - | 1 |
| Other | 2 | 1 | 4 | 1 | 2 | - |
| Total | 106 | 79 | 74 | 76 | 59 | 36 |
| Rank 1 | 106 | | | 76 | | |
| Ranks 1 and 2 | | 185 | | | 135 | |
| Ranks 1, 2, and 3 | | | 259 | | | 171 |
| Libraries responding | | | ÷3 = 86 | | | ÷3 = 57 |

Source: Machlup, Leeson, and Associates.

place and a tie of two for second place: Chemistry (11 votes), Religion (10 votes) and Popular Adult Nonfiction (10 votes).

Taking all three ranks together and expanding the list of subjects nominated for these ranks to five on each side, we find the top-ranking subjects in the following order of gains and losses in 1976 subscriptions compared with 1970:

| *In Ranks 1, 2 or 3 as most significant gainers* | *In Ranks 1, 2 or 3 as most significant losers* |
| --- | --- |
| Environmental Sciences (32 votes) | Chemistry (14 votes) |
| Psychology (16 votes) | Popular Adult Nonfiction (13 votes) |
| Health Sciences (16 votes) | Engineering and Technology (12 votes) |
| Economics (15 votes) | Physics (11 votes) |
| Biology (13 votes) | Religion (10 votes) |

If we had expanded the list of subjects still further, we would have seen the same subjects on both sides, as most significant gainers and also as most significant losers — because some libraries added and others cut subscriptions for journals in the same subjects. A point worthy of notice regarding the "discriminatory" treatment of different subjects is that Natural Sciences and Technology are among the gainers as well as among the losers, whereas, apart from Religion, Humanistic subjects are among neither. If there were changes in priorities, they did not discriminate against the Humanities as far as periodicals are concerned. We recall that in book-buying the Humanities seemed at a serious disadvantage.

*Reasons for Changes in Periodical Subscriptions*

What reasons did the librarians say were influential in their decisions to change the numbers of periodicals for different subjects? Our questionnaire contained the same list of possible reasons that we had formulated for the explanation of changes in book-buying, and our respondents were asked to mark or state the appropriate ones. The two subjects favored by the greatest increases and the two subjects suffering the greatest reductions were to be selected and, for each of the four changes, any number of reasons could be given.

The tallies were added and entered for increases in subscriptions in Table 6.7.7 and for reductions in Table 6.7.8. There were 88 libraries giving reasons for the increases in

129

TABLE 6.7.7  *Reasons for Increased Subscriptions to Periodicals in the Relatively Two Most-Favored Subjects, 1976, by 88 Libraries*

Reasons for *significant increase* in periodical acquisition

| Fields | Number of responses | Relative change in under-graduate student enrollment | Relative change in graduate student enrollment | Relative change in number of faculty | Change in program emphasis |
|---|---|---|---|---|---|
| Astronomy | 1 | | | | 1 |
| Biology | 10 | 3 | 2 | 2 | 7 |
| Chemistry | 3 | 1 | 2 | 1 | 1 |
| Environmental sciences | 10 | 3 | 3 | 4 | 11 |
| Geology | 1 | | | 1 | 1 |
| Mathematics | 4 | | | | 1 |
| Physics | 1 | | | | 1 |
| Zoology | 3 | 1 | 1 | 1 | 2 |
| Engineering & technology | 8 | 5 | 4 | 5 | 5 |
| Agriculture | 1 | 1 | 1 | 1 | 1 |
| Anthropology | 4 | 1 | 1 | 2 | 4 |
| Economics | 13 | 6 | 3 | 5 | 9 |
| Geography | 1 | | | | |
| History | 4 | | | | |
| Political science | 2 | 1 | | 1 | 2 |
| Psychology | 11 | 3 | 2 | 3 | 6 |
| Sociology | 11 | 2 | 2 | 4 | 9 |
| Statistics | | | | | |
| Urban studies | 9 | 3 | 4 | 4 | 5 |
| Architecture | 4 | 2 | | 2 | 4 |
| Art | 4 | 1 | 1 | 1 | 3 |
| Archaeology | | | | | |
| Classics | 1 | | | | |
| Language & literature | 8 | 2 | 2 | 2 | 3 |
| Music | 4 | 1 | 1 | | 2 |
| Philosophy | 1 | | | | |
| Religion | 2 | 1 | 1 | 1 | 1 |
| Health sciences | 22 | 8 | 6 | 7 | 13 |
| Law | 4 | 1 | 1 | 2 | 1 |
| Education | 4 | | 1 | 1 | 1 |
| Bibliography & library science | 5 | | | | 2 |
| Interdisciplinary subjects | 8 | 4 | 1 | 2 | 5 |
| Popular adult nonfiction | 5 | | | | 1 |
| Adult fiction | 1 | | | | |
| Juvenile fiction & nonfiction | 1 | | | | |
| Other | 5 | — | 1 | 1 | 3 |
| Total | 88 × 2 = 176 | 50 | 40 | 53 | 105 |
| Per cent of total | | 11.1% | 8.8% | 11.6% | 23.2% |

Reasons for *significant increase* in periodical acquisition

| Change in number of programs | Increase in relative price of books | Increase in relative price of serials | Change in external private funding | Change in external federal funding | Change in state or local funding | Change in internal library funding priority | Change in funding priority of supporting institutions | Other |
|---|---|---|---|---|---|---|---|---|
| 3 | 1 | 1 | 2 | | | 1 | 1 | 2 | 3 |
| 1 | 1 | 1 | | | | 1 | | 1 |
| 5 | | | | | 1 | | | 10 |
| | | | | | | 1 | | |
| 1 | | | 2 | | | 1 | 1 | 1 |
| 1 | | | | | | 1 | | |
| 2 | 1 | 1 | | | 1 | | | |
| 1 | | | | | | 1 | | |
| 2 | | | | | 1 | 1 | | 4 |
| | | | | | | | | 1 |
| 1 | | | | | 1 | 2 | 1 | |
| 1 | | | | | | | | |
| | | | | 2 | 1 | 1 | | 7 |
| 5 | | | | 1 | | 1 | | 2 |
| 4 | | | | 1 | | 2 | | 3 |
| 2 | | | 1 | | 2 | 1 | 1 | 1 |
| | | | 1 | 1 | 1 | 1 | 1 | |
| | | | 1 | | | | | |
| 2 | | 1 | | | 2 | 2 | | 6 |
| 1 | | | | 1 | 1 | 1 | 1 | |
| | | | | | | | | 2 |
| 1 | 1 | 1 | | | | | | |
| 11 | 2 | 2 | 1 | 1 | 2 | 2 | 2 | 5 |
| 1 | | | | | | | | 3 |
| 1 | | | | | 1 | 1 | | 1 |
| | | | | | 1 | 3 | | 2 |
| 4 | | | | | 1 | 2 | | 2 |
| | | | | | 2 | 3 | | 5 |
| | 1 | | | | | 1 | | |
| | | | | | 1 | 1 | | |
| 2 | − | − | 1 | − | − | 1 | 1 | 1 |
| 52 | 7 | 7 | 9 | 7 | 20 | 32 | 10 | 60 |
| 11.5% | 1.6% | 1.6% | 2.0% | 1.6% | 4.4% | 7.1% | 2.2% | 13.3% |

Source: *Machlup, Leeson, and Associates.*

TABLE 6.7.8  Reasons for Reduced Subscriptions to Periodicals in the Two Most Disadvantaged Subjects, 1976, by 63 Libraries

| Fields | Number of responses | Relative change in undergraduate student enrollment | Relative change in graduate student enrollment | Relative change in number of faculty | Change in program emphasis | Change in number of programs | Increase in relative price of books | Increase in relative price of serials | Change in external private funding | Change in external federal funding | Change in state or local funding | Change in internal library funding priority | Change in funding priority of supporting institutions | Other |
|---|---|---|---|---|---|---|---|---|---|---|---|---|---|---|
| | | | | | | | *Reasons for significant decrease in periodical acquisition* | | | | | | | |
| Astronomy | 9 | 2 | 4 | 2 | 3 | | 1 | 3 | | | | 6 | 1 | 3 |
| Biology | 9 | | | | | | 1 | 5 | | | | 3 | 1 | 2 |
| Chemistry | 11 | 1 | | | 1 | | 2 | 10 | | | | 1 | | 3 |
| Environmental sciences | | | | | | | | | | | | | | |
| Geology | 4 | 1 | | | | | 3 | 3 | 1 | 2 | 1 | 1 | 1 | |
| Mathematics | | | 2 | | | | 2 | 5 | 2 | 2 | 1 | 1 | | 2 |
| Physics | 8 | 1 | 2 | 1 | 3 | 1 | 2 | 2 | | | | 2 | | |
| Zoology | 5 | | 2 | | 1 | 1 | 3 | 3 | | | | 2 | | 2 |
| Engineering & technology | 7 | 2 | 1 | 1 | 2 | 2 | 2 | 1 | | 1 | 1 | 1 | | |
| Agriculture | 3 | | | | 1 | | | | | | | | | |
| Anthropology | 1 | | | | 1 | | | | | | | 1 | | |
| Economics | | | | | | | | | | | | | | |
| Geography | | 1 | 1 | 1 | 1 | | 1 | 1 | | | | | | |
| History | 2 | 2 | | | | | | 2 | | | 1 | | | |
| Political science | 1 | | | | | | | 1 | | | | | | 1 |
| Psychology | 3 | | | | 2 | | 1 | 2 | 1 | | | 2 | | 1 |
| Sociology | 3 | | | 1 | | | | 1 | | | | | | |
| Statistics | 2 | | | | | | | | | | | | | |
| Urban studies | | | | | | | | | | | | | | |
| Architecture | | | | | | | | | | | | | | |
| Art | 4 | | 1 | 1 | 1 | | 2 | 2 | 1 | | 1 | 1 | | |
| Archaeology | | | | | | | | | | | | | | |
| Classics | 3 | 2 | 1 | | | | | 1 | 1 | | | 2 | | 1 |
| Language & literature | 3 | | | 3 | 1 | 1 | | 1 | | | 1 | 1 | 2 | 1 |
| Music | 2 | | | | | | | 1 | | 1 | | 1 | | 9 |
| Philosophy | 3 | | 1 | | 1 | | | 2 | | | 2 | 4 | | 3 |
| Religion | 7 | | | | | 1 | | 5 | | | 1 | 2 | 3 | 3 |
| Health sciences | 2 | 1 | | | | | 3 | | | | | 1 | | 1 |
| Law | | | | | | | | | | | | | | 9 |
| Education | 7 | 2 | 1 | | 2 | 3 | | 2 | | | | 1 | | 2 |
| Bibliography & library science | 4 | | | | | | | 1 | | | | 1 | | |
| Interdisciplinary subjects | | | | | | | | | | | | 2 | | 3 |
| Popular adult nonfiction | 11 | 1 | 1 | | 1 | 1 | 1 | 9 | | | 2 | 2 | | 1 |
| Adult fiction | 4 | 1 | | 1 | 1 | | 1 | 1 | | | | 1 | | |
| Juvenile fiction & nonfiction | | | | | | | | | | | | | | |
| Other | 3 | 1 | | | 1 | | | 2 | | | | 1 | 1 | 2 |
| **Total** | 63 × 2 = 126 | 17 | 12 | 11 | 29 | 12 | 24 | 54 | 3 | 6 | 14 | 44 | 8 | 37 |
| **Per cent of total** | | 6.3% | 4.4% | 4.1% | 10.7% | 4.4% | 8.9% | 19.9% | 1.1% | 2.2% | 5.2% | 16.2% | 3.0% | 13.7% |

*Source: Machlup, Leeson, and Associates.*

each of the two most-favored subjects, hence a total of 176 reports in Table 6.7.7. Only 63 libraries gave their reasons for cutting the number of subscriptions in each of the two most disadvantaged subjects, which means 126 reports in Table 6.7.8. Horizontal additions of the figures entered in the subject-rows of the two tables bear no relation to the number of responding libraries, because each library could mark as many reasons as it deemed appropriate for each of the two subjects it had singled out as the most significantly affected ones.

The vertical additions in the two tables show the relative frequencies with which the different reasons were mentioned as the ones that influenced the decisions to increase or decrease the number of subscriptions. If, in examining Table 6.7.7, we combine the first three reasons — changes in student enrollment and faculty size — we see that these were mentioned 143 times, or in 32 per cent of all reasons for increases in subscriptions to periodicals. Change in program emphasis was mentioned 105 times, or in 23 per cent of the total of reasons marked by the librarians. There were no less than 60 "other" reasons for increased subscriptions stated; they included both increased supply and increased demand. The actual phrases were "increases in the number of new journals" or "increase in serials published," on the one hand, and "increased use," "more requests," and "change in public reading tastes," on the other.

To explain reductions in subscriptions, the increase in the prices of serials was mentioned most often, 54 times, or almost 20 per cent of the total of reasons marked, according to Table 6.7.8. The reason second in frequency (44 times or 16 per cent) was "change in internal library funding priority," which may well be a consequence of the budget constraint aggravated by the increase in prices. Again, other reasons than those pre-formulated by us were stated by librarians. They include such things as "lack of interest," "basic collection satisfies need," "agreement with neighboring institution," and "proliferation of competing titles."

Looking at particular subjects and the reasons given for increasing subscriptions (Table 6.7.7), we see that "change in program emphasis" and "change in the number of programs" were mentioned most frequently for Health Sciences, Environmental Sciences, Sociology, Economics, and Biology. Increased enrollment, undergraduate as well as graduate, was mentioned most often for Health Sciences, Engineering, and Economics. In Table 6.7.8, showing the frequencies of the reasons given for the sharpest reductions in subscriptions, we find only one entry remarkable: the figure 10 in the row for Chemistry and in the column "increase in the relative price of serials."

# A PERCENTAGE DISTRIBUTION AMONG FIELDS

Our attempts in the two preceding sections to quantify nonquantitative information about library acquisitions of books and journals did of course not succeed in producing numerical data on acquisitions classified by subject. The numbers we were able to present were merely counts of frequencies of answers in terms of "more" or "less," "significant" or "slight," and "for this reason" or "for that reason." We do not mean to deprecate the value of this information furnished by librarians with painstaking diligence and analyzed by us with considerable care. But we must not claim that we have gained the insights wanted: how the numbers of books and journals acquired by libraries on different subjects or fields have changed in recent years, possibly over the last ten years. Having learned that absolute numbers of books and periodicals classified by field are absolutely unavailable, we made an attempt to obtain something between absolute counts and non-numerical impressions, namely, *estimates of the percentage distributions* of books purchased and journals subscribed to over broadly defined fields.

## *Thirteen Fields or Subject Groups*

Instead of asking for estimates of acquisitions classified by 36 subjects, as in the previous questions, we asked the librarians for their estimates of the *percentage shares* of 13 more *broadly defined subject groups* or fields in the total of volumes of books purchased and periodicals subscribed to by the libraries in 1976. In order to get an idea of changes over time we also requested, in the case of books, analogous estimates of the percentage share of these 13 subject groups in the accumulated holdings. A comparison of the distribution of acquisitions with that of holdings can inform us about an ongoing change in the composition of the holdings.

The 13 subject groups were partly traditional, partly novel, which caused uneasiness among some librarians. Since, however, the overwhelming majority of them had neither shelf-list counts nor acquisitions counts by LC, Dewey, or other classification systems, to estimate relative shares would hardly be easier for traditional subject classes than for novel ones. We included such novel subjects as Health Sciences and Computer Science because we had learned that these were favored in the current acquisiton policy of many libraries and we might not get any idea about them if we used a traditional classification. We decided also to add three classes

134

of little importance for academic libraries but of great importance for public libraries. The following 13 subject groups were selected for this exercise:

1. Natural Sciences (traditionally composed of Astronomy, Biology, Chemistry, Environmental Sciences, Geology, Mathematics, Physics, and Zoology)

2. Engineering and Technology (including Aeronautical, Chemical, Civil, Electrical, and Mechanical Engineering)

3. Agriculture

4. Social Sciences (including Anthropology, Economics, Geography, History, Political Science, Psychology, Sociology, Statistics, Urban Studies)

5. Humanities (including Architecture, Art, Archaeology, Classics, Language and Literature, Linguistics, Music, Philosophy, Religion)

6. Health Sciences

7. Law

8. Education

9. Bibliography and Library Science

10. Computer Science

11. Popular Adult Nonfiction (for example, Recreation, Travel, Hobbies, etc.)

12. Adult Fiction

13. Juvenile Fiction and Nonfiction

This grouping of subjects offends our philosophical taste at least as much as it displeases many librarians, but it proved sufficiently pragmatic to produce considerable response rates. We received complete answers on the distribution of volumes in the book collections from 118 libraries, on the distribution of volumes of book acquisitions from 105 libraries, and on the distribution of periodical subscriptions from 119 libraries.

*Relative Shares of Subject Groups in Holdings and Acquisitions of Books*

To serve our purposes fully, the estimates of the percentage shares of the 13 subject groups in the total holdings and acquisitions of books have to be of identical libraries. Some responding libraries, however, supplied their estimates only for their holdings, others only for their acquisitions. Thus we had 118 estimates of the distribution of book holdings in 1976, 105 estimates of the distribution of book acquisitions in 1976, but only 89 estimates of both distributions for the same libraries. Table 6.7.9 presents all four distributions. Since the larger samples contain the smaller ones the differences are not very large, but still sufficient to give some false clues regarding the directions of change deduced by comparing the percentage shares of a subject group in total acquisitions with those in total holdings. For example, holdings of books in the Humanities would appear to be on the increase if one compared the 29.7 per cent share in acquisitions for the 105 libraries with the 29.0 per cent share in holdings for the 118 libraries. After clearing both samples of the non-comparable members and limiting them to the same 89 libraries, we see that the share of the Humanities in acquisitions, 28.8 per cent, falls short of their 30.1 per cent share in holdings, which indicates a falling trend in relative holdings. A similar false clue is given for Adult Fiction if the non-comparable samples are compared.

Even for the identical sample the comparisons of the shares in acquisitions with those in holdings are not necessarily reliable. Apart from the fact that the reported percentage shares are mere estimates based on impressions (since recorded data are available in only a few libraries), the weighted averages we calculated for the entire sample are somewhat questionable. For example, the estimates for acquisitions were reported as shares in the total of book volumes added to the collections but, as the total numbers of volumes were not reported for most libraries (because they are not known), we decided to weight the reported percentage shares by the dollar expenditures for books in 1976. These expenditures were for some mix of expensive and inexpensive books, and the mix may have been very different in different libraries. Whether the use of expenditure data as proxy for volumes-added data can significantly distort the picture is difficult to judge — but most statisticians have little compunction about substituting such closely related proxies for the real thing.

The large shares of the Social Sciences and the Humanities in both the holdings and the acquisitions of books, compared with the small shares of the Natural Sciences and Engineering and Technology would suggest that we further develop a theme first introduced in Chapter 6.6. There commented on the fact that it is much easier to build a book collection in Natural-Science subjects to the research level or even to the comprehensive level than it is in most of the subjects in the Social Sciences or in the Humanities. There are fewer books in the Natural Sciences. This is brought home most effectively by a look at Table 6.7.9, for example, at the last column:

136

TABLE 6.7.9  *Estimates of Percentage Shares of 13 Subject Groups in Total Holdings and in Total Acquisitions of Book Volumes in 1976, for 118, 105 Libraries, Respectively, and for the Same 89 Libraries*

| | Per cent of total holdings of book volumes, 1976[1] | | Per cent of total acquisitions of book volumes, 1976[2] | |
|---|---|---|---|---|
| | 118 Libraries | 89 Libraries | 105 Libraries | 89 Libraries |
| Natural sciences | 10.8% | 8.8% | 8.7% | 8.5% |
| Engineering & technology | 4.7% | 4.6% | 5.0% | 5.1% |
| Agriculture | 1.8% | 1.6% | 1.6% | 1.7% |
| Social sciences | 26.8% | 26.9% | 28.8% | 28.4% |
| Humanities | 29.0% | 30.1% | 29.7% | 28.8% |
| Health sciences | 6.1% | 7.2% | 5.3% | 5.9% |
| Law | 4.7% | 5.3% | 3.8% | 4.5% |
| Education | 4.1% | 4.1% | 4.1% | 4.1% |
| Bibliography & library science | 2.7% | 2.5% | 3.1% | 3.5% |
| Computer science | 0.4% | 0.3% | 0.4% | 0.4% |
| Popular adult non-fiction | 2.4% | 2.6% | 2.8% | 3.1% |
| Adult fiction | 2.9% | 2.6% | 3.0% | 2.5% |
| Juvenile fiction & nonfiction | 3.6% | 3.4% | 3.7% | 3.5% |
| Total | 100.0% | 100.0% | 100.0% | 100.0% |

[1]The estimates of the percentage shares in total holdings reported for each subject group by each library are weighted by its "total number of book volumes in collection" in 1976, as reported in reply to our question II-1.

[2]The estimates of the percentage shares in total acquisitions reported for each subject group by each library are weighted by its "expenditures for books" in 1976, as reported in reply to our question I-2.

*Source:  Machlup, Leeson, and Associates.*

the share of the Natural Sciences is shown as 8.5 per cent of
the books acquired, while the shares of the Social Sciences
and the Humanities are 28.4 and 28.8 per cent respectively, or
57.2 per cent together.  We shall see later that that the
situation with regard to journals is very different.

As to differences between shares of acquisitions and
shares of holdings, that is, between the figures in the fourth
and second columns, we notice increasing accretions in Engineering and Technology (5.1 versus 4.6 per cent), in the
Social Sciences (28.4 versus 26.9 per cent), Bibliography and
Library Science (3.5 versus 2.5 per cent), and Popular Adult
Nonfiction (3.1 per cent versus 2.6 per cent).  Some of these
"findings" contradict, or at least do not confirm, "findings"
from reported impressions discussed earlier in this chapter,
when we saw in Table 6.7.2 that Engineering had been voted
both a gainer and a loser in new acquisitions, and when we saw
in Table 6.7.1 that book-buying in Popular Adult Nonfiction
had been reported more often as having been reduced than as
having been increased.

Where shares in total acquisitions are lower than the
shares in total holdings, one may suspect a declining trend.
The figures in the fourth and second columns of Table 6.7.9
suggest such a trend for the Natural Sciences (8.5 versus 8.8
per cent) and for the Humanities (28.8 versus 30.1 per cent).
These suggestions are not in conflict with what one may have
concluded from Tables 6.7.1 and 6.7.2 with regard to some of
the subjects contained in the larger subject groups distinguished in Table 6.7.9.


*Relative Shares of Subject Groups in Subscriptions
to Periodicals*

We used the same classification of 13 subject groups in
our request to libraries that they estimate the relative
shares of these groups in current subscriptions to periodicals.
We did not, however, ask them for relative shares in their
collections of old journals.  Such estimates would be too
complicated and almost meaningless as a standard against which
current subscriptions could be judged.  The holdings of back
issues of journals in complete or incomplete sets cannot be
used as a benchmark for increases or reductions in current
subscriptions.  The only meaningful comparison would be between the numbers of subscriptions now and at some time in the
not too distant past; but, in the absence of good statistical
records, librarians could not be expected to remember the dis-

tribution of journal subscriptions, say in 1970, among subject groups. Thus, there is only a single column of percentage shares in Table 6.7.10.

What this column of figures can help us realize are the great differences between journals and books regarding their distribution among subject groups. The share of the Natural Sciences in total periodical subscriptions by 119 libraries in 1976 was 22.1 per cent, which is more than the 21.1 per cent share of Social Sciences and much more than the 15.7 share of the Humanities. The combined share of Social Sciences and Humanities in total subscriptions was 36.8 per cent, against their 57.2 per cent share in the acquisition of books. To look at other combinations, the Natural Sciences, Engineering and Technology, and the Health Sciences together commanded a share of 40.0 per cent in subscriptions to periodicals, but their combined share in the acquisition of books was only 19.5 per cent.

These differences in the proportions between books and journals are of course not a new discovery. The greater use of books has been at the bottom of the designation of the Humanities and the Social Sciences as the "reading departments" of the British universities. The results of experiments and of new techniques in the laboratories of universities and industrial workshops, or in the wards and operating rooms of hospitals, are more efficiently and expeditiously reported in periodicals. Thus, the differences in the roles of books and journals in different fields or subjects are neither artificial nor arbitrary, but are inherent in the working methods appropriate to the fields in question.

*Further Analysis*

The estimates of relative shares of subject groups in the total holdings and acquisitions of books and in total subscriptions to periodicals were presented in the last three tables without breakdown by type of library or size of library. A tentative computation indicated that the percentage distribution may be quite different in libraries of different types and sizes. For example, it seems that among academic libraries those with the largest budgets hold over 37 per cent of their book collections in the Humanities, while the academic libraries in the third budget stratum have only less than 24 per cent of their books in humanistic subject areas. These tentative computations were made with a smaller sample, but with a more appropriate technique of computing the averages weighted by the total number of book volumes held by the reporting libraries.

139

TABLE 6.7.10  Estimates of Percentage Shares
of 13 Subject Groups in Total Subscriptions
to Periodicals, 1976, for 119 Libraries

| | Per cent of total subscriptions to periodicals,[1] 1976 |
|---|---|
| Natural sciences | 22.1 |
| Engineering & technology | 7.7 |
| Agriculture | 4.0 |
| Social sciences | 21.1 |
| Humanities | 15.7 |
| Health sciences | 10.2 |
| Law | 5.6 |
| Education | 4.2 |
| Bibliography & library science | 3.6 |
| Interdisciplinary subjects | 3.5 |
| Popular adult nonfiction | 1.7 |
| Adult fiction | 0.3 |
| Juvenile fiction & nonfiction | 0.3 |
| Total | 100.0% |

[1]The estimates of the percentage shares in the total number
of subscriptions reported for each subject group by each
library are weighted by its "expenditures on all serials" in
1976, as reported in reply to our question I-2.

Source:  Machlup, Leeson, and Associates.

The same kind of analysis of variation in the distribution among subject groups can be made for periodicals subscribed to by the libraries which reported their estimates in reply to our questionnaire. Again, we consider it likely that significant differences can be found among libraries of different type. Tentative calculations indicate, for example, that journals in the Social Sciences represent over 20 per cent of all periodicals subscribed to by academic libraries, but only less than nine per cent by public libraries and, understandably, less than 0.5 per cent by special libraries. On the other hand, a breakdown of the subscriptions by academic libraries according to their size seems to show that the relative shares of journals in the Social Sciences are larger in academic libraries of the second and third size strata than they are in the largest.

We hope to extend this kind of analysis as soon as funds and time are available. The computer files remain available to us, and we plan to program the computer to yield the desired breakdown of the field distributions of books and periodicals by type and size of library.


OUR QUEST FOR NUMERICAL DATA

We cannot be proud of the mental contortions and statistical magics which we had to use in order to squeeze a few tentative conclusions out of the reported guesses and impressions of our cooperative respondents. We would much rather have collected numerical data from existing records — if such records existed. We made a special effort to find out what kinds of numerical information, broken down by subject or field, *might* be obtained, preferably in the form of time series, of expenditures for library materials, book volumes added to library collections, and periodicals subscribed to by libraries. In this section we report on the results of these inquiries.


*Subject Breakdown of Expenditures for Library Materials*

In the section on Library Expenditures in our questionnaire we asked the libraries to indicate for which years they could "generate a breakdown of total materials expenditures by subject field, with subjects corresponding to Dewey in 10s (e.g., 330, 880, 920, etc.), two-letter LC classes (e.g., HB, PR, KF, etc.), or some other formal subject-classification system." From the replies by 196 libraries we compiled an inventory of

141

potentially available data sources, which we arranged in ascending order from "none at all" to "all seven years from 1970 to 1976."

| Number of Libraries | Years for which data could be obtained |
|---|---|
| 171 | for no year |
| 1 | for one year,   1975 |
| 2 | for one year,   1976 |
| 1 | for two years,   1970-1971 |
| 1 | for two years,   1973-1974 |
| 3 | for two years,   1975-1976 |
| 1 | for three years, 1974-1976 |
| 1 | for six years,   1970-1975 |
| 1 | for six years,   1971-1976 |
| 14 | for seven years, 1970-1976 |
| Total   196 | |

The potential availability of 14 time series of expenditures broken down by subject gave us some hope, although we realized, of course, that a sample of 14 was very small indeed, compared with the population of 196 who had cared to answer our question, or the 223 who had returned our questionnaire, or the 778 whom we had selected for our random sample, or the 21,000 libraries in the United States. Still, 14 is better than one and we approached these most welcome sources of information and requested their data. We shall later report on the results of this effort.

*Subject Breakdown of Book Volumes Acquired*

In the section on Book Purchases our questionnaire had a request to libraries to indicate for which years they could "generate a breakdown of the number of book volumes added" by subject, corresponding to any of the formal classification systems. From the replies by 198 libraries we compiled an inventory of potential sources of data. It looks like this:

| Number of Libraries | Years for which data can be obtained |
|---|---|
| 139 | for no year |
| 1 | for one year,   1972 |
| 1 | for one year,   1974 |
| 1 | for one year,   1975 |

142

| Number of Libraries (continued) | Years for which data can be obtained (continued) |
|---|---|
| 2 | for one year, 1976 |
| 1 | for two years, 1970-1971 |
| 1 | for two years, 1973-1974 |
| 5 | for two years, 1975-1976 |
| 2 | for three years, 1970-1972 |
| 3 | for three years, 1974-1976 |
| 1 | for four years, 1970-1973 |
| 1 | for four years, 1972-1975 |
| 3 | for four years, 1973-1976 |
| 4 | for five years, 1972-1976 |
| 2 | for six years, 1970-1975 |
| 1 | for six years, 1971-1976 |
| 30 | for seven years, 1970-1976 |
| Total 198 | |

Some of these data sources could be combined if a year or more were to be sacrificed for the sake of a larger sample. For example, the sample of 30 could be enlarged to 32 for the period 1970-1975 (instead of 1976), to 34 for 1972-1976, or to 37 for 1973-1976, and so forth. Such a trade-off would hardly be beneficial, however, since the number of libraries added is too small to warrant the sacrifice of years in the time series.

For several reasons we did not request the data from the 30 libraries. We had seen the *National Shelflist Count*, the impressive project, undertaken under the direction of LeRoy D. Ortopan, of counting for two years the title holdings of 26 research libraries (see our description in Chapter 6.3). We surely were not equipped, neither with the experience nor with the funds required, to carry out an even larger project, encompassing seven years and 30 libraries. We could not be sure, moreover, that the data obtainable from the 30 libraries would be compatible and comparable. Their books may be classified according to different systems, not easily convertible into uniform LC or Dewey classes and subclasses. Finally, a few inquiries with librarians established the fact that the data from some libraries would be obtainable only at a cost (for computer programs, computer time, staff time), which we would have to assume.

An inspection of the list of the 30 libraries made it clear that this sample would be rather different from that of the National Shelflist Count. The group of 30 includes special, public, and Federal libraries, and a sprinkling of community-college libraries, in addition to university libraries. Such variety may reveal some interesting differences, but it

143

may also present obstacles to comparability. We must bear in mind also that the obtainable data refer to *volumes* of books not to *titles*, which again makes comparisons more difficult. Yet, it is good to know that at least 30 libraries may be able to generate seven-year series of book collections classified by subject, if it is found that an analysis of these data can be useful.

*Subject Breakdown of Periodicals Acquired*

In our questionnaire, in the section on Periodical Purchases, we asked the libraries to indicate for which years they could "generate a breakdown of the number of periodical titles added" to their collection, by subject, corresponding to any of the formal classification systems. Replies from 190 libraries were received. Our inventory of the potential data sources looks like this:

| Number of libraries | Years for which data could be obtained | |
| :---: | :--- | :--- |
| 150 | for no year | |
| 2 | for one year, | 1975 |
| 10 | for one year, | 1976 |
| 1 | for two years, | 1973-1974 |
| 6 | for two years, | 1975-1976 |
| 3 | for three years, | 1974-1976 |
| 1 | for four years, | 1970-1973 |
| 2 | for four years, | 1973-1976 |
| 1 | for five years | 1970-1974 |
| 1 | for six years, | 1971-1976 |
| 13 | for seven years, | 1970-1976 |
| Total 190 | | |

The number of libraries capable of generating a seven-year series of their acquisitions of periodical titles broken down by field is similar to that of libraries stating that they could generate a seven-year series of their expenditures for library materials by field, 13 versus 14. (The composition of the two groups is different.) In one respect, however, this inventory of potential statistical data looks more promising for future investigations, in as much as another 12 libraries state they can furnish shorter series including 1976 and another ten libraries seem to have started classified record-keeping in 1976. This would yield 35 possible sources of data for periodical subscriptions in 1976 and, we hope, from then on. This number represents 18.4 per cent of that of replies received to our question (190) and 15.7 per cent of the total number of questionnaire returns (223). Are we too optimistic if we have visions of an improved flow of data? We may well be mistaken in our hope that the possible availability of 1976 data signifies the beginning of a continuing series of annual data; perhaps the librarians merely meant that they could, if pressed, make a one-time effort to break down their subscriptions for the last year.

We have not approached the 13 libraries for their 1970-1976 series. Constraints of time and money barred us from tapping these sources of data. If these constraints are eased, we may go back and look into this small sample to see just what happened to the subscriptions to journals in different fields over the years.

*Examining the Data from 14 Libraries*

As we mentioned early in this section, 14 libraries had indicated that they could generate for seven years, 1970-1976, a breakdown of their expenditures for materials by subject fields according to some formal subject-classification system; and we approached these respondents regarding the availability of their data.

We found that some of the libraries could provide their data only at a cost (which we were not able to defray); that some libraries had collected the data only for book purchases, while others had them only for materials purchases, not separately for books and periodicals; that some were using classifications according to LC, some according to Dewey, others according to departmental organization and again others only by three or four major divisions. After considerable effort we had to conclude that at best six of the libraries could furnish compatible information in a shape usable, with some manipulation, for tabulating a distribution of expenditures for book acquisitions by subject groups. We could not afford to undertake this task.

THE USE OF ARCHIVAL TAPES

It may well be that an inquiry into library acquisitions classified by field is too expensive if the investigators have to go to individual libraries to find what information they happen to have compiled. It seems far more reasonable to turn to a central data bank that continuously receives and stores the information continuously sent to it by "on-line" computer facilities. The Ohio College Library Center (OCLC, in

145

Columbus, Ohio) is such a store of data for almost 1400
libraries.


## The OCLC Tapes

The participants of the OCLC report their acquisitions in
the process of cataloguing. Thus every new entry into the
catalog of the library becomes automatically an entry on that
library's computer file at OCLC (though most libraries work
through regional networks, such as that maintained by the
State University of New York [SUNY] in Albany). OCLC provides
the catalog cards for the card files of the participating
libraries. The time lag between request and delivery of the
catalog card is approximately one week, but the average response time for the electronic processing of the new entry is
less than six seconds. To illustrate the magnitude of the
undertaking, during a week in March 1977 participating libraries catalogued 202,789 books, for which OCLC produced
1,401,862 catalog cards. The system was first confined to
acquisitions of books but has recently begun to include
serials.
    The OCLC is a subscription service, designed for the more
efficient operations and management of the participating
libraries. As the number of participants increased, the
OCLC's archival tapes became sources for inquiries into the
collection development of a substantial part of the library
population.


## Collection Development Analysis

A pilot study of using the OCLC tapes for the analysis of
the development of library collection has recently been done.
In the words of Glyn T. Evans, "as more libraries across the
nation use the OCLC system, the OCLC-MARC Subscription Service
offers a medium for gathering data and performing (by machine)
statistical analyses by discipline, medium, library and sets
of libraries."[2]
    The Final Report on the project was published in November
1977. It covered the acquisitions of books by four libraries — Cornell University, SUNY Binghamton, SUNY Cortland, and

---

[2]*OCLC Newsletter*, No. 108, 29 April 1977, p. 3.

SUNY Oneonta — during a period of 12 weeks commencing January 10, 1977, which involved a total of 32,138 records.[3]  The project was meant to be a pilot study designed to develop the computer programs that could produce the information needed for an analysis of the acquisitions by individual libraries as well as for any group of libraries participating in the OCLC system.  Confined to twelve weeks in four libraries, the study, did of course not produce any findings to be reported by us; but it showed what could be done in the future.

---

[3]Glyn T. Evans *et al.*, *Collection Development Analysis Using OCLC Archival Tapes*, Final Report (Washington: Office of Education, U. S. Department of Health, Education, and Welfare, November 1977), p. 6.

CHAPTER 6.8

AUTOMATED RECORDING AND REPORTING SYSTEMS


Record-keeping and continuous maintenance of up-to-date
statistical data have been made much easier by the development
of automatic, electronic data-processing (EDP) systems.  The
installation of computerized control and information systems
is expensive and may for a while be out of reach for the smaller libraries.  For larger institutions, however, EDP will be
indispensable for efficient management and collection development.  This is not to say that manual record-keeping — using
ink and pen to write numbers in the appropriate columns of
large books — would be impossible, but it takes a particular
bent of mind to do it methodically, accurately and consistently, and not many people have a taste for it.  As a matter of
fact, few library managers have done it, as we have found out.


THE LITERATURE

The literature on "library automation" is extensive and
has grown at a quick pace.  The American Library Association
has published bibliographies which attest to that growth.
Thus, the compilers listed 377 items published from 1962 to
1967, 393 items from 1967 to 1968, and 713 items from 1969 to
1971.  All these bibliographies were selective, covering only
readily accessible sources such as English-language journals,
trade publications, monographs, technical reports and other
documents.[1]  These compilations show increasing outputs:  in

---

[1]Lois C. McCune and Stephen R. Salmon, comps., "Bibliography
of Library Automation," *ALA Bulletin*, Vol. 61 (No. 6, June
1967), pp. 674-694; Charlene Mason, comp., "Bibliography of Library Automation" (ERIC/CLIS Bibliography) *ALA Bulletin*, Vol.
63 (No. 8, September 1969), pp. 1117-1134; Alice Billingsley,
comp., "Bibliography of Library Automation" (ERIC/CLIS Series
3), *American Libraries*, Vol. 3 (March 1972), pp. 289-312.
A more recent bibliography was published by the LARC (Library Automation Research and Consulting) Association, *A Bibliography of Literature on Planned or Implemented Automated
Library Projects*, [Vol. 10 of World Survey Series] (Peoria,
Ill.:  LARC Press, 1973).

the first six years an average of 63 publications per year, in the subsequent two years an average of 197 publications, and in the next three years an average of 238 publications. A specialized quarterly, *The Journal of Library Automation*, provides for a continuing flow of information on electronic data processing in our libraries.[2]

Encouraged by this evidence of interest in the adoption of new data-processing and control technologies, we were curious to find out how far the libraries in our sample had gone in automating their operations. Moreover, we realized that the replies to our substantive questions would not supply us with enough numerical data needed for our research and, hence, we wanted to know which libraries might be able to generate the required information from their computer files. We decided that it would be appropriate to ask the librarians to what extent and in what year they had automated the record-keeping and data-processing in their activities. We also asked them to tell us what kind of time series of detailed information about their collections they would be able to "generate from data already in machine-readable form." In this chapter we report on the replies to our questions.

AUTOMATED SYSTEMS

Automation (computerization) may apply to a variety of library operations, and in fact came to be established only in a piecemeal fashion, beginning with accounting and aggregate-inventory controls and gradually extended to other functions. We asked the librarians to tell us for which functions they were using automated systems on a regular basis and since when. We listed in our questionnaire the following systems:

   (a) ordering system for books,
   (b) ordering system for serials,
   (c) cooperative cataloguing system (e.g., Ohio College Library Center),
   (d) circulation system,
   (e) accounting control system, and
   (f) inventory control system (e.g., automated shelflist).

---

[2] We have also benefited from the article by Peter Simmons, "Library Automation," *Annual Review of Information Science and Technology*, Vol. 8, 1973 (Washington, D.C.: American Society for Information Science, 1973), pp. 167-201.

Table 6.8.1 summarizes the replies received.  Only 152 of the 223 libraries that returned our questionnaire reported that they had installed any automated system for any of the listed purposes.  The last three rows in the table show the number of libraries that were using in 1976 an automated system for the purpose shown in the captions, the percentage which this number represents of the 152 libraries that had installed a computerized system for at least one of the purposes, and the percentage of the 223 libraries that had returned usable questionnaires.  The rows above the totals give a breakdown by the years in which their systems were installed.

By 1970 only eleven of the 152 libraries were using automated inventory-control systems, but we do not know whether these were of the shelflist type, classified by catalog codes. Even by 1976 only twenty reporting libraries, or 13 per cent of those who had *some* computerized systems, had automated inventory controls.

Only 17 libraries had, by 1970, automated ordering systems for books, and probably few, if any, of these systems provided breakdowns by the subject, field, or department which the books were designed to serve.  By 1976 the number of libraries with automated ordering of books had risen to 41, or 18.4 per cent of the libraries that returned our questionnaire. Automation progressed most conspicuously with respect to cooperative cataloguing; second and third in the rate of adoptions are accounting controls and circulation controls, but we do not know how many, if any, of these systems are capable of supplying machine-readable data classified by subject or subject group.

While the number of libraries with computerized data processing was very small, according to the reports from our respondents, we have been informed that a good many libraries were in the process of installing automated systems.  Another census of libraries, in a few years from now, should show a more promising growth in this area of machine-made knowledge.


DETAILED SERIES OF MACHINE-READABLE DATA

In a sense, the question most important for further research on library holdings, acquisitions, and circulation of books and serials was about the capabilities of libraries to generate time series of pertinent data from their EDP systems. We were not thinking of future research but of data for the present inquiry; and hence we asked about data possibly obtainable "from data already in machine-readable form."  And,

TABLE 6.8.1 *Number of Libraries Using Computerized Systems,*
*by Function and Time of Installation, for 152 Reporting Libraries, 1950-1976*

| | Number of libraries using automated systems for | | | | | |
|---|---|---|---|---|---|---|
| System installed | Ordering of books | Ordering of serials | Cooperative cataloguing | Circulation | Accounting control | Inventory control |
| Before 1964 | 1 | 1 | 1 | 2 | 3 | 1 |
| Between 1964 and 1967 | 7 | 5 | - | 8 | 9 | - |
| 1968 | 4 | 2 | - | 5 | 4 | 2 |
| 1969 | 4 | 2 | 1 | 7 | 2 | 3 |
| 1970 | 1 | - | 1 | 6 | 6 | 5 |
| 1971 | 3 | 4 | 3 | 2 | 2 | - |
| 1972 | 4 | 4 | 6 | 4 | 8 | 1 |
| 1973 | 4 | 3 | 4 | 5 | 6 | - |
| 1974 | 1 | 19 | 4 | 2 | 2 | - |
| 1975 | 4 | 2 | 35 | 1 | 4 | 2 |
| 1976 | 3 | 2 | 28 | 6 | 3 | 3 |
| Year not reported | 5 | 2 | 8 | 7 | 7 | 3 |
| Total use in 1976 | 41 | 46 | 97 | 55 | 56 | 20 |
| Per cent of 152 libraries using computer for some purposes | 27.0% | 30.3% | 59.9% | 36.2% | 36.8% | 13.2% |
| Per cent of 223 libraries returning our questionnaire | 18.4% | 20.6% | 40.8% | 24.7% | 25.1% | 9.0% |

*Source: Machlup, Leeson, and Associates.*

since we intended to examine the data for any observable trends, we asked also for the beginning year of the time series possibly generated.

## Eleven Lists Proposed

In the questionnaire we enumerated eleven lists that seemed interesting for our purposes. Three of the lists referred to the libraries' holdings, three to their acquisitions, and four to the circulation of their holdings. The order in which these lists were enumerated in the questionnaire was somewhat unsystematic; we take the liberty of rearranging them for the sake of a clearer presentation in this report.

Not that we asked the librarians to furnish us with any of these lists; our question was merely designed to find out whether the data-processing systems used in the libraries were equipped to generate the data required for the lists.

The three lists of holdings would contain

- all book titles (held in the collection) by subject
- book titles in special collections
- all serial titles (held in the collection)
  by subject

The three lists of acquisitions would contain

- all book titles (added to the collection)
  by subject
- all serial titles (currently received) by subject
- book and serial titles combined, by subject

The four lists concerning circulation would contain

- the book titles with the number of times they were checked out during the year,
- the book titles, by year of publication, with the number of times they were checked out since the book was acquired
- the book titles by the year it was checked out for the last time
- the book and serial titles by type of borrower
- all items by type (books, serials, microform, records, etc.)

153

TABLE 6.8.2  Number of Libraries Capable of Furnishing Information on Holdings, Acquisition, and Circulation from Data Available in Machine-Readable Form, by Specified Details and Length of Time Series, for 147 Reporting Libraries, 1951-1976

| Time series beginning | Holdings of | | | Acquisitions of | | | Circulation of | | | | |
|---|---|---|---|---|---|---|---|---|---|---|---|
| | All book titles by subject | Book titles in special collections by subject | Serial titles by subject | Book titles by subject | Serial titles by subject | Book and serial titles combined by subject | Book titles with number of times checked out in year | Book titles by year of publication with times checked out since acquisition | Book titles by year checked out last time | Book and serial titles by type of borrower | All items by type (books, serials, microform, record, etc.) |
| Before 1964 | 2 | 2 | 2 | 2 | 2 | - | - | - | - | - | 2 |
| Between 1964 and 1967 | - | - | 2 | 2 | 2 | - | 2 | - | - | 5 | 2 |
| 1968 | 2 | - | 3 | - | 3 | - | 2 | - | - | 2 | - |
| 1969 | 2 | 2 | 2 | 2 | 2 | 2 | 3 | - | 2 | 5 | 3 |
| 1970 | 3 | 2 | 2 | 4 | 3 | 2 | 3 | 2 | 2 | 4 | 2 |
| 1971 | 2 | 2 | 2 | 2 | 2 | 2 | 2 | - | 2 | 4 | 2 |
| 1972 | 2 | - | 2 | 2 | 2 | 2 | - | - | - | 2 | 2 |
| 1973 | - | 2 | 2 | 2 | 2 | - | 4 | 2 | 2 | 4 | 2 |
| 1974 | 2 | 3 | 6 | 3 | 6 | 2 | - | - | - | 2 | - |
| 1975 | 5 | 2 | 2 | 10 | 7 | 3 | - | - | - | - | - |
| 1976 | - | 2 | 2 | 12 | 7 | 2 | 6 | - | 2 | 4 | 2 |
| Beginning year not reported | 4 | 3 | 7 | 12 | 7 | 3 | 3 | 2 | 2 | 13 | 4 |
| Total obtainable for 1976 | 21 | 16 | 27 | 50 | 41 | 12 | 23 | 4 | 8 | 43 | 16 |
| Per cent of 147 libraries with automated systems | 14.3% | 10.9% | 18.4% | 34.0% | 27.9% | 8.2% | 15.6% | 2.7% | 5.4% | 29.3% | 10.9% |
| Per cent of 223 libraries returning our questionnaire | 9.4% | 7.2% | 12.1% | 22.4% | 18.4% | 5.4% | 10.3% | 1.8% | 3.6% | 19.3% | 7.2% |

Source: Machlup, Leeson, and Associates.

In Table 6.8.2 we summarize the replies received from 147 libraries regarding their capacity to supply any of these lists from data already in machine-readable form from as far back as possible. The table shows that lists for the period 1970-1976 could be obtained for only a handful of libraries, two for only a single library and none for more than 15 libraries (namely, lists of books and serial titles by type of borrower. It should be clear that to the numbers of libraries whose data go back to 1970 we must add the numbers of those whose data go back still farther.) Even for as short a period as the four years from 1973 to 1976, the number of libraries that could supply lists would not be much larger. Lists with a breakdown by type of borrower could now be furnished by 24 libraries; but lists of holdings of all serials titles by subject could be generated by only eleven libraries, and lists of book titles by year of publication with the number of times they were checked out since they were acquired could be generated by only two libraries (of the 147 who reported on the capacities of their data-processing systems).

The numbers in the three bottom lines refer to the libraries that could generate the various lists for 1976. The numbers are still too small to yield representative samples, but there is hope that the continuing automation of data recording and processing will soon increase the libraries' capacities to furnish reports for meaningful statistical computations.

When we asked our questions, we still considered the possibility of actually requesting some of the lists which the libraries would say they *could* generate. When we eventually found that the numbers of potentially obtainable lists were small and the cost of actually preparing the lists from the libraries' data files was much too high to be defrayed out of the funds at our disposal, we resigned ourselves to the fact that the data were beyond our reach.

APPENDIX TO PART SIX

## PRELIMINARY QUESTIONNAIRE

## --THIS IS NOT A REQUEST FOR DATA--

### Instructions

Through the attached questionnaire we hope to obtain your evaluation of the level of difficulty and costs involved in gathering annual statistical data about your library for the period 1970 through 1975. Please select the response which best describes the accessibility of the various types of information listed and enter the corresponding code in the appropriate box. The responses are as follows:

| Code | Response |
|------|----------|
| 1 | Data are available at little or no cost (under 1 man-hour). |
| 2 | Data are obtainable at moderate cost (1 man-hour to 1 man-day). |
| 3 | Data are obtainable at substantial cost (1 man-day to 1 man-week). |
| 4 | Data are obtainable at excessive cost (more than 1 man-week). |
| 5 | Data are not obtainable. |

Where possible, we would like to be able to obtain the data broken down into the following broad subject areas:

| Subject Area | Corresponding Library of Congress Classification |
|--------------|--------------------------------------------------|
| Science | Q |
| Engineering & Technology | T |
| Medicine | R |
| Other Sciences | S, U-V |
| Social Sciences | C,D,E,F,H,J |
| Humanities | B,G,M,N,P |
| Rare Books | |
| Law | K |
| Education | L |
| Other | A,Z |

For some of the data such a breakdown may be easier to obtain than for others. Hence, for each of the years shown, please indicate your judgment of the degree of difficulty if the requested data were to be derived (A) without a further breakdown into subject area and (B) with a further breakdown into subject area.

Finally, in those instances where data are available in computer form, please circle your response.

An example appears on the next page.

E X A M P L E

Preliminary Questionnaire

Name of Library _____

Name and Position of Individual
Completing this Form _____

I. Size of Collection:

(a) Number of book titles

| | YEAR | | | | | | | | | | |
|---|---|---|---|---|---|---|---|---|---|---|---|
| | 1970 | | 1971 | | 1972 | | 1973 | | 1974 | | 1975* |
| | Not Broken Down (A) | Broken Down By Subject Area (B) | Not Broken Down (A) | Broken Down By Subject Area (B) | Not Broken Down (A) | Broken Down By Subject Area (B) | Not Broken Down (A) | Broken Down By Subject Area (B) | Not Broken Down (A) | Broken Down By Subject Area (B) | Not Broken Down (A) | Broken Down By Subject Area (B) |
| | 2 | 3 | 2 | 3 | 1 | 3 | ① | 2 | ① | ② | ① | ① |

In this example, for 1973, the response indicates that to obtain the number of book titles for that year by subject area would entail a moderate cost, while obtaining the number of book titles without breaking them down by subject area would involve little or no cost. The response also indicates that the latter information is obtainable either from printed computer output that may be on file or directly from a computer system.

*When available.

159

Preliminary Questionnaire

Name of Library_____

Name and Position of Individual
  Completing this Form_____
_____

| | YEAR | | | | | | | | | | | |
|---|---|---|---|---|---|---|---|---|---|---|---|---|
| | 1970 | | 1971 | | 1972 | | 1973 | | 1974 | | 1975* | |
| | Not Broken Down | Broken Down By Subject Area | Not Broken Down | Broken Down By Subject Area | Not Broken Down | Broken Down By Subject Area | Not Broken Down | Broken Down By Subject Area | Not Broken Down | Broken Down By Subject Area | Not Broken Down | Broken Down By Subject Area |
| | (A) | (B) | (A) | (B) | (A) | (B) | (A) | (B) | (A) | (B) | (A) | (B) |
| **I. Size of Collection:** | | | | | | | | | | | | |
| (a) Number of book titles | | | | | | | | | | | | |
| (b) Number of book volumes | | | | | | | | | | | | |
| (c) Number of serial titles | | | | | | | | | | | | |
| (d) Number of serial volumes | | | | | | | | | | | | |
| (e) Number of indexing and abstracting titles | | | | | | | | | | | | |
| (f) Number of indexing and abstracting volumes | | | | | | | | | | | | |
| (g) Number of theses and dissertations | | | | | | | | | | | | |
| **II. Annual Increase in Size of Collection:** | | | | | | | | | | | | |
| (a) Number of book titles | | | | | | | | | | | | |
| (b) Number of book volumes | | | | | | | | | | | | |
| (c) Number of serial titles | | | | | | | | | | | | |
| (d) Number of serial volumes | | | | | | | | | | | | |
| (e) Number of indexing and abstracting titles | | | | | | | | | | | | |
| (f) Number of indexing and abstracting volumes | | | | | | | | | | | | |
| (g) Number of theses and dissertations | | | | | | | | | | | | |

*When available.

160

|  | YEAR | | | | | | | | | | | |
|---|---|---|---|---|---|---|---|---|---|---|---|---|
|  | 1970 | | 1971 | | 1972 | | 1973 | | 1974 | | 1975* | |
|  | Not Broken Down | Broken Down By Subject Area | Not Broken Down | Broken Down By Subject Area | Not Broken Down | Broken Down By Subject Area | Not Broken Down | Broken Down By Subject Area | Not Broken Down | Broken Down By Subject Area | Not Broken Down | Broken Down By Subject Area |
|  | (A) | (B) | (A) | (B) | (A) | (B) | (A) | (B) | (A) | (B) | (A) | (B) |
| III. Purchases ($ figures) of Books and Back Issues of Serials: | | | | | | | | | | | | |
| (a) Broken down into purchases from | | | | | | | | | | | | |
| (i) University Presses | | | | | | | | | | | | |
| (ii) Commercial Publishers | | | | | | | | | | | | |
| (iii) Government | | | | | | | | | | | | |
| (iv) Wholesalers and Jobbers | | | | | | | | | | | | |
| (v) Special Dealers | | | | | | | | | | | | |
| (b) A total figure not broken down as in (a) above. | | | | | | | | | | | | |
| IV. Serial Subscriptions: | | | | | | | | | | | | |
| (a) Total Number | | | | | | | | | | | | |
| (b) Number Dropped | | | | | | | | | | | | |
| (c) Number Added | | | | | | | | | | | | |
| V. Materials Received at No Charge: | | | | | | | | | | | | |
| (a) Numbers broken down by: | | | | | | | | | | | | |
| (i) Books (Volumes) | | | | | | | | | | | | |
| (ii) Books (Titles) | | | | | | | | | | | | |
| (iii) Serials (Subscriptions) | | | | | | | | | | | | |
| (iv) Serials (Volumes) | | | | | | | | | | | | |
| (v) Microform (Items) | | | | | | | | | | | | |
| (b) Numbers not broken down as in (a) above | | | | | | | | | | | | |

*When available.

161

| | YEAR | | | | | | | | | | | |
|---|---|---|---|---|---|---|---|---|---|---|---|---|
| | 1970 | | 1971 | | 1972 | | 1973 | | 1974 | | 1975* | |
| | Not Broken Down | Broken Down By Subject Area | Not Broken Down | Broken Down By Subject Area | Not Broken Down | Broken Down By Subject Area | Not Broken Down | Broken Down By Subject Area | Not Broken Down | Broken Down By Subject Area | Not Broken Down | Broken Down By Subject Area |
| | (A) | (B) | (A) | (B) | (A) | (B) | (A) | (B) | (A) | (B) | (A) | (B) |
| VI. Rates of Loss of Books and Serials (Please note whether your library has prepared any reports dealing with this subject). | | | | | | | | | | | | |
| VII. Users of Library Materials -- outside circulation (other than interlibrary loan): | | | | | | | | | | | | |
| (a) Number of borrowers who are | | | | | | | | | | | | |
| (i) Undergraduates | | | | | | | | | | | | |
| (ii) Graduate students | | | | | | | | | | | | |
| (iii) Faculty | | | | | | | | | | | | |
| (iv) Other - faculty family | | | | | | | | | | | | |
| (v) Other - non-university | | | | | | | | | | | | |
| VIII Interlibrary Borrowing and Lending: | | | | | | | | | | | | |
| (a) Books | | | | | | | | | | | | |
| (b) Serials | | | | | | | | | | | | |
| IX. Staff Analysis -- number of professional, nonprofessional, full-time, and part-time employees. (Please indicate at the end of this questionnaire how you are defining the term "professional.") | | | | | | | | | | | | |
| X. Salaries and Benefits -- broken down into the above categories given in IX above. | | | | | | | | | | | | |
| XI. Costs Other than Salaries: | | | | | | | | | | | | |
| (a) Binding | | | | | | | | | | | | |

*When available.

162

| | YEAR 1970 | | 1971 | | 1972 | | 1973 | | 1974 | | 1975* | |
|---|---|---|---|---|---|---|---|---|---|---|---|---|
| | Not Broken Down (A) | Broken Down By Subject Area (B) | Not Broken Down (A) | Broken Down By Subject Area (B) | Not Broken Down (A) | Broken Down By Subject Area (B) | Not Broken Down (A) | Broken Down By Subject Area (B) | Not Broken Down (A) | Broken Down By Subject Area (B) | Not Broken Down (A) | Broken Down By Subject Area (B) |
| (b) Equipment | | | | | | | | | | | | |
| (c) General and Administrative | | | | | | | | | | | | |
| XII. Funding | | | | | | | | | | | | |
| (a) Broken down by sources, such as | | | | | | | | | | | | |
| (i) General Funds | | | | | | | | | | | | |
| (ii) Income from Endowments | | | | | | | | | | | | |
| (iii) Federal Aid | | | | | | | | | | | | |
| (iv) State Aid | | | | | | | | | | | | |
| (v) Local Aid | | | | | | | | | | | | |
| (vi) Gifts | | | | | | | | | | | | |
| (vii) Other | | | | | | | | | | | | |
| (b) Total funding not broken down as in (a) above. | | | | | | | | | | | | |

Definition of "professional" staff:

*When available.

163

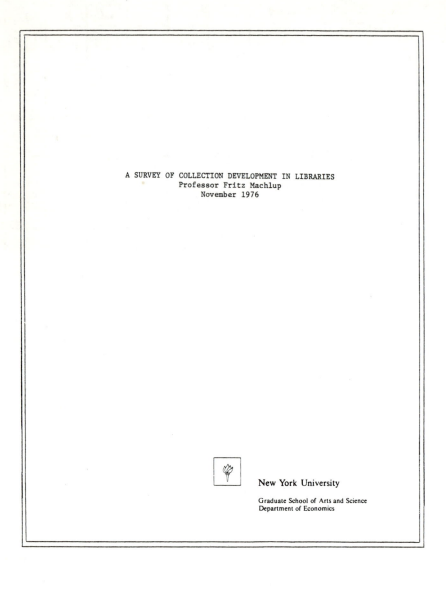

A SURVEY OF COLLECTION DEVELOPMENT IN LIBRARIES
Professor Fritz Machlup
November 1976

**New York University**

Graduate School of Arts and Science
Department of Economics

164

Page 1

| INTRODUCTION |
| --- |

- The following questionnaire is divided into five sections:

        Section I      Library Expenditures
        Section II     Book Purchases
        Section III    Periodical Purchases
        Section IV     Collection Assessment
        Section V      Availability of Automated Files

- The sections are physically separable so that you can distribute portions to appropriate staff. The cover sheet of each section requests, for purposes of follow up, the name, title, and phone number of the respondent if different from the name of the principal respondent identified below. Definitions also appear in each section. In several cases, questions in Sections II and III refer back to tables in Section I.

- Each library will be assigned a unique number to assure anonymity, hence the blank box at the top of each section.

- Please urge your staff to estimate all answers when exact figures or percentages are not available.

- Place all estimates in brackets [    ].

- If you are not able to provide data, or if you cannot estimate, please indicate with "NA" (Not Available).

- Ignore the numbers in parentheses down the right hand column on each page. They are for keypunching purposes only.

- We have enclosed a stamped, self-addressed envelope for return of the questionnaire. Please return the questionnaire to:

        Professor Fritz Machlup
        347 Fifth Avenue
        Room 1110
        New York, New York 10016

- The deadline for return is *February 15, 1977*. If you have any questions, please feel free to call Professor Machlup's office in New York at 212-683-2050 (call collect).

- We hope that you will be able to respond by answering in terms of *all* libraries in your system as we wish the data to be as inclusive as possible. We are aware, however, that for some libraries this request is unrealistic. Consequently, we have asked in each section which organizational units are included and which are excluded in your answers.

- Please enclose a complete list of all libraries/organizational units in your system so that we have a checklist.

- Please circle the number of the type of your library. *(Circle 1, 2, 3, or 4):*

  Academic . . 1  Public . . 2  Special (Excluding Federal) . . 3  Federal . . 4      (9-10)

- Please indicate which is your twelve month reporting year. *(Circle 1, 2, or 3):*

  Calendar . . 1  Academic . . 2  Fiscal . . 3
                              └─→ Beginning_____ Ending_____      (11-12.)
                                      (month)           (month)

- If you changed your reporting year between 1970 and 1976, please indicate the year(s) in which the change(s) took place: _____

_____

| |
| --- |
| Name and Title of Principal Respondent _____ |
| Name of Library _____  Phone No._____ |
|                                          (area code) |
| Address _____ |

165

SECTION I - LIBRARY EXPENDITURES

This section of the survey is devoted to your library's expenditures between 1970 and 1976, especially those expenditures associated with collection development.

- Please place all estimates between brackets. [ ]
- If you are unable to provide data, or if you cannot estimate, please indicate with "NA" (Not Available).
- Please indicate at the end of this section which organizational units are excluded in your responses.

Please fill in your name, title, and phone number if different from the principal respondent:

Name: _____

Title: _____

Phone Number: _____
(area code)-

If you have any questions, please feel free to call Professor Machlup's office in New York: (212) 683-2050 (call collect)

- Definitions:

Book: All catalogued monographs and catalogued government documents. Excludes bound volumes of periodicals and newspapers, annuals, society journals, and proceedings.

Serial: An inclusive term for publications issued in successive parts bearing numerical or chronological designations and intended to be continued indefinitely. Includes periodicals, newspapers, annuals, society journals and proceedings.

Periodical: A serial publication usually published at regular or stated intervals over an indefinite period, each issue of which contains separate articles. Includes society journals, excludes newspapers, annuals, and proceedings.

Microform: Material that has been photographically reduced in size and which is too small to be read without magnification. Includes microfilm, microfiche, microcard and microtext.

Other Materials: Includes audio recordings, film strips, movies, slides, maps, charts, etc. Excludes books, serials and microforms.

Title: A bibliographic unit, whether issued in one or several volumes, reels, discs, slides or parts.

Volume: A physical unit that has been catalogued. Excludes microforms and "other materials".

Domestic Publication: Book or serial published in the United States.

Foreign Publication: Book or serial published outside the United States.

## I-1 TOTAL LIBRARY EXPENDITURES

Please break down your library's total *expenditures* (i.e., dollars spent) as requested
in columns (a) through (e) for the years 1970 through 1976. Report plant operation and
maintenance in column (d) if it is part of your library's expenditures. Please do not
report building construction funds in this table:

| Year | TOTAL LIBRARY EXPENDITURES (in dollars) | | | | | | |
|---|---|---|---|---|---|---|---|
| | Books, Serials, Micro-forms, and Other Materials (a) | Salaries & Wages Including Fringe Benefits (b) | Binding (c) | Plant Operation & Mainte-nance (d) | All Other (Supplies, Equipment, etc.) (e) | Total (sum of columns a through e) (f) | |
| 1976 | | | | | | | (8-67.) |
| 1975 | | | | | | | (8-67.) |
| 1974 | | | | | | | (8-67.) |
| 1973 | | | | | | | (8-67.) |
| 1972 | | | | | | | (8-67.) |
| 1971 | | | | | | | (8-67.) |
| 1970 | | | | | | | (8-67.) |

## I-2 MATERIALS EXPENDITURES

Please break down your library's materials *expenditures* (i.e., dollars spent) from
column (a) above into books, serials, microforms, and other materials. If possible,
separate expenditures for Periodicals from expenditures for Other Serials. Columns
(g) through (1) below should sum to column (a) above:

| Year | MATERIALS EXPENDITURES (in dollars) | | | | | | |
|---|---|---|---|---|---|---|---|
| | Books (g) | Serials | | | Microforms (Both Books and Serials) (k) | Other Materials (1) | |
| | | Periodicals (h) | Other Serials (i) | Total Serials (j) | | | |
| 1976 | | | | | | | (8-67.) |
| 1975 | | | | | | | (8-67. |
| 1974 | | | | | | | (8-67.) |
| 1973 | | | | | | | (8-67.) |
| 1972 | | | | | | | (8-67.) |
| 1971 | | | | | | | (8-67.) |
| 1970 | | | | | | | (8-67.) |

I-3  In Question number I-2, please indicate how you treated *numbered monographic series*. *(Circle one number)*:

Monographic Series treated as BOOKS (column f) . . . . . . . . 1

Monographic Series treated as PERIODICALS (column g) . . . . . 2

Monographic Series treated as OTHER SERIALS (column h) . . . . 3    (8-9)

Monographic Series treated as TOTAL SERIALS (column i) . . . . 4

I-4  MICROFORM EXPENDITURES

Please break down your library's microform *expenditures* (i.e., dollars spent) from column k in Question number I-2 into expenditures for *microform books* and for *microform serials*:

| Year | MICROFORM EXPENDITURES (in dollars) | | |
|---|---|---|---|
| | Microform Books (m) | Microform Serials (n) | |
| 1976 | | | (10-26) |
| 1975 | | | (27-43) |
| 1974 | | | (44-60.) |
| 1973 | | | (8-24) |
| 1972 | | | (25-41) |
| 1971 | | | (42-58.) |
| 1970 | | | (8-24) |

I-5  Please indicate the approximate age of your library by estimating for how many years your library has been regularly purchasing library materials. *(Circle one response)*:

Less than 10 Years . . . . 1

10-19 Years . . . . . . . 2

20-49 Years . . . . . . . 3    (25-26)

50 Years or More . . . . . 4

I-6  Indicate what percent of your 1976 book expenditures was for books published prior to 1970. *(Insert percent in box)*: . . . . . . . . . .  [    %  ]    (27-31)

I-7  Indicate what percent of your 1976 periodical expenditures was for back issues published prior to 1976. *(Insert percent in box)*: . . . . .  [    %  ]    (32-35.)

I-8 During 1976, your library may have experienced budget pressures which had an impact on your collection development and maintenance activities.  If this is so, please circle the code numbers of the items below which correspond to the specific actions your library took to relieve this budget pressure.  *(Circle the code corresponding to all applicable responses.  If you have circled any codes 1 through 6, please indicate how many subscriptions were affected.  If your library did not experience budget pressures which had an impact on your collection development and maintenance activities, circle 22):*

| Action | Item | Code | For How Many Subscriptions | |
|---|---|---|---|---|
| Dropped Duplicate Subscriptions to | Periodicals<br>Newspapers<br>Indexing/Abstracting Services | 1<br>2<br>3 | _____<br>_____<br>_____ | (8-17)<br>(18-27)<br>(28-37) |
| Dropped the Only Subscriptions to | Periodicals<br>Newspapers<br>Indexing/Abstracting Services | 4<br>5<br>6 | _____<br>_____<br>_____ | (38-47)<br>(48-57)<br>(58-67.) |
| Added Fewer New Subscriptions to | Periodicals<br>Newspapers<br>Indexing/Abstracting Services | 7<br>8<br>9 | | (8-9)<br>(10-11)<br>(12-13) |
| Added No New Subscriptions to | Periodicals<br>Newspapers<br>Indexing/Abstracting Services | 10<br>11<br>12 | | (14-15)<br>(16-17)<br>(18-19) |
| Purchased Microform of Periodical in lieu of | Original<br>Binding | 13<br>14 | | (20-21)<br>(22-23) |
| Reallocated Budget to Periodicals at the Expense of | Books<br>Binding<br>Supplies/Equipment<br>Salaries<br>Other (specify)\_\_\_\_ | 15<br>16<br>17<br>18<br>19 | | (24-25)<br>(26-27)<br>(28-29)<br>(30-31)<br>(32-33) |
| Other Actions Taken | (specify)\_\_\_\_<br>(specify)\_\_\_\_ | 20<br>21 | | (34-35)<br>(36-37) |
| No Action Taken | | 22 | | (38-39) |

I-9 Please indicate which cost-reducing action from the above list was most effective in reducing budget pressures experienced during the last year.  *(Insert code number in box.  Insert 22 if you circled 22 above):* . . . . . . . . [    ]  (40-41)

169

I-10   Please indicate for which years your library can generate a breakdown of total materials expenditures by *subject* field, with subjects corresponding to Dewey in 10's (e.g., 330, 880, 920, etc.), two-letter L.C. classes (e.g., HB, PR, KF, etc.), or some other formal subject classification system. *(Circle all applicable years, circling 8 if all years apply or 9 if none apply):*

| | | | |
|---|---|---|---|
| 1976 . . . . . . . | 1 | 1972 . . . . . . . | 5 |
| 1975 . . . . . . . | 2 | 1971 . . . . . . . | 6 |
| 1974 . . . . . . . | 3 | 1970 . . . . . . . | 7 |
| 1973 . . . . . . . | 4 | All of the above | 8 |
| | | None of the above | 9 |

I-11   If your library *cannot* generate a breakdown of total materials expenditures by a formal subject classification system, please indicate how and for which years non-subject breakdowns can be made available. *(Examples of such breakdowns would be by academic division or by library department. Please describe each breakdown and indicate for which years it can be generated:*

Non-Subject Breakdown for
Materials Expenditures:              Years Available:

Describe: _____    _____

Describe: _____    _____

Describe: _____    _____

I-12   Please indicate how many separate organizational units with collections are covered in this section of the questionnaire. *(Insert number in box):* . . ☐     (42-44)

• Does this number include all the organizational units with collections which are part of your library or library system? *(Circle 1 or 2):*

           Yes . . . . 1          No . . . . 2     (45-46.)

• IF NO: What are the names of the excluded units? *(list):*

_____    _____

_____    _____

_____    _____

_____    _____

• Please enclose a complete list of libraries in your system if you have not already done so.

┌─────────────────────────────┐                    ┌──────────────┐
│ SECTION II - BOOK PURCHASES │                    │              │
└─────────────────────────────┘                    └──────────────┘

This section of the questionnaire is devoted to your library's book purchases between 1970 and 1976.

- Please place all estimates between brackets [   ].

- If you are unable to provide data, or if you cannot estimate, please indicate with "NA" (Not Available).

- Please indicate at the end of this section which organizational units are excluded in your responses.

┌───────────────────────────────────────────────────────────────────────┐
│ Please fill in your name, title, and phone number if different from the │
│ principal respondent:                                                   │
│                                                                         │
│         Name: _____                 │
│                                                                         │
│         Title: _____                │
│                                                                         │
│         Phone Number: _____                  │
│                              (area code)-                               │
│ If you have any questions, please feel free to call Professor Machlup's │
│ office in New York:  (212) 683-2050 (call collect)                      │
└───────────────────────────────────────────────────────────────────────┘

- Definitions:

  **Book:**  All catalogued monographs and catalogued government documents.  Excludes bound volumes of periodicals and newspapers, annuals, society journals, and proceedings.

  **Serial:**  An inclusive term for publications issued in successive parts bearing numerical or chronological designations and intended to be continued indefinitely. Includes periodicals, newspapers, annuals, society journals and proceedings.

  **Periodical:**  A serial publication usually published at regular or stated intervals over an indefinite period, each issue of which contains separate articles.  Includes society journals, excludes newspapers, annuals, and proceedings.

  **Microform:**  Material that has been photographically reduced in size and which is too small to be read without magnification.  Includes microfilm, microfiche, microcard and microtext.

  **Other Materials:**  Includes audio recordings, film strips, movies, slides, maps, charts, etc.  Excludes books, serials and microforms.

  **Title:**  A bibliographic unit, whether issued in one or several volumes, reels, discs, slides or parts.

  **Volume:**  A physical unit that has been catalogued.  Excludes microforms and "other materials".

  **Domestic Publication:**  Book or serial published in the United States.

  **Foreign Publication:**  Book or serial published outside the United States.

171

II-1  BOOK COLLECTION TRENDS

In the following table, please include all catalogued books, both foreign and domestic.  Exclude uncatalogued items.  If you cannot distinguish between purchases and gifts and exchanges, use columns (c) and (e) to report the volumes and titles added.

| Year | Total Number of Book Volumes in Collection (a) | Total Number of Book Titles in Collection (b) | Number of Book Volumes *Added* through: | | Number of Book Titles *Added* through: | | |
|---|---|---|---|---|---|---|---|
| | | | Purchase (c) | Gift & Exchange (d) | Purchase (e) | Gift & Exchange (f) | |
| 1976 | | | | | | | (8-58.) |
| 1975 | | | | | | | (8-58.) |
| 1974 | | | | | | | (8-58.) |
| 1973 | | | | | | | (8-58.) |
| 1972 | | | | | | | (8-58.) |
| 1971 | | | | | | | (8-58.) |
| 1970 | | | | | | | (8-58 ) |

II-2  Of your library's *total book expenditures* for 1976, as reported in column (g), question number I-2, please estimate the percent of these expenditures that went for the purchase of volumes published outside the U.S.  *(Insert percent in box):* . . . . . . . . . . . . . . . . . . . . . . . . . . . . . . . . . %(59-63)

II-3  Of the total number of *book volumes* added to your library in 1976, as reported in columns (c) & (d) in question II-1 above, please estimate what percent of these volumes was published outside the U.S.  *(Insert percent in box):*  (64-68)

172

II-4  BREAKDOWN OF BOOK VOLUMES BY SUBJECT

In column (a) estimate the percentage of book volumes currently *in your collection* that fall into each of the general subjects listed below. Also, please estimate in column (b) the percentage of book volumes *added* during 1976 in each subject.

|  | Percent of Total Book Volumes in Collection (a) | Percent of Book Volumes *Added* During 1976 (b) |
|---|---|---|
| • Natural Sciences[1] | _____ ( 8-12) | _____ ( 8-12) |
| • Engineering & Technology[2] | _____ (13-17) | _____ (13-17) |
| • Agriculture | _____ (18-22) | _____ (18-22) |
| • Social Sciences[3] | _____ (23-27) | _____ (23-27) |
| • Humanities[4] | _____ (28-32) | _____ (28-32) |
| • Health Sciences | _____ (33-37) | _____ (33-37) |
| • Law | _____ (38-42) | _____ (38-42) |
| • Education | _____ (43-47) | _____ (43-47) |
| • Bibliography & Library Science | _____ (48-52) | _____ (48-52) |
| • Computer Science | _____ (53-57) | _____ (53-57) |
| • Popular Adult Non-Fiction[5] | _____ (58-62) | _____ (58-62) |
| • Adult Fiction | _____ (63-67) | _____ (63-67) |
| • Juvenile Fiction & Non-Fiction | _____ (68-72.) | _____ (68-72.) |
| • TOTAL | 100% | 100% |

[1] Including Astronomy, Biology, Chemistry, Environmental Sciences, Geology, Mathematics, Physics, Zoology

[2] Including Aeronautical, Chemical, Civil, Electrical and Mechanical Engineering

[3] Including Anthropology, Economics, Geography, History, Political Science, Psychology, Sociology, Statistics, Urban Studies

[4] Including Architecture, Art, Archaeology, Classics, Language and Literature (and Linguistics) Music, Philosophy, Religion

[5] For example, Recreation, Travel, Hobbies, etc.

II-5  CHANGES IN BOOK-BUYING PATTERNS BY SUBJECT, 1970-1976

On the scale below, compare your library's buying patterns by subject in 1976 with the buying patterns by subject in 1970 (for book volumes). For example, if you are "buying significantly more" Chemistry book volumes now than in 1970, you would circle "1" next to the Chemistry heading. If you do not collect materials in a given field, circle "6" for "Not Applicable". If there has been no change since 1970, circle "3". *(Please circle one item on the scale for each subject):*

| Subjects | Buying Significantly More | Buying Slightly More | No Change | Buying Slightly Less | Buying Significantly Less | Not Applicable | |
|---|---|---|---|---|---|---|---|
| **Natural Sciences** | | | | | | | |
| Astronomy | 1 | 2 | 3 | 4 | 5 | 6 | (8-9) |
| Biology | 1 | 2 | 3 | 4 | 5 | 6 | (10-11) |
| Chemistry | 1 | 2 | 3 | 4 | 5 | 6 | (12-13) |
| Environmental Sciences | 1 | 2 | 3 | 4 | 5 | 6 | (14-15) |
| Geology | 1 | 2 | 3 | 4 | 5 | 6 | (16-17) |
| Mathematics | 1 | 2 | 3 | 4 | 5 | 6 | (18-19) |
| Physics | 1 | 2 | 3 | 4 | 5 | 6 | (20-21) |
| Zoology | 1 | 2 | 3 | 4 | 5 | 6 | (22-23) |
| Engineering & Technology | 1 | 2 | 3 | 4 | 5 | 6 | (24-25) |
| Agriculture | 1 | 2 | 3 | 4 | 5 | 6 | (26-27) |
| **Social Sciences** | | | | | | | |
| Anthropology | 1 | 2 | 3 | 4 | 5 | 6 | (28-29) |
| Economics | 1 | 2 | 3 | 4 | 5 | 6 | (30-31) |
| Geography | 1 | 2 | 3 | 4 | 5 | 6 | (32-33) |
| History | 1 | 2 | 3 | 4 | 5 | 6 | (34-35) |
| Political Science | 1 | 2 | 3 | 4 | 5 | 6 | (36-37) |
| Psychology | 1 | 2 | 3 | 4 | 5 | 6 | (38-39) |
| Sociology | 1 | 2 | 3 | 4 | 5 | 6 | (40-41) |
| Statistics | 1 | 2 | 3 | 4 | 5 | 6 | (42-43) |
| Urban Studies | 1 | 2 | 3 | 4 | 5 | 6 | (44-45) |
| **Humanities** | | | | | | | |
| Architecture | 1 | 2 | 3 | 4 | 5 | 6 | (46-47) |
| Art | 1 | 2 | 3 | 4 | 5 | 6 | (48-49) |
| Archaeology | 1 | 2 | 3 | 4 | 5 | 6 | (50-51) |
| Classics | 1 | 2 | 3 | 4 | 5 | 6 | (52-53) |
| Language & Literature (including Linguistics) | 1 | 2 | 3 | 4 | 5 | 6 | (54-55) |
| Music | 1 | 2 | 3 | 4 | 5 | 6 | (56-57) |
| Philosophy | 1 | 2 | 3 | 4 | 5 | 6 | (58-59) |
| Religion | 1 | 2 | 3 | 4 | 5 | 6 | (60-61) |
| Health Sciences | 1 | 2 | 3 | 4 | 5 | 6 | (62-63) |
| Law | 1 | 2 | 3 | 4 | 5 | 6 | (64-65) |
| Education | 1 | 2 | 3 | 4 | 5 | 6 | (66-67) |
| Bibliography and Library Science | 1 | 2 | 3 | 4 | 5 | 6 | (68-69) |
| Interdisciplinary Subjects | 1 | 2 | 3 | 4 | 5 | 6 | (70-71) |
| (specify)_____ | 1 | 2 | 3 | 4 | 5 | 6 | (8-9) |
| (specify)_____ | 1 | 2 | 3 | 4 | 5 | 6 | (10-11) |
| **Popular Adult Non-Fiction** (e.g., Recreation, Travel, Hobbies, etc.) | 1 | 2 | 3 | 4 | 5 | 6 | (12-13) |
| Adult Fiction | 1 | 2 | 3 | 4 | 5 | 6 | (14-15) |
| Juvenile Fiction & Non-Fiction | 1 | 2 | 3 | 4 | 5 | 6 | (16-17) |
| Other (specify)_____ | 1 | 2 | 3 | 4 | 5 | 6 | (18-19) |
| Other (specify)_____ | 1 | 2 | 3 | 4 | 5 | 6 | (20-21) |

II-6  RANKING OF SIGNIFICANT CHANGES IN BOOK-BUYING PATTERNS

From your answers to question II-5 above, please *select* and *rank* the three subjects for which you are buying significantly more and the three subjects for which you are buying significantly less:

a) Rank the three subjects for which you are buying *significantly more:*

_____  1st

_____  2nd

_____  3rd

b) Rank the three subjects for which you are buying *significantly less:*

_____  1st

_____  2nd

_____  3rd

II-7  REASONS FOR CHANGES IN BOOK-BUYING PATTERNS BY SUBJECT

Please characterize reasons for change in book acquisitions from the list below. Select four (4) subjects from your ranked responses in Question II-6 above. Insert the names of these subjects in the boxes at the top of each column and circle *all* the appropriate responses that describe reasons for change. If you wish to add additional reasons, please do so in the blanks provided:

| Reasons for Changes in Book-Buying: | Subjects with Most Significant *Increases:* | | Subjects with Most Significant *Decreases:* | | |
|---|---|---|---|---|---|
| | | | | | (22-41) |
| 1. Relative change in undergraduate student enrollment . . . . . . . . . . . . . . . | 1 | 1 | 1 | 1 | (42-49) |
| 2. Relative change in graduate student enrollment . . . . . . . . . . . . . . . | 2 | 2 | 2 | 2 | (50-57) |
| 3. Relative change in number of faculty . . . | 3 | 3 | 3 | 3 | (58-65.) |
| 4. Change in program emphasis . . . . . . . . | 4 | 4 | 4 | 4 | (8-15) |
| 5. Change in number of programs . . . . . . . | 5 | 5 | 5 | 5 | (16-23) |
| 6. Increase in relative price of books . . . | 6 | 6 | 6 | 6 | (24-31) |
| 7. Increase in relative price of serials . . | 7 | 7 | 7 | 7 | (32-39) |
| 8. Change in external private funding . . . . | 8 | 8 | 8 | 8 | (40-47) |
| 9. Change in external federal funding . . . . | 9 | 9 | 9 | 9 | (48-55) |
| 10. Change in state or local funding . . . . . | 10 | 10 | 10 | 10 | (56-63) |
| 11. Change in internal library funding priority . . . . . . . . . . . . . . . . . | 11 | 11 | 11 | 11 | (64-71.) |
| 12. Change in funding priority of supporting institution · · · · · · · · · · · · · | 12 | 12 | 12 | 12 | (8-15) |
| 13. Other (specify) _____ · | 13 | 13 | 13 | 13 | (16-23) |
| 14. Other (specify) _____ · | 14 | 14 | 14 | 14 | (24-31) |
| 15. Other (specify) _____ · | 15 | 15 | 15 | 15 | (32-39) |

175

II-8  DOMESTIC BOOK VOLUMES ADDED *(BY TYPE OF PUBLISHER)*

Of the total number of domestic (U.S. published) book volumes added by your library in 1976, please estimate what percent were *published by* the following type of *publisher:*

| Type of Domestic *Publisher* | Percent of Total Book Volumes Added in 1976 | |
|---|---|---|
| a.  Commercial Presses (e.g., Doubleday, Random House, etc.) . . . . . . . . . . | _____ % | (40-44) |
| b.  University Presses (e.g., Harvard University Press, The University of Minnesota Press, etc.). . . . . . . . . . | _____ % | (45-49) |
| c.  Societies & Associations (e.g., American Medical Association, Modern Language Association, etc.) . . . . . . . . . . . | _____ % | (50-54) |
| d.  U.S. Federal & State Governments (e.g., the Government Printing Office, Dept. of Labor, City of San Francisco, Maricopa County, etc.) . . . . . . . . . . . . . . . . | _____ % | (55-59) |
| e.  Other Publishers . . . . . . . . . . . . . . . . . . . . | _____ % | (60-64.) |
| f.  TOTAL . . . . . . . . . . . . . . . . . . . . . | 100 % | |

II-9  DOMESTIC BOOK VOLUMES ADDED *(BY TYPE OF SOURCE)*

Of the total number of domestic (U.S. published) book volumes added by your library in 1976, please estimate what percent were *purchased from* the following types of *sources/vendors:*

| Type of *Source* | Percent of Total Book Volumes Added in 1976 | |
|---|---|---|
| Direct from: | | |
| a)  Commercial & University Presses . . . . . . . . . . | _____ % | (8-12) |
| b)  Societies & Associations . . . . . . . . . . . . . . | _____ % | (13-17) |
| c)  Federal & State Governments . . . . . . . . . . . . | _____ % | (18-22) |
| Through Intermediaries: | | |
| d)  Wholesalers/Jobbers . . . . . . . . . . . . . . . . | _____ % | (23-27) |
| e)  Bookstores . . . . . . . . . . . . . . . . . . . . . | _____ % | (28-32) |
| f)  Special Dealers (2nd hand, Out of Print) . . . . . . | _____ % | (33-37) |
| g)  Other Publishers . . . . . . . . . . . . . . . . . . | _____ % | (38-42) |
| h)  TOTAL . . . . . . . . . . . . . . . . . . . . . . . | 100 % | |

II-10 Does your library now use any of the following book purchasing plans: approval plans, standing orders, or blanket orders? *(Circle 1 or 2. Consider an "approval plan" to be a profile of your library's acquisitions needs which is matched regularly against a wholesaler's inventory. For our purposes, "standing order" and "blanket order" are synonymous):*

Yes . . . . . . . 1  *(Continue with Question number II-11)*

No  . . . . . . . 2  *(Skip to Question number II-15)*     (43-44)

II-11 Please estimate what percent of your *domestic* (U.S. published) *book expenditures* in 1976 and 1970 were made through purchasing plans, and what percent through single order purchases:

|  | Percent of Domestic 1976 Book Expenditures | Percent of Domestic 1970 Book Expenditures |  |
|---|---|---|---|
| a) Percent of domestic book expenditures via approval plans, standing orders, blanket orders, etc. . . . . . . . . | % | % | (45-54) |
| b) Percent of domestic book expenditures via single order purchases . . . . . | % | % | (55-64.) |
| c) TOTAL book expenditures . . . . . | 100  % | 100  % | |

II-12 Estimate what percent of your *foreign book expenditures* in 1976 and 1970 were made through purchasing plans, and what percent through single order purchases:

|  | Percent of Foreign 1976 Book Expenditures | Percent of Foreign 1970 Book Expenditures |  |
|---|---|---|---|
| a) Percent of foreign book expenditures via approval plans, standing orders, blanket orders, etc. . . . . . . . . | % | % | (8-17) |
| b) Percent of foreign book expenditures via single order purchases . . . . . | % | % | (18-27) |
| c) TOTAL book expenditures . . . . . | 100  % | 100  % | |

II-13 If you are currently purchasing *domestic (U.S. published)* books through an approval plan, please list the name of the company or companies which handle your approval plan(s):

| (name of wholesaler) | (city) | (state) | (year service began) |
|---|---|---|---|

| (name of wholesaler) | (city) | (state) | (year service began) |
|---|---|---|---|

II-14 If during the last five years, you dropped a U.S. based wholesaler's approval plan, please list the name(s) of the(se) wholesaler(s):

| (name of wholesaler) | (city) | (state) | (year service began) |
|---|---|---|---|

| (name of wholesaler) | (city) | (state) | (year service began) |
|---|---|---|---|

177

II-15 Please indicate for which years your library can generate a breakdown of number of book volumes *added by subject* field with subjects corresponding to Dewey in 10's (e.g., 330, 880, 920, etc.), two-letter L.C. classes (e.g., HB, PR, KF, etc.), or some other formal subject classification system. *(Circle all applicable years, circling 8 if all years apply or 9 if none apply):*

| | | | |
|---|---|---|---|
| 1976 . . . . . . . | 1 | 1972 . . . . . . . | 5 |
| 1975 . . . . . . . | 2 | 1971 . . . . . . . | 6 |
| 1974 . . . . . . . | 3 | 1970 . . . . . . . | 7 |
| 1973 . . . . . . . | 4 | All of the above | 8 |
| | | None of the above | 9 |

II-16 If your library *cannot* generate a breakdown of number of book volumes added by a formal subject classification system, please indicate how and for which years non-subject breakdowns can be made available. *(Examples of such breakdowns would be by academic division or by library department. Please describe each breakdown and indicate for which years it can be generated):*

|  Non-Subject Breakdown for Book Volumes Added: | Years Available: |
|---|---|
| Describe: _____ | _____ |
| Describe: _____ | _____ |
| Describe: _____ | _____ |

II-17 Please indicate how many separate organizational units with collections are covered in this section of the questionnaire. *(Insert number in box):* . . [    ]   (28-30)

- Does this number include all the organizational units with collections which are part of your library or library system? *(Circle 1 or 2):*

          Yes . . . . 1        No . . . . 2        (31-32.)

- IF NO: What are the names of the excluded units? *(list):*

_____    _____
_____    _____
_____    _____
_____    _____
_____    _____

SECTION III - PERIODICAL PURCHASES

This section of the questionnaire is devoted to your library's periodical purchases between 1970 and 1976. We are also interested in the sources from which you obtain your periodicals, such as subscription agencies and publishers.

- Please place all estimates between brackets [ ] .
- If you are unable to provide data, or if you cannot estimate, please indicate with "NA" (Not Available).
- Please indicate at the end of this section which organizational units are excluded in your responses.

Please fill in your name, title, and phone number if different from the principal respondent:

Name: _____

Title: _____

Phone Number: _____
(area code)-

If you have any questions, please feel free to call Professor Machlup's office in New York: (212) 683-2050 (call collect)

- Definitions:

Book: All catalogued monographs and catalogued government documents. Excludes bound volumes of periodicals and newspapers, annuals, society journals, and proceedings.

Serial: An inclusive term for publications issued in successive parts bearing numerical or chronological designations and intended to be continued indefinitely. Includes periodicals, newspapers, annuals, society journals and proceedings.

Periodical: A serial publication usually published at regular or stated intervals over an indefinite period, each issue of which contains separate articles. Includes society journals, excludes newspapers, annuals, and proceedings.

Microform: Material that has been photographically reduced in size and which is too small to be read without magnification. Includes microfilm, microfiche, microcard and microtext.

Other Materials: Includes audio recordings, film strips, movies, slides, maps, charts, etc. Excludes books, serials and microforms.

Title: A bibliographic unit, whether issued in one or several volumes, reels, discs, slides or parts.

Volume: A physical unit that has been catalogued. Excludes microforms and "other materials".

Domestic Publication: Book or serial published in the United States.

Foreign Publication: Book or serial published outside the United States.

179

III-1  PERIODICALS COLLECTION TRENDS

Please fill in data about your library's periodical *subscriptions* for 1970 - 1976 in columns (a) through (h) below. If you are unable to distinguish between purchases and gifts and exchanges, use columns (e) and (g) to report periodical subscriptions added and periodical titles added.

If you cannot separate periodical titles from total serials, please base numbers on total serials reported in column (j), Question number I-2, and check (√) the box at right: . . . . . . . . . . . . . . . . . .   (8-9.)

| Year | Total Number of Periodical *Subscriptions* (a) | Number of Periodical *Titles* excluding duplicate copies (b) | Number of Periodical *Subscriptions* cancelled (c) | Number of Periodical *Titles* cancelled (d) | Number of Periodical *Subscriptions Added* through: | | Number of Periodical *Titles Added* through: | |
| | | | | | Purchase (e) | Gift & Exchange (f) | Purchase (g) | Gift & Exchange (h) |
|---|---|---|---|---|---|---|---|---|
| 1976 | | | | | | | | | (8-71.) |
| 1975 | | | | | | | | | (8-71.) |
| 1974 | | | | | | | | | (8-71.) |
| 1973 | | | | | | | | | (8-71.) |
| 1972 | | | | | | | | | (8-71.) |
| 1971 | | | | | | | | | (8-71.) |
| 1970 | | | | | | | | | (8-71.) |

III-2  Of the total *periodical expenditures* for 1976 (as reported in column (h), Question number I-2), please estimate the percent of these expenditures which went for the purchase of subscriptions published outside the U.S. *(Insert percent in box)*: . . . . . . . . . . . . . . . . . . . . . . . . . . . . . . . . .  % (8-12)

III-3  Of the total *number of periodical subscriptions* received by your library in 1976, (as reported in (a), Question number III-1), please estimate what percent were published outside the U.S. *(Insert percent in box)*: . . . . . . . .  % (13-17)

III-4  BREAKDOWN OF PERIODICAL SUBSCRIPTIONS BY SUBJECT

Please estimate in percentage terms the breakdown of your currently received *1976 periodical subscriptions* using the broad subjects below. *(Include duplicate copies in making your percent estimates):*

|  | Percent of 1976 Periodical Subscriptions Currently Received |
|---|---|
| ● Natural Sciences[1] | _____ ( 8-12) |
| ● Engineering & Technology | _____ (13-17) |
| ● Agriculture | _____ (18-22) |
| ● Social Sciences[2] | _____ (23-27) |
| ● Humanities[3] | _____ (28-32) |
| ● Health Sciences | _____ (33-37) |
| ● Law | _____ (38-42) |
| ● Education | _____ (43-47) |
| ● Bibliography & Library Science | _____ (48-52) |
| ● Interdisciplinary Subjects[4] | _____ (53-57) |
| ● Popular Adult Non-Fiction[5] | _____ (58-62) |
| ● Adult Fiction | _____ (63-67) |
| ● Juvenile Fiction & Non-Fiction | _____ (68-72.) |
| ● TOTAL | 100 % |

---

[1] Astronomy, Biology, Chemistry, Geology, Mathematics, Physics, Zoology

[2] Anthropology, Economics, Geography, History, Political Science, Psychology, Sociology, Statistics

[3] Architecture, Art, Archaeology, Classics, Language & Literature (including Linguistics) Music, Philosophy, Religion

[4] For example, Environmental Science, Urban Studies, etc.

[5] For example, Recreation, Travel, Hobbies, etc.

III-5  CHANGES IN PERIODICAL SUBSCRIPTIONS BY SUBJECT, 1970-1976

On the scale below, compare by subject the number of your library's subscriptions in 1976 with your subscriptions in 1970.  For example, if your current number of subscriptions to Psychology journals is "significantly less" than the number in 1970, circle "5" next to the Psychology heading.  If you do not subscribe to any journals in a given field, circle "6" for "Not Applicable".  If there has been no change, circle "3".  *(Circle one item on the scale for each subject):*

| Subjects | Buying Significantly More | Buying Slightly More | No Change | Buying Slightly Less | Buying Significantly Less | Not Applicable | |
|---|---|---|---|---|---|---|---|
| **Natural Sciences** | | | | | | | |
| Astronomy | 1 | 2 | 3 | 4 | 5 | 6 | (8-9) |
| Biology | 1 | 2 | 3 | 4 | 5 | 6 | (10-11 |
| Chemistry | 1 | 2 | 3 | 4 | 5 | 6 | (12-13 |
| Environmental Sciences | 1 | 2 | 3 | 4 | 5 | 6 | (14-15 |
| Geology | 1 | 2 | 3 | 4 | 5 | 6 | (16-17 |
| Mathematics | 1 | 2 | 3 | 4 | 5 | 6 | (18-19 |
| Physics | 1 | 2 | 3 | 4 | 5 | 6 | (20-21 |
| Zoology | 1 | 2 | 3 | 4 | 5 | 6 | (22-23 |
| Engineering & Technology | 1 | 2 | 3 | 4 | 5 | 6 | (24-25 |
| Agriculture | 1 | 2 | 3 | 4 | 5 | 6 | (26-27 |
| **Social Sciences** | | | | | | | |
| Anthropology | 1 | 2 | 3 | 4 | 5 | 6 | (28-29 |
| Economics | 1 | 2 | 3 | 4 | 5 | 6 | (30-31 |
| Geography | 1 | 2 | 3 | 4 | 5 | 6 | (32-33 |
| History | 1 | 2 | 3 | 4 | 5 | 6 | (34-35 |
| Political Science | 1 | 2 | 3 | 4 | 5 | 6 | (36-37 |
| Psychology | 1 | 2 | 3 | 4 | 5 | 6 | (38-39 |
| Sociology | 1 | 2 | 3 | 4 | 5 | 6 | (40-41) |
| Statistics | 1 | 2 | 3 | 4 | 5 | 6 | (42-43) |
| Urban Studies | 1 | 2 | 3 | 4 | 5 | 6 | (44-45) |
| **Humanities** | | | | | | | |
| Architecture | 1 | 2 | 3 | 4 | 5 | 6 | (46-47) |
| Art | 1 | 2 | 3 | 4 | 5 | 6 | (48-49) |
| Archaeology | 1 | 2 | 3 | 4 | 5 | 6 | (50-51) |
| Classics | 1 | 2 | 3 | 4 | 5 | 6 | (52-53) |
| Language & Literature (including Linguistics) | 1 | 2 | 3 | 4 | 5 | 6 | (54-55) |
| Music | 1 | 2 | 3 | 4 | 5 | 6 | (56-57) |
| Philosophy | 1 | 2 | 3 | 4 | 5 | 6 | (58-59) |
| Religion | 1 | 2 | 3 | 4 | 5 | 6 | (60-61) |
| Health Sciences | 1 | 2 | 3 | 4 | 5 | 6 | (62-63) |
| Law | 1 | 2 | 3 | 4 | 5 | 6 | (64-65) |
| Education | 1 | 2 | 3 | 4 | 5 | 6 | (66-67) |
| Bibliography and Library Science | 1 | 2 | 3 | 4 | 5 | 6 | (68-69) |
| Interdisciplinary Subjects | 1 | 2 | 3 | 4 | 5 | 6 | (70-71) |
| (specify)_____ | 1 | 2 | 3 | 4 | 5 | 6 | (8-9) |
| (specify)_____ | 1 | 2 | 3 | 4 | 5 | 6 | (10-11) |
| Popular Adult Non-Fiction (e.g., Recreation, Travel, Hobbies, etc.) | 1 | 2 | 3 | 4 | 5 | 6 | (12-13) |
| Adult Fiction | 1 | 2 | 3 | 4 | 5 | 6 | (14-15) |
| Juvenile Fiction & Non-Fiction | 1 | 2 | 3 | 4 | 5 | 6 | (16-17) |
| Other (specify)_____ | 1 | 2 | 3 | 4 | 5 | 6 | (18-19) |
| Other (specify)_____ | 1 | 2 | 3 | 4 | 5 | 6 | (20-21) |

III-6  RANKING OF SIGNIFICANT CHANGES IN PERIODICAL SUBSCRIPTIONS BY SUBJECT

From your answers to Question III-5 above, please *select* and *rank* the three subjects for which you are buying significantly more and the three subjects for which
you are buying significantly less:

a) Rank the three subjects for which       b) Rank the three subjects for which
you are buying *significantly more:*          you are buying *significantly less:*

_____ 1st                 _____ 1st

_____ 2nd                 _____ 2nd

_____ 3rd                 _____ 3rd

III-7  REASONS FOR CHANGES IN SUBSCRIPTIONS BY SUBJECT

Please characterize reasons for change in periodical acquisitions from the list
below.  Select any four (4) subjects from your ranked responses in Question III-6.
Insert the names of these subjects in the boxes at the top of each column and
circle *all* the appropriate responses which describe reasons for change.  If you
wish to add additional reasons, please do so in the blanks provided.

| Reasons for Change in Subscriptions: | Subjects with Most Significant *Increases:* | | Subjects with Most Significant *Decreases:* | | (22-41) |
|---|---|---|---|---|---|
| 1. Relative change in undergraduate student enrollment . . . . . . . . . . . . . . . . . 1 | 1 | | 1 | 1 | (42-49) |
| 2. Relative change in graduate student enrollment . . . . . . . . . . . . . . . . 2 | 2 | | 2 | 2 | (50-57) |
| 3. Relative change in number of faculty . . . . 3 | 3 | | 3 | 3 | (58-65.) |
| 4. Change in program emphasis . . . . . . . . . 4 | 4 | | 4 | 4 | (8-15) |
| 5. Change in number of programs . . . . . . . . 5 | 5 | | 5 | 5 | (16-23) |
| 6. Increase in relative price of books . . . . 6 | 6 | | 6 | 6 | (24-31) |
| 7. Increase in relative price of serials . . . 7 | 7 | | 7 | 7 | (32-39) |
| 8. Change in external private funding . . . . . 8 | 8 | | 8 | 8 | (40-47) |
| 9. Change in external federal funding . . . . . 9 | 9 | | 9 | 9 | (48-55) |
| 10. Change in state or local funding . . . . . . 10 | 10 | | 10 | 10 | (56-63) |
| 11. Change in internal library funding priority . . . . . . . . . . . . . . . . . 11 | 11 | | 11 | 11 | (64-71.) |
| 12 Change in funding priority of support-ing institution · · · · · · · · · · · · · · 12 | 12 | | 12 | 12 | (8-15) |
| 13. Other (specify) _____ · · 13 | 13 | | 13 | 13 | (16-23) |
| 14. Other (specify) _____ · · 14 | 14 | | 14 | 14 | (24-31) |
| 15. Other (specify) _____ · · 15 | 15 | | 15 | 15 | (32-39) |

183

III-8  DOMESTIC PERIODICAL SUBSCRIPTIONS *(BY TYPE OF PUBLISHER)*

Of the total number of domestic (U.S. published) periodical subscriptions received
by your library in 1976, please estimate what percent were published by the following types of *publishers.* *(If you are not able to separate periodicals from the
rest of your serial subscriptions, please make estimates based on total serials,
and check (✓) the box at right):* . . . . . . . . . . . . . . . . . . . . .  (40-41)

| Type of Domestic *Publisher* | Total Periodical Subscriptions in 1976 | |
|---|---|---|
| a) Commercial Presses (e.g., McGraw-Hill, Williams & Wilkins, etc.) . . . . . . . . . | _____ % | (42-46) |
| b) University Presses (e.g., University of Chicago Press, Princeton University Press, etc.) . . . . . . . . . . . . . . . | _____ % | (47-51) |
| c) Societies & Associations (e.g., American Chemical Society, American Philosophical Society, etc.) . . . . . . . . . . . . | _____ % | (52-56) |
| d) U.S. Federal & State Governments (e.g., Government Printing Office, National Bureau of Standards, New York City, Dade County, etc.) . . . . . . . . . . . . . . . | _____ % | (57-61) |
| e) Other Publishers . . . . . . . . . . . . . . . . . . . | _____ % | (62-66.) |
| f) TOTAL . . . . . . . . . . . . . . . . . . . . . . . . . | 100 % | |

III-9  DOMESTIC PERIODICAL SUBSCRIPTIONS *(BY TYPE OF SOURCE)*

Of the total number of domestic (U.S. published) periodical subscriptions received
by your library in 1976, estimate what percent were purchased from the following
sources:

| Type of Subscription *Source* | Percent of Subscriptions Received in 1976 | |
|---|---|---|
| Direct from: | | |
| a) Commercial & University Presses . . . . . . . . . . . . . | _____ % | (8-12) |
| b) Societies & Associations . . . . . . . . . . . . . . . . | _____ % | (13-17) |
| c) Federal & State Governments . . . . . . . . . . . . . . . | _____ % | (18-22) |
| Through Intermediary: | | |
| d) Serial Subscription Agents . . . . . . . . . . . . . . . | _____ % | (23-27) |
| e) TOTAL . . . . . . . . . . . . . . . . . . . . . . . . . | 100 % | |

184

III-10  Please indicate for which years your library can generate a breakdown of number of periodical titles added by subject field, with subjects corresponding to Dewey in 10's (e.g., 330, 880, 920, etc.), two-letter L.C. classes (e.g., HB, PR, KF, etc.), or some other formal subject classification system.  *(Circle all applicable years circling 8 if all years apply or 9 if none apply):*

|  |  |
|---|---|
| 1976 . . . . . . . 1 | 1972 . . . . . . . 5 |
| 1975 . . . . . . . 2 | 1971 . . . . . . . 6 |
| 1974 . . . . . . . 3 | 1970 . . . . . . . 7 |
| 1973 . . . . . . . 4 | All of the above . 8 |
|  | None of the above  9 |

III-11  If your library *cannot* generate a breakdown of number of periodical titles added by a formal subject classification system, please indicate how and for which years non-subject breakdowns can be made available.  *(Examples of such breakdowns would be by academic division or by library department.  Please describe each breakdown and indicate for which years it can be generated):*

|  | Non-Subject Breakdown for Periodical Titles Received | Years Available: |
|---|---|---|
| Describe: | _____ | _____ |
| Describe: | _____ | _____ |
| Describe: | _____ | _____ |

III-12  Please indicate how many separate organizational units with collections are covered in this section of the questionnaire.  *(Insert number in box):* . .  ☐  (28-30)

- Does this number include all the organizational units with collections which are part of your library or library system?  *(Circle 1 or 2):*

     Yes . . . . 1          No . . . . 2          (31-32.)

- IF NO:  What are the names of the excluded units?  *(list):*

| | |
|---|---|
| _____ | _____ |
| _____ | _____ |
| _____ | _____ |
| _____ | _____ |
| _____ | _____ |

| SECTION IV - COLLECTION ASSESSMENT | |
|---|---|

This section of the survey raises questions involving your assessment of such factors as collection level and subject emphasis.

- Please indicate at the bottom of this page which organizational units are excluded in your responses.

- Please read the definitions on the next page before answering Question number IV-2.

> Please fill in your name, title, and phone number if different from the principal respondent:
>
> Name: _____
>
> Title: _____
>
> Phone Number: _____
>                (area code)-
>
> If you have any questions, please feel free to call Professor Machlup's office in New York:  (212) 683-2050 (call collect)

IV-1  Please indicate how many separate organizational units with collections are covered in this section of the questionnaire.  *(Insert number in box):* . . ☐  (8-10)

- Does this number include all the organizational units with collections which are part of your library or library system? *(Circle 1 or 2):*

   Yes . . . . 1          No . . . . 2          (11-12.)

- IF NO:  What are the names of the excluded units? *(list):*

_____     _____
_____     _____
_____     _____
_____     _____
_____     _____

- Definitions of Collection Levels:

The following definitions of collection levels are based on a preliminary edition
of *Guidelines for the Formulation of Collection Development Policies* prepared by
the Collection Development Committee, Resources Section, RTSD, of the American
Library Association, March 1976.  These definitions have been designed to provide
an objective basis for collection assessment.

It is quite likely that very few libraries will hold "comprehensive level" collections in any area.  Similarly public, undergraduate and community college libraries
which are not oriented toward specialized research may not have any "research level"
collections.

(a) Comprehensive level

> Collecting all significant works of recorded knowledge; the aim,
if not the achievement, is exhaustiveness.

(b) Research level

> Collecting the major source materials required for pure and applied
research; the aim is to include all important reference works and abstracting and indexing services, a wide selection of specialized monographs
and extensive journal collections.

(c) Study level

> Collecting a wide range of basic monographs (with complete collections
of important writers and selections from secondary writers), a selection of
representative journals and basic subject-related reference and bibliographical
tools; the aim is to support the collection at the equivalent of undergraduate
or graduate coursework, but at less intensity than the research level.

(d) Basic level

> Collecting highly selective introductory materials, including major
dictionaries and encyclopedias, selected important works and surveys, a few
major periodicals and bibliographies; the aim is to define the subject and
to indicate the varieties of information available elsewhere.

(e) Minimal level

> Collecting only a few primary materials and the basic reference tools;
the subject is out of scope of the collection.

## IV-2  ASSESSMENT OF COLLECTION LEVEL

From the list of definitions on the previous page, please select the "collection level" which *best describes* the completeness of each of these subjects in your library's collection.

For example, if your music collection is at the basic level, (see definition) circle "4" next to the Music heading or if your library has no adult fiction, circle "6", "Not Applicable" next to "Adult Fiction" near the bottom of the list.

| Subjects | Comprehensive (virtually exhaustive) | Research Level | Study Level | Basic Level | Minimal Level | Not Applicable | |
|---|---|---|---|---|---|---|---|
| **Natural Sciences** | | | | | | | |
| Astronomy | 1 | 2 | 3 | 4 | 5 | 6 | (8-9) |
| Biology | 1 | 2 | 3 | 4 | 5 | 6 | (10-11) |
| Chemistry | 1 | 2 | 3 | 4 | 5 | 6 | (12-13) |
| Environmental Sciences | 1 | 2 | 3 | 4 | 5 | 6 | (14-15) |
| Geology | 1 | 2 | 3 | 4 | 5 | 6 | (16-17) |
| Mathematics | 1 | 2 | 3 | 4 | 5 | 6 | (18-19) |
| Physics | 1 | 2 | 3 | 4 | 5 | 6 | (20-21) |
| Zoology | 1 | 2 | 3 | 4 | 5 | 6 | (22-23) |
| Engineering & Technology | 1 | 2 | 3 | 4 | 5 | 6 | (24-25) |
| Agriculture | 1 | 2 | 3 | 4 | 5 | 6 | (26-27) |
| **Social Sciences** | | | | | | | |
| Anthropology | 1 | 2 | 3 | 4 | 5 | 6 | (28-29) |
| Economics | 1 | 2 | 3 | 4 | 5 | 6 | (30-31) |
| Geography | 1 | 2 | 3 | 4 | 5 | 6 | (32-33) |
| History | 1 | 2 | 3 | 4 | 5 | 6 | (34-35) |
| Political Science | 1 | 2 | 3 | 4 | 5 | 6 | (36-37) |
| Psychology | 1 | 2 | 3 | 4 | 5 | 6 | (38-39) |
| Sociology | 1 | 2 | 3 | 4 | 5 | 6 | (40-41) |
| Statistics | 1 | 2 | 3 | 4 | 5 | 6 | (42-43) |
| Urban Studies | 1 | 2 | 3 | 4 | 5 | 6 | (44-45) |
| **Humanities** | | | | | | | |
| Architecture | 1 | 2 | 3 | 4 | 5 | 6 | (46-47) |
| Art | 1 | 2 | 3 | 4 | 5 | 6 | (48-49) |
| Archaeology | 1 | 2 | 3 | 4 | 5 | 6 | (50-51) |
| Classics | 1 | 2 | 3 | 4 | 5 | 6 | (52-53) |
| Language & Literature (including Linguistics) | 1 | 2 | 3 | 4 | 5 | 6 | (54-55) |
| Music | 1 | 2 | 3 | 4 | 5 | 6 | (56-57) |
| Philosophy | 1 | 2 | 3 | 4 | 5 | 6 | (58-59) |
| Religion | 1 | 2 | 3 | 4 | 5 | 6 | (60-61) |
| Health Sciences | 1 | 2 | 3 | 4 | 5 | 6 | (62-63) |
| Law | 1 | 2 | 3 | 4 | 5 | 6 | (64-65) |
| Education | 1 | 2 | 3 | 4 | 5 | 6 | (66-67) |
| Bibliography and Library Science | 1 | 2 | 3 | 4 | 5 | 6 | (68-69) |
| Interdisciplinary Subjects | 1 | 2 | 3 | 4 | 5 | 6 | (70-71.) |
| (specify)_____ | 1 | 2 | 3 | 4 | 5 | 6 | (8-9) |
| (specify)_____ | 1 | 2 | 3 | 4 | 5 | 6 | (10-11) |
| Popular Adult Non-Fiction (e.g., Recreation, Travel, Hobbies, etc.) | 1 | 2 | 3 | 4 | 5 | 6 | (12-13) |
| Adult Fiction | 1 | 2 | 3 | 4 | 5 | 6 | (14-15) |
| Juvenile Fiction & Non-Fiction | 1 | 2 | 3 | 4 | 5 | 6 | (16-17) |
| Other (specify)_____ | 1 | 2 | 3 | 4 | 5 | 6 | (18-19) |
| Other (specify)_____ | 1 | 2 | 3 | 4 | 5 | 6 | (20-21.) |

188

---

SECTION V - AVAILABILITY OF AUTOMATED FILES

---

In this section of the questionnaire we are interested in finding out the extent to which your library is able to generate listings based on data already on file in machine-readable form.

---

NOTE: If your library does not use, on a regular basis, any computerized or automated system which contains data associated with your library's books or serials, check (✓) the box at right and skip this section of the questionnaire . . . . . .  (8-9)

---

Please fill in your name, title, and phone number if different from the principal respondent:

Name: _____

Title: _____

Phone Number: _____
           (area code)-

If you have any questions, please feel free to call Professor Machlup's office in New York: (212) 683-2050 (call collect)

---

V-1  REGULARLY-USED AUTOMATED SYSTEMS

Indicate which of the following automated systems your library or institution now uses on a regular basis. *(Circle 1 or 2 to denote yes or no. If you circle 1 for yes, please note the year begun):*

| Does your library regularly use a(n): | Yes | No | First Year Begun | |
|---|---|---|---|---|
| a) Automated ordering system for books . . . . . . | 1 | 2 | _____ | (10-16) |
| b) Automated ordering system for serials . . . . . | 1 | 2 | _____ | (17-23) |
| c) Cooperative cataloging system (e.g., OCLC) . . . | 1 | 2 | _____ | (24-30) |
| d) Automated circulation system . . . . . . . . . . | 1 | 2 | _____ | (31-37) |
| e) Automated accounting control system . . . . . . | 1 | 2 | _____ | (38-44) |
| f) Automated inventory control system (e.g., automated shelf list) . . . . . . . . . . . . . | 1 | 2 | _____ | (45-51) |

189

V-2  AVAILABLE DATA LISTINGS

Indicate which of the following lists of data you can generate from data already in machine-readable form. *(Circle 1 or 2 to denote yes or no. If you circle 1 for yes, please note the year begun):*

| | | Yes | No | First Year Begun | |
|---|---|---|---|---|---|
| a) | A list of book titles with number of times circulated each year . . . . . . . . . . . . . . . | 1 | 2 | _____ | (52–58) |
| b) | A list of book titles by date of publication with number of times circulated . . . . . . . . . | 1 | 2 | _____ | (59–65) |
| c) | A list of new book titles by subject . . . . . . . . . . . . . . . . . . . . . | 1 | 2 | _____ | (66–72.) |
| d) | A list of current serials titles by subject . . . | 1 | 2 | _____ | (8–14) |
| e) | A list of all book titles by subject . . . . . . . | 1 | 2 | _____ | (15–21) |
| f) | A combined list of current serial titles and new books by subject . . . . . . . . . . . . . . | 1 | 2 | _____ | (22–28) |
| g) | A complete list of all book holdings in special collections . . . . . . . . . . . . . . . | 1 | 2 | _____ | (29–35) |
| h) | A complete list of all serial holdings by subject . . . . . . . . . . . . . . . . . . . . | 1 | 2 | _____ | (36–42) |
| i) | A list of book titles by last time circulated . . | 1 | 2 | _____ | (43–49) |
| j) | Circulation by type of borrower . . . . . . . . . | 1 | 2 | _____ | (50–56) |
| k) | Circulation by type of item (book, microform, serial, etc.) . . . . . . . . . . . . . . . . . | 1 | 2 | _____ | (57–63) |

V-3  **Please indicate how many separate organizational units with collections** are covered **in this section of the questionnaire.** *(Insert number in box):* . . [ ]   (64–66)

- Does this number include all the organizational units with collections which are part of your library or library system? *(Circle 1 or 2):*

  Yes . . . . 1      No . . . . 2      (67–68.)

- IF NO:  What are the names of the excluded units? *(list):*

_____    _____
_____    _____
_____    _____
_____    _____
_____    _____

190

V-3   RELATIVE CHANGES IN ACQUISITION LEVEL 1970-1976

To reflect changes in buying patterns *within your own library* since 1970, please
compare subject categories in terms of the amount of library materials purchased
(i.e., numbers of volumes). For each subject indicate the change by circling
the appropriate code number. For example, if you feel your library is purchasing
significantly fewer volumes in the field of agriculture, circle "5" next to the
Agriculture heading. If you do not collect materials in a given field, circle
"6" for "Not Applicable". If there has been no change, circle 3.

| Subjects | Comprehensive (virtually exhaustive) | Research Level | Study Level | Basic Level | Minimal Level | Not Applicable | |
|---|---|---|---|---|---|---|---|
| **Natural Sciences** | | | | | | | |
| Astronomy . . . . . . . . . . . . . . | 1 | 2. | 3 | 4 | 5 | 6 | ( ) (8-9) |
| Biology . . . . . . . . . . . . . . | 1 | 2 | 3 | 4 | 5 | 6 | ( ) (10-11) |
| Chemistry . . . . . . . . . . . . . | 1 | 2 | 3 | 4 | 5 | 6 | ( ) (12-13) |
| Environmental Sciences . . . . . . . . | 1 | 2 | 3 | 4 | 5 | 6 | ( ) (14-15) |
| Geology . . . . . . . . . . . . . . | 1 | 2 | 3 | 4 | 5 | 6 | ( ) (16-17) |
| Mathematics . . . . . . . . . . . . . | 1 | 2 | 3 | 4 | 5 | 6 | ( ) (18-19) |
| Physics . . . . . . . . . . . . . | 1 | 2 | 3 | 4 | 5 | 6 | ( ) (20-21) |
| Zoology . . . . . . . . . . . . . . | 1 | 2 | 3 | 4 | 5 | 6 | ( ) (22-23) |
| Engineering & Technology . . . . . . . . . | 1 | 2 | 3 | 4 | 5 | 6 | ( ) (24-25) |
| Agriculture . . . . . . . . . . . . . | 1 | 2 | 3 | 4 | 5 | 6 | ( ) (26-27) |
| **Social Sciences** | | | | | | | |
| Anthropology . . . . . . . . . . . . | 1 | 2 | 3 | 4 | 5 | 6 | ( ) (28-29) |
| Economics . . . . . . . . . . . . . . | 1 | 2 | 3 | 4 | 5 | 6 | ( ) (30-31) |
| Geography . . . . . . . . . . . . . | 1 | 2 | 3 | 4 | 5 | 6 | ( ) (32-33) |
| History . . . . . . . . . . . . . . | 1 | 2 | 3 | 4 | 5 | 6 | ( ) (34-35) |
| Political Science . . . . . . . . . . . | 1 | 2 | 3 | 4 | 5 | 6 | ( ) (36-37) |
| Psychology . . . . . . . . . . . . . | 1 | 2 | 3 | 4 | 5 | 6 | ( ) (38-39) |
| Sociology . . . . . . . . . . . . . | 1 | 2 | 3 | 4 | 5 | 6 | ( ) (40-41) |
| Statistics . . . . . . . . . . . . . | 1 | 2 | 3 | 4 | 5 | 6 | ( ) (42-43) |
| Urban Studies . . . . . . . . . . . . | 1 | 2 | 3 | 4 | 5 | 6 | ( ) (44-45) |
| **Humanities** | | | | | | | |
| Architecture . . . . . . . . . . . . . | 1 | 2 | 3 | 4 | 5 | 6 | ( ) (46-47) |
| Art. . . . . . . . . . . . . . . . . | 1 | 2 | 3 | 4 | 5 | 6 | ( ) (48-49) |
| Archaeology . . . . . . . . . . . . . | 1 | 2 | 3 | 4 | 5 | 6 | ( ) (50-51) |
| Classics . . . . . . . . . . . . . . | 1 | 2 | 3 | 4 | 5 | 6 | ( ) (52-53) |
| Language & Literature (including Linguistics) | 1 | 2 | 3 | 4 | 5 | 6 | ( ) (54-55) |
| Music . . . . . . . . . . . . . . . | 1 | 2 | 3 | 4 | 5 | 6 | ( ) (56-57) |
| Philosophy . . . . . . . . . . . . . | 1 | 2 | 3 | 4 | 5 | 6 | ( ) (58-59) |
| Religion . . . . . . . . . . . . . . | 1 | 2 | 3 | 4 | 5 | 6 | ( ) (60-61) |
| Health Sciences. . . . . . . . . . . . . | 1 | 2 | 3 | 4 | 5 | 6 | ( ) (62-63) |
| Law. . . . . . . . . . . . . . . . . | 1 | 2 | 3 | 4 | 5 | 6 | ( ) (64-65) |
| Education. . . . . . . . . . . . . . . | 1 | 2 | 3 | 4 | 5 | 6 | ( ) (66-67) |
| Bibliography and Library Science . . . . . . | 1 | 2 | 3 | 4 | 5 | 6 | ( ) (68-69) |
| Interdisciplinary Subjects . . . . . . . . . | 1 | 2 | 3 | 4 | 5 | 6 | ( ) (70-71. |
| (specify)_____ | | | | | | | (8-9) |
| (specify)_____ . . . . | 1 | 2 | 3 | 4 | 5 | 6 | ( ) (10-11) |
| Popular Adult Non-Fiction (e.g., Recreation, Travel, Hobbies, etc.). . | 1 | 2 | 3 | 4 | 5 | 6 | ( ) (12-13) |
| Adult Fiction. . . . . . . . . . . . . . | 1 | 2 | 3 | 4 | 5 | 6 | ( ) (14-15) |
| Juvenile Fiction & Non-Fiction . . . . . . . | 1 | 2 | 3 | 4 | 5 | 6 | ( ) (16-17) |
| Other (specify)_____ . . . | 1 | 2 | 3 | 4 | 5 | 6 | ( ) (18-19) |
| Other (specify)_____ . . . | 1 | 2 | 3 | 4 | 5 | 6 | ( )(20-21.) |

191

# Our Libraries:
# Can We Measure Their Holdings and Acquisitions

*Fritz Machlup*

Reprinted from
**AAUP Bulletin**
Autumn, 1976

We are a "knowledge society," a society that devotes a large and ever-increasing part of its gross national product to the production and distribution of knowledge. The "knowledge industry" has been growing at a faster rate than most other sectors of the economy, and the number of people working in "knowledge occupations" is between two fifths and one half of our potential labor force. Statements of this sort were advanced fifteen years ago, and statistical research on "knowledge production" has been going forth ever since.[1] Yet, on some rather elementary questions regarding "knowledge embodied in print" we know so little that we must admit deep embarrassment.

Knowledge contained in books and journals has in fact been the earliest object of measurement in this area. The size and growth of our library collections have been taken to be the most reliable and most easily obtainable indicators of our engagement in knowledge production. For decades apodictic statements have been passed around to the effect that "knowledge" stored on the shelves of our libraries has been doubling every ten years, or every seven years, or some such number. A few of us have been skeptical about the meaning of such assertions; we have asked, for example, whether one hundred books really represented twice as much knowledge as fifty books, and whether fifteen journals really conveyed thrice as much information as five journals. But we have not questioned the physical meaning of the measurement. We have not questioned the reported "facts" about the rate at which the numbers of books and journals on the shelves in our libraries have been increasing. We believed the stories about the doubling every few years, because we had not known that the librarians themselves were so very unsure about the collections under their control. Now I know a little more about the extent of my ignorance and I want to share it with others. By sharing the

realization of my ignorance I may relieve my conscience as an investigator of the dissemination of information.

## Simple Questions, But No Answers

I set out to get answers to what appeared to me as rather simple questions. Relying on the most widely used classification systems employed in library collections—say, the system of the Library of Congress—I wanted to find out the size of the libraries' total holdings, and the annual acquisitions, of books and journals in the various fields. Concerned with the economics of library services, I also wanted to find out how much the libraries have been spending each year for acquiring various kinds of materials in the different fields. Call it the scholar's optimism or call it the fool's naïveté, but I thought that all I had to do to get answers to my questions was to ask the librarians. Alas, the librarians did not have the answers, and the most I have learned from them is why the answers were not available and how enormously difficult, if not impossible, it would be to obtain them.

At first I was perplexed. If a grocery store can know how much were the year's purchases of sugar, flour, vegetables, beer, bread, and all the rest, why should a librarian not know his expenditures for books and journals in physics, biology, mathematics, English literature, art history, and so forth? What differences are there in keeping such records in a commercial business and in a research library?

*FRITZ MACHLUP, a former President of the Association, is Professor of Economics at New York University.*

---

[1] Fritz Machlup, *The Production and Distribution of Knowledge in the United States* (Princeton: Princeton University Press, 1962). Since the publication of this book, several other researchers have attempted to update the statistical findings. I myself, under grants from the National Science Foundation and the National Endowment for the Humanities, have been engaged in an inquiry to bring the study up to date. The present phase of my study focuses on publishing and library services.

At last it dawned upon me that differences in the mental habits of men of learning and men of business may be at the root of their different practices regarding accounts and statistical records. In contrast with businessmen, the custodians of our scholarly publications are not under any legal obligation to file annual returns to income-tax authorities, who may be curious to know the details of the expenditures and losses of the enterprise. The keepers of our books in the libraries are not bookkeepers, and the subscriptions they pay for learned journals are not entered into such lined journals and ledgers as are the bookkeepers' daily concern.

There may be another difficulty behind the lack of statistical records in library administration: the absence of an operational unit of measurement, apart from dollar expenditure. While groceries are bought in pounds and tons, pecks and bushels, quarts and gallons, such units do not apply to books and journals. Bewildering problems have to be solved before one can say how many "volumes" or "journals" are in the stacks of a library and how many have been added in any particular year.

**The Units of Measurement**

The most usual description of the size of a library collection, as we find it in the leaflets, bulletins, and reports of the institutions, is in terms of the number of volumes. The curious, surely, will immediately ask whether a two-volume edition of Adam Smith's *Wealth of Nations* is counted as two volumes while the Modern Library edition is only one volume. And since the *Encyclopaedia of the Social Sciences* is available in eight fat volumes but also in fifteen slimmer volumes, should it be counted as eight or fifteen volumes, or as just *one* reference work? Many libraries used to bind several paper-covered pamphlets by different authors of the nineteenth century—if they were addressing related subject-matters—into one hard-cover volume; should the number of pamphlets be counted or the number of bound volumes? If the library had bought multiple copies of a book that was assigned in an undergraduate course with large enrollment, should all the duplicates be included in the total? If a succession of administrators over the last fifty or hundred years had been keeping "accurate records" of acquisitions but had answered these questions differently, some counting the number of different titles acquired, some the number of bound books, some the number of pamphlets joined between hard covers, and so forth, the "accuracy" of the records would be of no avail and, if a consistent count of the total collection were wanted, a new stocktaking would be necessary—at a cost hardly justified by the benefits expected from knowing the "accurate" measure.

The problem of operational definitions is perhaps even more serious in the case of the serials: the journals, magazines, newsletters, newspapers, and other periodical publications. The library may have subscribed to a magazine or paper and put the issues into hard bindings, some annually, others semi-annually. Should the number of issues be counted or the number of the bound volumes, or perhaps simply the number of subscriptions? But what if the library does not have the complete set from the first issue of Volume I to the present? How should it count its collection of a journal if it possesses only Volumes XII to XXXII and again Volumes XLIV to LXI?

All these questions can of course be answered by some generally agreed convention. But can a library which has not kept consistent records afford the cost of taking a complete inventory? With library budgets so stringent that not all the wanted journals can be subscribed to and only a part of the wanted books can be purchased, should the allocation of funds for acquisitions be further encroached upon by expenditures for a stock-taking operation? Even a very curious researcher in library science or in information science could not have his priorities so distorted that he would vote for *measuring* rather than for *increasing* the stock of books and serials available in the stacks. We do not want to impede growth by an attempt to find out how fast it has been and how far it has gotten us.

I have deliberately drawn an excessively dark picture of the task of measuring the physical contents of our libraries. Readers quite unfamiliar with the problems of library operations may thereby be helped in shedding some of their illusions. But they should be told that some less expensive techniques of estimating the size of library collections have been developed. They include counts of the titles, copies, and serials as they appear in cards in the catalogue of the library. Since these cards are by author, title, and subject matter (often more than one subject for a single book), an estimate of the most likely multiple counting has to be made if estimates of the numbers of cards in the trays are used as the bases of the inventorization. Unfortunately, these techniques, though helpful to estimate the total number of titles held by the library, rarely help ascertain what the library possesses in the various fields of knowledge. Only specialized libraries, for example, a chemistry library, will be able by a simple count of catalogue cards to estimate its collection in the field of specialization.

**Fields of Knowledge**

My aim of obtaining information on the total holdings and annual acquisitions by our libraries of printed materials in the different fields of knowledge is not motivated by idle curiosity. Important questions of national policy may be raised by such information. If annual library budgets, though increasing in dollars appropriated, can buy only fewer journals and fewer books at the faster increasing subscription rates and list prices, are the unavoidable retrenchments in real acquisitions equally distributed among the fields of learning? Or are the priorities such that some fields are given preferred treatment and other fields shut out in the process? Are, for example, current acquisitions in the social sciences being throttled, and acquisitions in the humanities stopped, in order to allow the physical sciences to be kept up to date? Since we know that subscription rates for most journals in the natural sciences have been raised at a spectacular pace—some by as much as 400 percent over the last six years—and that, as a result, the number of books purchased by libraries had to be reduced, how has this curtailment affected the different fields of knowledge? Clearly, these are not idle questions; we should do our best to get the answers.

In consultation with various authorities, public and private, my research associates classified books and journals published in recent years into thirty-one fields and have been trying to develop accordingly disaggregated data on new publications. Theoretically, the use of call numbers in the libraries, for example, under the Library of Congress classification, could yield an even finer breakdown by subject areas, subareas, and subsubareas. In actual fact, however, we would be lucky if we were able to get a breakdown of library acquisitions by no more than ten areas. Thus we have approached the members of the Association of Research Libraries regarding the feasibility of the following broad classes: Science (Library of Congress class Q), Engineering and Technology (T), Medicine (R and S), Other Sciences (U and V), Social Sciences (C,D,E,F,H, and J), Humanities (B,G,M,N, and P), Law (K), Education (L), Other (A and Z), and Rare Books. In our innocence, we thought that this rather general classification would be practicable without undue cost or effort.

Our hope was to obtain, from as many research libraries as possible, information, broken down by the ten areas, on the size of their collection, annual increases in size since 1970, annual purchases from various channels of distribution, serial subscriptions, materials received at no charge—and a few other things, such as outside circulation, rates of loss, interlibrary borrowing and lending, and sources of funding.

## He Who Asketh Too Much Will Get Nothing

I lost my innocence in my first interviews with the most knowledgeable librarians and learned of the limits of the information they could furnish. I discarded the carefully designed pages of an excessively nosy questionnaire that I had drafted. I realized that the administrators of libraries, like most other human beings, would not undertake to complete a questionnaire that asked too many unanswerable questions. I took a vow of modesty and decided not to request any data before I found out how easy or how difficult it would be for my respondents to respond to a request for information.

In line with this game plan, my research associates, aided by officers and staff of the Association of Research Libraries, developed a "Preliminary Questionnaire," with the subtitle in capital letters: "THIS IS NOT A REQUEST FOR DATA." The instructions read as follows:

Through the attached questionnaire we hope to obtain your evaluation of the level of difficulty and costs involved in gathering annual statistical data about your library for the period 1970 through 1975. Please select the response

which best describes the accessibility of the various types of information listed and enter the corresponding code in the appropriate box. The responses are as follows:

| Code | Response |
|------|----------|
| 1 | Data are available at little or no cost (under 1 man-hour). |
| 2 | Data are obtainable at moderate cost (1 man-hour to 1 man-day). |
| 3 | Data are obtainable at substantial cost (1 man-day to 1 man-week). |
| 4 | Data are obtainable at excessive cost (more than 1 man-week). |
| 5 | Data are not obtainable. |

The questionnaire was sent to ninety-nine librarians; returns were received from sixty-seven—which I regard as a good rate of response. I may take this opportunity to commend the respondents for their cooperation and to thank them for their understanding and helpfulness. The findings, however, give no cause for enthusiasm; the scores show that most of the data will be either unobtainable or obtainable only at excessive cost. I have never seen so many 5s on a computer printout: 72 percent of all boxes exhibited this number, conveying the message "data are not obtainable." Only 7.6 percent of the boxes showed the figures 1 or 2, indicating that the data would be available at little or moderate cost.

As a matter of fact, these percentages still exaggerate the availability of information, because they include the boxes for responses regarding "data not broken down" by various subcategories, such as channels of acquisition, sources of funds, and, especially, subject areas. If we focus only on responses regarding the availability of data "broken down by subject areas," we see the figures 4 and 5—standing for virtual or actual unobtainability—in no less than 82 percent of the boxes. This seems to close the door to the researcher who wants to find out what has been happening to the libraries as buyers and lenders of books and journals in different fields of science and scholarship.

This may sound like excessive defeatism. Yet it undoubtedly bars an inquiry that may answer such relatively simple questions as these: How are the book collections of our research libraries divided among natural sciences, social sciences, and the humanities? How many journals in each of these areas are being subscribed to by the largest and by the medium-sized libraries? How many book titles in science, in medicine, in technology, in the social sciences, in the humanities were acquired in each of the last five years? What trend in book acquisitions can be observed and what would happen if the trend continued for another five years? How have the library budgets been reallocated in recent years? Have acquisitions of books or subscriptions to learned journals been maintained in certain fields at the expense of other fields, regarded as less important or of lower priority or urgency?

Of course, we shall not give up so easily. If only a dozen of the large research libraries will be able to produce the data required for our research, we shall have to do with that small sample. Perhaps some sampling techniques will permit us to do some legitimate "blowing up" of small samples and obtain reasonable information about the "total population" of libraries. And, surely, if we cannot learn all that we ought to know about our libraries, we shall be able to learn a good deal about the few libraries that have managed to keep good records.

## The Next Steps in Our Research

Our first reaction was *not* to bother many librarians with questionnaires on which they would be unable to answer most of the questions. The response rate would be so small that the whole inquiry might become worthless. It had become clear to us that different questionnaires have to be designed for libraries equipped with different systems of record-keeping and data-processing. Unfortunately, the libraries cannot be easily sorted into a few classes defined by degrees of availability of data. Most of the respondents to our feasibility test have indicated that they might furnish information on certain types of questions, but not on others, but the replies showed not only great inequality in the distribution of knowledge but also a wide dispersion in the distribution of hopelessness among different institutions regarding different questions. To fit each questionnaire exactly to the individual librarian's knowledgeability or ingenuity would help to get the highest rate of response, but would be quite unhelpful in providing comparable data for any meaningful analysis.

We tentatively concluded to design three questionnaires, one for the most knowledgeable of our respondents (ten or twelve), one for the middle class of about another twenty library administrators, and a third for the remaining seventy institutions from which we can and hope to get more than a minimum of information useful in our inquiry. If the response rate were high in all three classes, we would at least know how significant the answers of our first-class respondents would be in the total population of research libraries. Thus, the value of the detailed information obtained from the most promising providers of data would depend partly on the degree of cooperation by the members of the groups who can complete only the less demanding of our questionnaires.

The final decision on our procedures will be made in consultation with hardnosed librarians, seasoned specialists and experienced researchers in the field.

vant data, broken down in any way desired. But will they take full advantage of the physical capability of their equipment?

In a survey of university libraries in the United States with responses from 116 institutions (59 percent of those queried), a researcher back in 1969 found that 51 percent of the respondents had installed automated systems of some sort. Most of these systems, however, were used only for some "listings" and other isolated pieces of information.[2] Only a few libraries have developed computerized systems for all major operations: acquisition procedures, cataloging, serial records and controls, and circulation records.[3] And even those that have do not in general seek answers to all the questions which curious outsiders believe they need for their research.

There are no very stringent physical limitations imposed by the computer systems; the actual limitations lie partly in the interests and imagination of the administrators and their programmers, but chiefly in the time, effort, and money that can be allocated to the development of a comprehensive information program. Practically every additional piece of information increases the cost of the system, for its hardware, software, and for current operation. More expensive equipment may be needed to meet the increased demands for information, and each transaction in the various departments—acquisitions, cataloging, etc.—may require extra time for feeding the data into the system. Are the benefits from additional or more detailed information worth its cost? An outside researcher may be convinced that the answer is in the affirmative, whereas the library administrator, struggling hard to keep within his budget and, especially, to keep administrative expenses from increasing much faster than the cost of acquisitions, may have serious doubts or may even have concluded that the potential benefits of the additional information are *not* worth the incremental cost.

In these circumstances it will be necessary to embark on some realistic benefit-and-cost analysis for information systems of various dimensions. I suspect that the crunch due to fast-rising costs of urgently needed materials (journals and books) and more slowly rising appropriations will call for decisions which cannot be made wisely in the absence of better information than is now available. The budget crunch may, conceivably, suggest to some the desirability of economizing in "unproductive" record-keeping and data-processing but, more likely, will impress decision makers that they need bet-

## Improvements in Library Record-Keeping

Techniques for better record-keeping have been developed and tried out by a number of libraries. Some large institutions which in our feasibility test had to report only 4s and 5s—indicating that they are not equipped to answer our questions for detailed data—have installed or ordered computerized information systems with the capability of yielding virtually all rele-

[2] James H. Byrn, "Automation in University Libraries: The State of the Art," *Library Resources and Technical Services,* 13 (Fall, 1969), pp 520-530. The report suggests that the sample may have been unrepresentative, as libraries with well-known computerized systems had not responded to the questionnaire.

[3] Ralph H. Parker, "Library Automation," *Annual Review of Information Science and Technology,* 8 (1970), pp. 193-222.

ter information in order to make wiser decisions. As long as ample funds are available for buying all the books and serials that look desirable, librarians may find it useless to spend time and money on information systems just to satisfy the idle curiosity of statisticians, economists, and operations researchers. But when funds get so scarce that every journal subscription crowds out the acquisition of several books, and every purchase of a book on physical chemistry shuts out the purchase of a book on literary criticism, then it may be deemed imperative to know the comparative needs and desires of students, faculty members, and other constituents of the college or university community for materials wanted for teaching and research. The librarian, in such circumstances, may wish to know how much he has been spending for books and journals in different fields and what use has been made of the collections on his shelves.

We can trust the economic forces in operation to make library administrators realize that the old saying "ignorance is bliss" does not apply any longer to their management techniques.

# Controversy

Reprinted from
**AAUP Bulletin**
November 1977

*In this section, the Bulletin will from time to time present debates which are too extended to carry in the Correspondence section.*

## More on "The Production and Distribution of Knowledge in the United States"

### Short Shoelaces: Machlup Looks at Library Statistics

*From David W. Heron*

It is pleasing to a librarian-member of AAUP to find the lead article in the Autumn issue of the *Bulletin* devoted to academic libraries,[1] and all the more so that it is by the dean of American economists, Fritz Machlup. His landmark book, *The Production and Distribution of Knowledge in the United States*, disregarded libraries as a part of the knowledge chain, and this article compensates, to some degree, for that omission.

My title comes from one delightful passage less apposite here than to some other parts of his second chapter titled "Types of Knowledge and Knowledge Production":

A great deal of practical knowledge is not based on anything that can be attributed to science or scholarship of any sort; for example, where I can shop at lowest prices, which is the fastest route from my home to my office, how I can tie my shoelaces if they are too short, at what time the last train for Princeton leaves Pennsylvania Station.[2]

Short shoelaces are a quantitative problem in a sense,

and thus have some similarity to unsatisfactory statistics, but both problems have qualitative aspects which are more interesting than measurement. Libraries lend themselves in some ways to measurement, but their books reflect the amazing diversity of human perception suggested by this passage about practical knowledge. This diversity makes library measurement complicated and somewhat uncertain.

The two central questions which he has asked of librarians are simple and reasonable: (1) What is the composition of our research library collections, and (2) How is it changing?

"Alas," he says, "the librarians did not have the answers, and the most that I have learned from them is why the answers were not available and how enormously difficult, if not impossible, it would be to obtain them. . . ."[3]

From the initial questions which he tested on the Association of Research Libraries and from the responses which he had, he concluded that very few libraries make the effort to measure their performance, concluding with reference to examining "the few libraries that have managed to keep good records."

In the second twenty-six page questionnaire which has since emerged, with the hesitant endorsement of the prestigious Association of Research Libraries, he has offered the delinquents a model for measuring their performance which, like Leonardo's flying machines, is not likely to fly, but is likely to provide some stimulus to the pedestrians who leave flying to the birds, bees, and cherubim. As a matter of fact, librarians tend to spend quite a lot of time counting their books and what they have done to them, although excesses are more evident in such activities as accounting and processing than in those library services concerned with teaching people the uses of bibliography and answering specific questions from reference books. The Association of Research Libraries, the American Library Association, and the U.S. Office of Education's ubiquitous National Center

---

[1] Fritz Machlup, "Our Libraries: Can We Measure Their Holdings and Acquisitions?" *AAUP Bulletin*, 62 (October, 1976), pp. 303-307.

[2] Fritz Machlup, *The Production and Distribution of Knowledge in the United States* (Princeton: Princeton University Press, 1962), p. 17.

[3] Machlup, "Our Libraries. . . ," p. 303.

for Education Statistics, all publish substantial clutches of academic library statistics. On a couple of recent occasions in its annual request for academic library statistics, the Office of Education has even asked for collection analysis by subject, although the results have yet to be published.[4]

The most important difficulties in Professor Machlup's search for a crisp quantitative analysis of academic library development aren't lazy librarians, a lack of good statistical models, or unwillingness to use them. The principal problem is simply in establishing categories of things to count.

"If a grocery store can know how much were the year's purchases of sugar, flour, vegetables, beer, bread, and all the rest, why should a librarian not know his expenditure for books and journals in physics, biology, mathematics, English literature, art history and so forth?" Machlup asks. His response is to charge librarians with lack of responsibility and lack of quantitative standards, then to present them with an inventory model in which there is more "and so forth" than either grocer or librarian could possibly use.

The fact is that academic libraries *don't* have satisfactory standards for collection analysis. But then a book is not a loaf of bread; a poem is not a potato. The ten categories of knowledge which Machlup chose in his first questionnaire, by combinations (some of them new) of the classifications used in the Library of Congress classification scheme, have been abandoned in the second questionnaire in favor of a list similar to that used in the book trade's *Publisher's Weekly*, of thirteen categories unrelated to the Library of Congress classification, and another with thirty-five categories possibly derived from an Office of Education scheme.

The Library of Congress classification has been fairly generally adopted by American academic libraries. Richard Angell has described it by saying:

> The development of the Library of Congress classificaton began in the early years of this century for the purpose of disposing in useful subject groupings the collection of monographs and serials of what was in fact if not in name a great national library. . . .
> The schedules are based entirely on the collections. When a new work requires a new class number, developments in the particular field of knowledge are borne in mind in deciding on its placement; but no class number is added to a schedule until a work requires it. The scope of the LC classification, in a word, is coextensive with the Library's acquisition policy which, while extremely broad, is not exhaustive in all fields. Accordingly, the LC classification cannot be characterized as "universal."[5]

It is useful to academic libraries because it has grown out of a collection like theirs but larger, which leaves them "room to grow."

If the LC classification isn't perfect, Melville Dewey's is less so, as are those of Ranganathan, Bliss, and Richardson, but they can be used (and have been used) for rough analysis of library collections. The Office of Education, in 1967, used a scheme for collection analysis using either LC or Dewey, more or less equating individual parts of both systems. This analysis scheme called for percentages expressed either in Dewey or LC classification, in five major categories and one miscellany as shown in Table 1.

One of the principal difficulties with Machlup's first classification (upon which the *Bulletin* article was based) was that it included a combination of religion, geography, music, and art (the LC scheme's B, G, M, and N categories)—actually a new and original classification. The schemes in the second questionnaire are just as hard to relate to library collections. Analysis of a book collection (and of its growth) must depend on one of these classification systems. It need not be Dewey's or LC's—but if you want to use a *new* one, any librarian can tell you it will be expensive.

To return for a moment to the grocery store: if the year's purchases of bread are neatly tallied, and the IGA analyst pops in one day and says he needs the total number of white loaves, rye loaves, bagels, and tortillas, the grocer will experience the New Questionnaire Syndrome.

Professor Machlup reported that three quarters of his ARL responses were, "Data are not obtainable." One possibility in that sort of response is that you have asked the wrong question; another is that you've asked a good question in such a way that it can't be answered. Regrettably he hasn't heard the phrase "not obtainable" for the last time yet.

He accuses librarians of a management philosophy of "ignorance is bliss," because they have not been able to produce an analytical inventory of a university library's collection using—in effect—two new classifications, and applying it with some degree of plausibility to large collections of books. Books don't, as a rule, fit neatly into classification schemes. Consider, for example, what the Library of Congress does to *The Production and Distribution of Knowledge*, which it assigns to "general history of knowledge and learning" (AZ505) with a Dewey number of 001, for the most general treatises of human knowledge. The University of California (Berkeley) used the number P91 (general philology and linguistics) although all the other UC campuses have used the LC number.[7]

Even if available classifications are uncritically accepted, as the Office of Education has done with its so-far unpublished surveys of 1966 and 1968, and the shelf-list (standard inventory file arranged in classifica-

---

[4] One important (although inconclusive) study of standards for library measurement is the International Federation of Library Associations' *International Standardization of Library Statistics*, London, 1968.

[5] Richard S. Angell, "On the Future of the Library of Congress Classification," in *Classification Research Proceedings of the Second International Study Conference*, Copenhagen, Munksgaard, 1965, pp. 103-4.

[7] University of California, Berkeley, *Author-Title Catalog* (Boston: GK Hall, 1963), and *National Union Catalog*, 1963. (Washington: Library of Congress, 1964-.)

**Table 1**
1967 Office of Education Scheme for Collection Analysis

| Area | Classification Dewey | Classification L. C. | % of Total Collection | % of Current Acquisitions |
|---|---|---|---|---|
| 1 | 2 | 3 | 4 | 5 |
| Humanities and General Works | 000, 100, 200, 400, 700, 800 | A, B, M, N, P, Z, | | |
| Social Sciences | 300, 900 | C, D, E, F, G, H, J, K*, L | | |
| Physical Sciences, Including Mathematics | 500–559 | Q–QE | | |
| Biomedical Sciences | 560–599 610–619 | QH–QR R, S | | |
| Technology (Engineering) | 600–609 620–699 | T, U, V | | |
| Unclassified materials (including unclassified bound periodicals) | | | | |

\* i.e., LAW (pending)

tion-number order) is used as the simplest measuring device—100 titles to the inch of cards—how significant are the results? It would certainly be important to know that the library's acquisitions in the humanities had declined 10 per cent in the last biennium, while those in the social sciences had increased 2 per cent, and in science and technology had increased 6 per cent. The broader these categories, the more credible the statistics, in a sense, but their credibility is still uncomfortable because the boundaries are indistinct between science and technology, between religion and anthropology (which shares the Library of Congress "G" classification with geography and recreation), and among some of the other areas in which perceptions of things are changing especially fast.

There are some other problems in the second Machlup Survey questionnaire which will detract from its response but serve, perhaps, as useful irritants. Although there are incipient national standards for differentiating books, serials, periodicals, and other publishers' aberrations, there are local traditions to be overcome before there is a reservoir of uniform statistics (Questionnaire, Section I). There will be some lack of uniformity in the inclusion of fringe benefits in salary totals (I,1,b) and in presentation of plant operation and maintenance as a category of library expenditure (I,1,d). There are relatively few libraries which have kept careful count of foreign books, as such (II,2-3), or of categories of publishers (II,8). A number of questions could be answered by rough estimates, but the answers would have to be so subjective as to be unreliable.

The use of computers in library catalogs and circulation (inventory) systems will (in fact, already do) make it easier to compile the kinds of statistics which would dispel the Machlup "ignorance is bliss" charge. As more library inventory, catalog, and use information is computerized, the extraction of the kind of data Professor Machlup asks will become feasible. The validity and value of these numbers, however, will still depend upon whether there is a common understanding of what they represent, and the classification question remains the principal problem in the Machlup Survey.

As a librarian I don't apologize for our problems with classification of books. They derive from the infinite capacity of the human mind.

DAVID W. HERON
*University Librarian*
*University of California, Santa Cruz*

## My Short Shoelaces and the Shortage of Library Data

*From Fritz Machlup*

I am grateful to David Heron for his response to my lament on library statistics. In my article, "Our Libraries: Can We Measure Their Holdings and Acquisitions?" I had described some of the difficulties of obtaining good statistical data classified by subject or discipline. My article elicited no less than twenty replies—addressed either to the editor of the *Bulletin* or to me directly—some expressing sympathy or irritation, others suggesting techniques by which librarians might be able to obtain the now unavailable data. One good-natured librarian told me that duly "classified" data on their stocks and accretions would become available only after their recently automated ordering systems, circulation systems, and inventory-control systems have been in operation for several years. His advice: "Come back in three years and we will have the answers to your questions."

A promise of data in the future is, of course, most welcome. However, for a diagnosis of problems of the present, knowledge of past developments and of the current situation is needed. My research project calls for information about any detectable trends during the last six or seven years, because various symptoms point to significant changes that seem to have taken place in that period.

My survey is part of an inquiry, sponsored jointly by the National Science Foundation and the National Endowment for the Humanities, into the dissemination of scientific, technical, and scholarly knowledge through books and journals. Libraries are the main purchasers of such publications. Book publishers do not know how their sales are distributed among the final purchasers of their products, because a large portion of total sales goes through wholesalers and jobbers. With one or two exceptions, these middlemen have no data broken down by subject matter or discipline. Hence, librarians remain the only ones who can know what they have acquired. In recent years, the subscription rates to scientific journals have increased so rapidly that increasing shares of library budgets had to be—or have been—devoted to maintaining unbroken collections of serial publications, leaving decreasing shares of the budgets for the purchase of books. As the prices of journals and books, and the number of book titles, have been increasing, the number of copies sold per title has been declining at an alarming rate. Yet this trend may not prevail in *all* subject areas, and surely the degree of change may have been different in different areas. The experience in, say, physics, chemistry, or engineering has probably been quite different from that in history, literature, or philosophy. But how can we tell if we cannot obtain records of these experiences? Such information, I am convinced, would be important not only for the publishers but also for librarians, university administrators, the research community, and perhaps for public-policy makers.

Bernard H. Holicky, Director of Library Services, Calumet Campus, Purdue University, in a sympathetic response to my article, confirmed my suspicions: "Our library forced the cancellation of subscriptions. Diplomatic arm twisting and the application of eighth-grade arithmetic convinced everyone that in a short time the Library would only have subscriptions and would not be adding any books if subscriptions were not cancelled." Another librarian agreed that "if good budget planning based on priorities is ever to occur, more viable statistics are needed."

In order to obtain such statistics we designed three consecutive questionnaires. The first, sent to the (then) ninety-nine members of the Association of Research

Libraries and answered by two thirds of them, was merely exploratory. It was supposed to tell us which of our questions could be answered by the librarians at reasonable cost. It was clear from the responses that the data we really needed—the size of the collections, the annual acquisitions, and the annual expenditures, all classified by subject—were either unobtainable or obtainable only at excessive cost, except in about a dozen libraries.

The second questionnaire was sent to 778 libraries of all types and sizes, selected to yield a representative sample. Alas for the purists in sampling techniques, the response rate was so different for different types and sizes of libraries that the sampling was largely for the birds. Altogether 223 replies with usable information were received. The questionnaire had been carefully designed with the advice of several librarians and library scientists. Having learned from the first survey, we left out the questions that could not be answered at reasonable cost. For example, instead of asking for a breakdown of holdings or acquisitions by field, we asked the respondent only for an indication of the *years* for which his library *could* generate a breakdown of total expenditures for materials by subject—with subjects corresponding to the Dewey classification in tens (e.g., 330, 880, 920, etc.), or to the LC classification in two letters (e.g., HB, PR, KF, etc.), or to any other formal subject-classification system. Regarding the composition of book collections, we abstained from requesting information about the number of volumes, and confined ourselves to asking for the librarians' *estimates* of the *percentage shares* of thirteen broad subject classes in their present collections and in their acquisitions in 1976; in addition we asked the librarians to *rank* the three subjects for which they are buying significantly *more*, and the three for which they are buying significantly *less*, than in the past. Similar questions were asked for periodicals. In three questions—concerning "book buying patterns," "periodical subscriptions by subject," and "assessment of collection level"—we listed thirty-five subjects, not for any numerical reports, but only to obtain the librarians' own assessments of any changes in their purchases and subscriptions and of the "completeness" of their holdings in each of these fields.

Mr. Heron finds that the subject breakdown used in these questionnaires would have caused the librarians too much trouble. Such trouble would arise (1) because our subject classes deviated from the classification schemes customarily used by librarians; (2) because these various schemes differ from one another; and (3) because cataloguers' judgments in classifying particular titles under any scheme may differ considerably.

The deviations of the first kind occurred because we added six categories: computer science, environmental sciences, and urban studies—which had become significant in the NSF taxonomy—and "popular adult nonfiction," "adult fiction," and "juvenile fiction and nonfiction"—categories that were needed for the nonacademic libraries in our sample. The latter three categories are likely to be important for public libraries in many small municipalities in the country. (It was felt necessary for our survey to include municipal libraries in the sample, besides academic libraries, special libraries and large research libraries.) We did not think that the addition of the six subject groups would cause serious difficulties to academic or other research libraries.

Regarding the differences among the LC, Dewey, Richardson, and other classification schemes, we are aware of the problems which the Shelf-List Count of some twenty participating academic libraries has been facing. We thought that our best strategy would be not to get embroiled in the controversy about the imperfect interconvertibility of LC and Dewey codes and therefore decided to list the subjects without prescribing the respective class codes. In two of the questions of the second questionnaire, asking for qualitative changes in journal subscriptions and total collection levels, we selected thirty-one subjects broadly corresponding to the two-digit level in Dewey or the two-letter level in LC (that is, we asked for physics, chemistry, etc., rather than natural science). I have already acknowledged the misdeed of adding a few nontraditional subjects, and have explained why this appeared appropriate. Another strong reason for including the unusual subjects was our attempt to make the *librarians'* data consistent with the *publishers'* data. One of the tasks of our research program is to reconcile the publishers' sales with the libraries' purchases. Since publishers do not use any of the customary classification schemes of the libraries, we felt compelled to make some adjustments in both the publishers' and the librarians' systems of classifying the books and journals that have gone from the publishing houses to the libraries.

Unquestionably, inconsistencies in classification lead to inaccuracies in the statistics. These inaccuracies will be added to those caused by defects and differences in the techniques of counting, measuring, or estimating the libraries' holdings and acquisitions. The question is how great the margins of error are likely to be and, if they are substantial, whether conclusions drawn from the "findings" are thereby vitiated. I submit that even relatively large margins of error in the figures supplied need not rule out the detection of major changes in the allocations of library budgets to different subjects.

With regard to the third apprehension concerning classification, I believe that the margins of error would not be increased to an intolerable degree by the judgmental differences in classifying individual titles. To be sure, there are many borderline cases, but it does not really matter for the purposes of our survey whether my book, *The Production and Distribution of Knowledge in the United States,* is catalogued under "general history of knowledge and learning," or "general philology and linguistics," or under "economics," "sociology," or "interdisciplinary subjects." Even if as many as 10 per cent of all books were put into different classes by different cataloguers, some of the differences would cancel out in the count of titles in the collections or acquisitions and, more importantly, these inconsistencies would hardly conceal significant changes in the composition of acquisitions or, obversely, would hardly point to changes that had not in fact occurred. Even if some librarians reported their acquisitions neither by LC nor by Dewey or other cataloguing systems, but instead reported them by departmental budget allocations, ordering records, or expenditure accounts, such subject breakdowns would still be better than none at all.

No doubt, counts by title, by volume, by dollars budgeted, and by dollars spent may yield different results, but any such data for a series of years would still be helpful in assessing the changes that have occurred. The fact that so many librarians reported that none of these data could be furnished induced me to write the article and the fact that several of the librarians who replied to the article believed that the data actually *were* readily available indicates to me that they agreed with my contention that they *ought to be* available. My third survey, which requests numerical data from only the few libraries indicating their preparedness to supply them, includes only about fifteen institutions. In addition we may also be able to use the Shelf-List Counts initiated by some highly enterprising librarians, and also the expenditure analysis recently undertaken by the California State University and Colleges.

May I close with a personal remark? David Heron made me blush by describing me as the "dean of American economists," which I interpreted as a highly flattering epithet. On second thought I realized that professors entertain a healthy disrespect for deans; and so I wondered whether I should feel flattered or insulted. I concluded that Heron and the other librarians who took the time to reply to my article were not really angry with me; by the same token, I did not mean to be scornful—I was merely trying to encourage the librarians in their efforts to obtain and supply better information on our treasures of recorded knowledge.

FRITZ MACHLUP
*Economics*
*New York University*

201

*Fritz Machlup*, born in 1902, received his doctorate in 1923 from the University of Vienna.  After spending ten years in industrial management, he came to the United States in 1933 on a research fellowship of the Rockefeller Foundation.  He was visiting professor at Harvard University in 1935, 1936, and 1939;  Goodyear Professor of Economics at the University of Buffalo, 1935-1947;  Hutzler Professor of Political Economy at the Johns Hopkins University, 1947-1960;  Walker Professor of Economics and International Finance at Princeton University, 1960-1971;  and he is now Professor of Economics at New York University.

Dr. Machlup holds six honorary degrees from American and European universities.  He served as president of the Southern Economic Association, the American Economic Association, the International Economic Association, and also the American Association of University Professors.  The list of his writings enumerates over 800 titles, of which 112 were articles in major economic journals, 28 were books of sole authorship, and 13 books of joint authorship, not counting the 3 volumes now being published.

*Kenneth Leeson* recently received his doctorate in economics from New York University and is currently research associate at the Center for Applied Economics at N.Y.U. Chief among his interests are the economics of knowledge and information, technology and technological change, industrial organization, and international trade and finance.  As Senior Research Associate on the project culminating in these three volumes on *Information through the Printed Word* he has spent the last three years directing the research activities of the staff that gathered and compiled the reported data.  He has authored or co-authored publications on, "The Economic Viability of Scientific and Scholarly Journals," "Major Journals in Economics:  A User Study," "Sources and Uses of Funds of Academic Libraries," and "The Effects of Innovations on the Demand for and Earnings of Factors of Production."